Hope *Ahead*

A Journey to Freedom After Sexual Abuse

Barb Mulvey and Cris Paulson

Copyright 2015 by Barb Mulvey and Cris Paulson.
The book author retains sole copyright to
their contributions to this book.
Published 2015.
Printed in the United States of America.

Second Edition.

All rights reserved. No portion of this book may be reproduced, stored in a retrieval system, or transmitted in any form or by any means – electronic, mechanical, photocopy, recording, scanning, or other – except for brief quotations in critical reviews or articles, without the prior written permission of the author.

ISBN 978-1-937862-86-2

Library of Congress Control Number 2015901475

Cover designed by Heath Ashburn, Hoffmantown Church
Hopeaheadthebook@gmail.com

Scripture quotes are from the NIV version, unless otherwise stated.
New International Version ® NIV ®
Copyright © 1973, 1978, 1984, 2011 by Biblica, Inc ®
Used by permission. All rights reserved worldwide.

*We want to dedicate this book to God, our Redeemer,
as the first-fruits of our work. Without Him there would be no book.*

Scripture quotations from THE MESSAGE.
Copyright © by Eugene H. Peterson 1993, 1994, 1995, 1996, 2000, 2001, 2002.
Used by permission of Tyndale House Publishers, Inc.

Scripture quotations taken from the New American Standard Bible®,
Copyright © 1960, 1962, 1963, 1968, 1971, 1972, 1973, 1975, 1977, 1995
by The Lockman Foundation. Used by permission. (www.Lockman.org)

Scripture quotations taken from the Amplified® Bible,
Copyright © 1954, 1958, 1962, 1964, 1965, 1987 by The Lockman Foundation.
Used by permission. (www.Lockman.org)

Scripture quotations marked (TLB) are taken from
The Living Bible Copyright © 1971.
Used by permission of Tyndale House Publishers, Inc., Carol Stream, Illinois 60188.
All rights reserved.

Table of Contents

Introduction………... 1

Chapter 1- Barb's Testimony… 9

Chapter 2- A New Road to a New Destination (Receiving Input)…....... 24

Chapter 3- Tips from the Tour Guide- Beware of Scammers
    (Truth and Deception)….. 41

Chapter 4- Get On the Train (Engaging Your Will)… 60

Chapter 5- What Drives You? (Flesh vs. Spirit Battle).…............................ 77

Chapter 6- Gifts for the Journey (God's Resources)….................................. 94

Chapter 7- Engine Trouble (Emotions)… 113

Chapter 8- Baggage Handling (Responsibility)…....................................... 136

Chapter 9- Your Permanent Traveling Companion (Renewing the Mind). 155

Chapter 10- Following the Map (Doing the Word)…................................ 173

Chapter 11- Destination: Forgiveness…... 193

Chapter 12- Mountain Passes (Practicing Forgiveness)…........................... 212

Chapter 13- Drawing Close (Sexual Intimacy)…....................................... 228

Chapter 14- Open Road Ahead (Freedom)….. 251

Appendix A- Glossary Language of Mercy.. 266

Appendix B- Permission to Behave Badly Card... 273

Appendix C- Psalm 18 (Terror)... 274

Introduction

My dear Christian, you may be opening this book with *hope* and with *fear*. Hope that somehow, someone can write something that will set you free from despair, and fear that this will be just another disappointment. I get that.

Hope and **Fear**:
Hope for a magic pill. Fear that it will work for everyone but me.
Hope that I can change. Fear that I never will.
Hope that Jesus will bind up my broken heart. Fear that I won't let Him.

I have also known the hope in hearing another thought and another concept that just might numb the pain of abuse. And the despair of another night wracked with shame and heartache, because the latest thing didn't help. I used to live like a hamster in a cage, frantically running but still trapped. Spinning but unable to find the way out of despair, anger, confusion, fear, hurt and shame. Until, Jesus, the true Healer—

>the One who came to set the captives free,
>the One who came to bind the broken-hearted,
>the One who came to show me His strong and gentle love,
>the One who knows everything about me—past, present and future,

—came into the prison of my sexual abuse, saving me from death, changing me from the inside out and setting my feet upon a solid rock, delivering me as He promised. (Isa.61)

>I am not the person I was when I began this journey….
>I am not how **man** made me to be….
>I'm not who **I** thought I would be….
>**I am who God made me to be.**

I'm not perfect now, but I have a great life. I love God and I live to proclaim His name. I am free and whole and I live in hope now. I am not a super-woman but I am a loved woman, loved by the King of Kings,[1] who redeemed me from the pit of despair and lead me to wisdom. I wanted a life of peace without pain, but since I received a new heart,[2] I have strength to handle both. I feel my feelings but they don't rule me.

---
[1] Romans 5:5
[2] Ezekiel 11:19-20

Come live where I live now—in the Land of Grace. It is unlike any place you have been before. It is a place without condemnation. It is a place of peace. It is a place of comfort and strength and hope. But you can't close your eyes and click your heels three times and get there. You can't sit on your couch and get there. You can't get there by demanding, or pouting, or expecting someone else to take you there. It takes faithful hard work.

Surveying the Damage

During my 20-year search for healing from sexual abuse, I found that most books took most of their chapters naming the damage, but only a few pages describing what to do next to overcome it. Like Nehemiah did with the ruins of Jerusalem, an honest survey of the damage must be made before the walls can be repaired.[3] If you still need to admit and accept how abuse has affected your life, you probably need to look to other resources.

This book is for those who know the realities of the damage and are ready to journey to freedom. Hope Ahead is not four more months of dissecting the pain. I want to show you a new way and a new future—life beyond abuse, shame and heartache, with the pain and the pit really behind you and a good future ahead.[4] Even though your life has been bumped off the original path, the new path will still lead you to God. Like the GPS lady who says, 'Recalculating...,' God will work **no matter where you are** to get you back on track. Even if it's hard, you know how to do hard, right? You have done hard your whole life. It will be easier than staying in your life as is. So what do you have to lose?

> Your pain?
> Your heartache?
> Your misery?
> Confusion?
> Shame?
> Anger?

But this book doesn't hold any quick fixes or magic formulas. (There are no such things. Let go of that fantasy now!) It may frustrate you, but it will also challenge you to change and grow. Our journey is mapped out, but it's okay if you need to look ahead and read out of order. We hope you will eventually read the whole book but we trust God to lead you. I hope you will not spend one more second on your past than you need to. I don't believe it takes years to get healthy. I believe you can be different by next week.

---
[3] Nehemiah 2:11-18
[4] Beth Moore, Get Out of That Pit, Thomas Nelson, Nashville, TN © 2009

"Be careful where you put your but"

I love that saying. Be careful, and let me tell you why. The "but" literally negates the first part of the sentence. The "but" has the last word. Look at the next two sentences and see where you stand:

> I am a Christian who loves God BUT I have been sexually abused
>
> —Or—
>
> I have been sexually abused BUT I am a Christian who loves God

Same words but completely different meanings—all because of where you put your "but." The "but" changes the direction of the sentence. Where did your "but" land you? Stuck in the pit of abuse or free for God?

For years I had my "but" in the wrong place. I read books, did support groups, and found some knowledge, but these didn't set me free. I wanted so much more. I didn't want to be known as the church lady who had been abused, I wanted to be known as the daughter of the King. But for years, my identity was "Sexual Abuse Victim." I went for SA groups and read SA books. I saw myself through the lens of that pain. Hope and fear; joy and hate; peace and torment; love and pain. Most of my life I tried to eliminate one and live in the other. I wanted either/or but God had bigger plans.

Bottom Lines

My nickname is Bottom-line Barb. Most people think it is because I am an accountant. (The bottom line of a financial statement shows whether a company is making or losing money.) But I simplify everything down to bottom lines. When I studied Jesus' words in the Gospels, I pared them down to "Love God and Love Others."[5] Once I realized that **love** was the common word, I had a big picture in a short phrase, one that I still live by today. There are lists of bottom lines that summarize concepts for every chapter, but please add your own. **My** bottom lines may not be **your** bottom lines!

Language Problems

My husband Jim and I were once stuck in a train station in Paris because of a national holiday that shut down all travel. We had both taken years of Canadian French in school,

---
5 Matthew chapters 5-7

but no matter how hard we tried to communicate, no one understood us. After hours of frustration, we left in disgust and boarded a train for Switzerland. We never saw Paris because we could not speak the language.

On our tour of the Land of Grace, you will hear a different language being spoken—the Language of Mercy. Mercy's words may sound like words you know, but their meanings are very different. I want us all to be on the same page, so I explain key words from <u>Noah Webster's 1828 Dictionary</u>, which used the Bible for its definitions.

Before the 1870's, the Bible was the universal standard of truth. Most people would have understood and defined common words the same way, based on their biblical usage. For example, the word "need" used to mean:

1. To be in want, in a pressing or urgent sense.
2. Not having some necessity; a state that requires supply or relief.
3. To be in need monetarily, to be poor; indigent, lacking necessities, to be in want.
4. To require, as supply or relief.[6]

It referred to basic needs for life like food, water, clothing, shelter, but also salvation. But since the 1880's, Freud and modern psychology have altered the meanings of words. A modern definition of "needs" is based on Maslow's Hierarchy of Needs theory,[7] which defines people's "basic bodily needs," as air, food, clothing, sex, sleep and excretion. Once those needs are met, people seek to satisfy groups of successively "higher needs." Once they have met their needs for safety, they can meet belongingness and self-esteem needs. The goal is to have the pyramid of needs met so they can be "an enlightened human being."

I hope you can see how different these two definitions are. You may need to check the Glossary in the back so we can start the same place with the words I use.

What's in a Bar?

My first counselor, Melanie, is a sweet Christian, a pastor's daughter and pastor's wife whose background and life were the opposite of mine. She often said that Psalm 16:6 portrayed her childhood: "The boundary lines have fallen for me in pleasant places; surely I have a delightful inheritance." I used Exodus 1:14 to describe mine: "They made their lives bitter…in all their hard labor the Egyptians used them ruthlessly." She has a sincere,

---

[6] <u>1828 Webster's Dictionary</u>, 1828.mshaffer.com/d/search/word, *need*
[7] From Wikipedia. Google "Maslow's Hierarchy of Needs" chart. It is read from the bottom to the top, saying these are all the things we need in order to be fully functional human beings.

life-long faithfulness to God. At age 33, I didn't even know who God was. She was kind and gentle. I was hard and angry. We were opposites who couldn't connect.

One day I demanded of her, "You have to define your terms." She looked at me strangely as I fumed, "I don't get what you are saying. You must mean something different than I do. Like, what is your first thought when I say the word 'bar'?"

Immediately she responded, "O' Henry chocolate bar."

"Exactly!" I said, "That's my point! The first thing that pops into my mind with the word 'bar' is a place to get drunk."

We had opposite definitions for most of the words that we used. For example, discipline was done in love in her home and in anger in mine; positive word for her, negative word for me. Authority, forgiveness, love and obedience were some of the words we struggled with.

I started using word pictures to tell her my story. I didn't have words to explain thoughts that were in my head, so I related them to simple things I **did** know and understand. They are shortcuts to help me explain concepts and explore feelings; simple descriptions, not perfect explanations. Hold them loosely, and allow them to be flexible. I pray my word pictures will help you understand God's truths.

NTK

As a child, Cris went on many great family vacations—trips to Disneyland, Washington, D.C., the Rose Bowl Parade, skiing at Vail—the kind we dream about. But her parents told the kids few details about the trip. They were on a "need-to-know" basis. They sat in the backseat of the car, sleeping, reading, sometimes fighting, but confident that this would be a wonderful vacation, trusting Dad to be true to his nature, knowing that good things were ahead. If they questioned their parents, they heard, "You don't need to know that now."

My friend, in life we are often on a NTK basis with God. There are things that we may not know in this world. I have a "Poofy" file in my head that holds questions I don't have answers to and things that make no sense to me. There are things I don't understand but hope to find one day. Some of the files are fifty years-old. When I get new information, I open my files to see if it resolves any of my questions. My Poofy files are much smaller than they used to be, but there are things that I won't know until heaven. I don't like not having all the answers. But if I wait until I have all the answers, I would waste my life.

Some of you are stuck in the quicksand of the abuse. You have wrestled and fought and analyzed and reviewed and talked and cried and pushed down and ignored and blown up, but you feel like you are worse off than when you started.

Some of you are stuck because you have a 'Why' question screaming in your head:

Why did this happen?
Why didn't my parents help me?
Why didn't God stop the abuse?

Some of you are stuck because a 'Where' question has haunted you for years:

Where were my parents?
Where was God?

You think if you could just get an answer to the question, you could move forward. I know it's hard, but could you put your questions in the back seat of the car and accept that you are on a "need-to-know" basis? Can you put those questions in a "Poofy" file, join me in the backseat of the car, and trust that our Father will be true to His nature? Perhaps you could write the questions in your Journal and read them again when you finish this book. Or tell a friend that you really want an answer, but you are going to set it aside for a while and ask other questions. I pray you will find lots of answers in this book. We give dozens of biblical responses to being sinned against in the area of sexual abuse.

<u>Hope Ahead</u> is different from most other books about sexual abuse because we don't look at the abuse (I call it "jump into the pool of pain") until you have tools to know how to walk through it. We don't want you to get stuck in the hurt; we want you to leave it behind and live in freedom.

Fellow Travelers

When brave pioneers and explorers first crossed the prairies and opened up the West, they cut new paths through unknown territories, forged alliances with natives, opened trade routes and drew maps. The later settlers had trials too, but their journey was easier because trails had been blazed and they knew about the dangers ahead.

The pioneers knew that their safety depended on a few crucial things: preparation, getting good counsel and staying with the group. Even though most women I've met want to travel this journey to freedom by themselves, I don't think you can do it alone. I encourage you to find a travel companion, someone you trust to talk with truthfully about God and your history. Start a small group of women to go through the book together. Pick a discipleship partner who will listen to your homework assignments and pray for you. Ask a friend with a similar history to go through the book together. Just find **someone** to walk with you. I can say without exaggerating that a few godly counselors have saved my life and connected me to God.

Bridge-Builder

God gave me my life's work when I attended a retreat for divorced, separated or widowed women. I had just left a session where I had asked the teacher if some of her marriage problems could have come from her childhood sexual abuse, which she rejected as a factor. Feeling out of place and stupid for opening my mouth, I headed down the stairs for lunch when I heard God clearly say from Proverbs 31:8:

"I'm going to use you to speak for those who can't speak for themselves, for the rights of those who are destitute, poor and needy, to judge fairly. I'm calling you to speak for those who have no voice."

Like Moses, I stammered, "Lord, this is Barb. Are you sure you have the right person?? I don't want to be here, and I'm running away from my husband." But He has confirmed and repeated this challenge to speak over the last twenty years. And like Moses, I probably will be in training for at least forty more years! Every year He adds more depth to the calling, but it has never wavered from 'Speak for those who have no voice.' This book is another facet of that calling.

I am also a trailblazer, hard-working, tenacious, stubborn and not a quitter. I think differently than most people (I call it "thinking sideways"), so I often come up with new solutions to old problems. Some people settle for life at a 4, but I won't quit until I get to a 10. My passion is to make life easier for those who come after me. For timid followers or weary fighters, I pray that this book will take years off your journey. I have simplified my 20-year trek, because I want YOU to be free of this by next year. This book is not about me so much as it's about God's work in my life. I hope what worked for me will help you too, and I believe God will use my story to write yours. Don't just look to me for help, draw closer to Him.

I am eternally grateful for my small group that meets every Wednesday morning for over two years. They eagerly await the latest and greatest idea that God has given me. This book could not have been written without their stellar input, steady encouragement and support. Cris, Dianne, Heather, Kathleen, Sara, Sylvia—I can't wait to see where God takes us next!

Worship Song: *God Will Make a Way* by Don Moen[8]

---

[8] © 1990 Integrity's Hosanna! Music (Admin. by Capitol CMG Publishing (IMI))

Chapter 1
A Shattered Life

How can I be happy? How do I get out of the pain? Most of my life had been a search to find answers to those two questions. *Are my questions too big or are their answers too small?* I wondered for the hundredth time. *Can I find answers before the dark fog of confusion smothers me?* Sexual abuse—my worst pain but not my oldest—left my soul feeling like a pile of shattered glass. No matter how I struggled to fit the pieces together, the shards cut me and everyone who came near. The church's band-aid fixes couldn't stop the bleeding; I doubted God Himself could rescue me from the mess that was my life.

My husband Jim was the latest casualty. We would have been okay if he did things my way, but no matter how much I had asked him to change, he ignored me. I treated Jim like my parents had treated each other; just anger and sarcasm. I yelled at him and demanded he lead in our marriage then mocked his choices. I berated him for mistakes then called him lazy when he stopped trying. When I tore into him, he lied to me then avoided me. But I had offered him the biggest sacrifice I could. When I drank enough to numb the pain in my body and heart, I could have sex with him. Why wasn't that enough to make us okay? Why did I feel like killing myself every time we were together? His answers to my two questions were: Just be happy; make love more.

I was sick of it all; sick of the fights and the problems, sick of his running away and sick of trying. I had forced Jim to prove his love to me every day for ten years. I wanted to be loved, so why did I drive him away? I always landed curled up on the bed, crying and hugging the dog. At least she still loved me. *You don't deserve to be loved*, the voice in my head mocked.

I had given it my best and got nothing back. Looking for a way out of the pain, I told God, "This marriage was a big mistake. You wouldn't be so cruel as to hold me to it, would You? I give up. Let me out, and I'll never do it again." My two answers were: Leave Jim and do things my way. I moved out and put our house on the market.

The Pain of My Way

A few years later, Melanie, the pastor's wife, taught a Bible study that I thought was about friendship but had changed to explore the roles of husbands and wives. The more she talked, the more tricked I felt. I was looking for help, but this sure wasn't was it. When the lesson was over, I jumped up and slammed the door going out. But I thought about it all night. I felt guilty enough to try doing my part before walking away from my marriage and the church. When I called her the next morning, she agreed to meet me.

After an emotional women's retreat, Melanie had offered to listen if I ever wanted to talk, but I had dried my tears and said no thanks. 'No one needs to know our business' was our old family rule. So a year later, when I found myself at the end of hope, jammed into the corner of her saggy couch, I was beyond angry. Arms crossed over my chest, scanning the living room for signs of danger, ready to run, I hammered myself. *What are you doing here? Why did you call her? You're too far gone* the voices in my head taunted. *You're weak, you're a failure.* I didn't trust Melanie and didn't think she could help, but desperation will make you do crazy things. *She already thinks you're crazy. You just going to sit there? How will you look if you tell her everything?*

I didn't really want God or my husband; I just wanted a way out of the pain. I wanted what the lyrics of my favorite song promised: "A rock feels no pain and an island never cries."[9] I was a master at running away from pain: I could ignore it, pretend it away, drink it into silence, dump it on others and sidestep around it. But I didn't know how to stop feeling it (my real answer to the second question). My zero-pain-tolerance plan had never worked. An elaborate system of self-protective walls locked pain in my heart, like a scorched desert inside a fortress. I didn't know how to keep people from hurting me, so I always ran away. But the Bible said I should love people, which drove me to them. Then my failures were exposed and pain burned me again, so I withdrew. Then I felt guilty, so I stumbled back toward people. I wondered if my love was poison that caused all the pain. Could I love people but never be with them? Would that make God happy? Melanie waited while a battle raged inside. *Let's get this over with and go.*

Words of Despair

In a few words, I told her I hated being married and I didn't know who I was angrier with, Jim or myself. We had never heard about roles in marriage, so we never had a chance. I was a natural leader and I just railroaded him. Could she teach me more about them? Could she help me change? Those words tasted bitter coming out of my mouth, but I needed help. I had no idea how to be a good wife or help Jim be a godly man. She agreed to counsel me once a week. *See, she thinks you're hopeless,* the ugly voice said.

---

9 *I am a Rock*, Simon and Garfunkel, from the album *Sounds of Silence*, Columbia Records, January 1966.

She asked about my childhood. I hid my face and shared the agony of incest. She tried to draw me to God's comfort, but my heart raged against her unskilled hand. She made no sense. When she talked about faith, I heard *you don't meet up to the standards*. When she talked about sin, I heard *you've sinned too much*. She spoke of love, life, and hope but I knew only abuse, death, and despair. She had no idea what lies were in my head—*you'll never be free; you are beyond help; you'll never be a woman.* I believed them and thought everyone else did too.

Then she explained how she saw me. I was surprised that her normally soft voice was firm as she confronted me. No pity or coddling, no agreement that my hard life gave me the right to stay mad. I expected the sweet pastor's wife with an easy life to offer me quick-fix Bible verses. I didn't expect God to use my despair to get my attention. I didn't expect an answer to my two questions. And I didn't expect to hear the words that started my journey to maturity:

"Barb, you are the most bitter, angry woman I have ever met."

I glared at her, daring her to take it back. *How is this helping? This is not love, it's just judgment. I don't need this.* I felt like screaming "Leave me alone!" I wanted to run away, but something in my heart knew she was bang-on. While she prayed silently, I fought the truth of her words as pictures flashed in my mind. Bitter and angry woman. How did I get this way?

Snapshot 1: My family, age 5. Mom is always sick, even before she got pregnant with me at 42. I am unwanted, another drain on a poor family. Dad works, comes home, drinks beer and passes out on the couch, TV blaring. On hard stuff, he turns violent. I hate his anger and cruelty, the screaming fights. When he hits Mom, my sister gets her to her room. My job is to distract him. I become the target and turn off the feelings in my body. Mom hides in her room, takes tranquilizers to escape; says, "Just say he's right, don't argue." Learn how to live in chaos; lie, keep secrets, thrive at school.

Snapshot 2: Christmas Eve, age 8. Dad, drunk on hard stuff, comes into my room, says he has a gift I will really like. I see a hungry look in his eyes, and feel him pushing my knees apart. Later, I "come to," hiding in the closet, sobbing under a pile of clothes. My soul starts shattering. Start to burn between my legs with scalding water in the bathtub. Start humping my stuffed penguin. Start hearing voices in my head, pouring condemnation:

> *If only you could keep him from being angry, he wouldn't hurt you.*
> *If only you could keep him from drinking, he wouldn't hurt you.*
> *If only you had been born a boy, this would never have happened.*

If only you could keep your legs together, he wouldn't force himself on you. It's all your fault.

Snapshot 3: The Game, age 9. Try everything to keep the abuse from happening. My new answers are: keep Dad happy, tune out. *You can win, just figure out the rules*. I make it go fast, so I am winning. I'm ready for him; nightgown up, panties down. He says, "Don't ever tell. If you do, it will kill Mom." I don't tell. Keep Mom alive. *You don't have a right to exist.* Abuse ends at age 11. Don't know why. Maybe because my sister and I share a room. My period starts; maybe he was afraid I'd get pregnant. Hear the condemning voice for twenty years.

Snapshot 4: Childhood killed, age 11. Playing guns in summer with best friend and his cousin, they hold me down, pull down my clothes, and run their hands all over my body. Abuse is "out there" too, not just at home. There are no safe places. Furious at being used by everyone, not able to stop it, I vow I will never be stupid or vulnerable again, never be used again, never be a sexual being. Childhood is for sissies. Lock myself in bedroom all summer, refuse to eat, make nooses and hang my stuffed animals from the ceiling. I'm terrified of boys, confused about life as a girl. The voice plays a tape loop in my head: *You're not normal.*

Snapshot 5: Mean girl, teens. Forget the past, throw myself into sports. Wear baggy boy's clothes and control my own body. On the court or the field, anger shows up with a vengeance. Rage is success, intimidation and protection. *Yah, I'm only 5 feet tall, but I'll take you on; don't mess with me.* People call it passion and praise me for scoring goals and shutting down opponents. Anger makes things happen. Become top athlete at school as a junior. I like the approval. Graduate with honors, 1st in my class. I must be perfect. I now answer the two questions: Keep moving. Outrun the pain.

Snapshot 6: Summer job, age 19. Work with a Christian (another Barb). She invites me to church; I spike her o.j. with vodka. Sick of hearing about her Jesus. Challenge her to an all-or-nothing talk about God. "Give it your best shot," I say. Mom begs me not to listen. "I raised you to think for yourself, Barbara." Barb says her youth group is praying for me—that's unfair. She shows from the Bible that God loves me, will forgive all my sins and give me new life. Somebody loves me! I want that; I pray, give God my life. That week, filled with restless joy, I drive out into the country, and by my headlights, dance and sing to God with a clean heart. Share that with Sunday school class, see stony faces. Get lectured that dancing is a sin not tolerated in the church, and I should find more acceptable ways of proving my faith. I learn that God loves me but church ladies don't. Must be perfect here too? Have to keep secrets in church like at home? Are grace or rules more important? I thought giving my life to God would make me happy and take my pain away.

Snapshot 7: Trying on Normal, age 19. Start dating Jim, who knows Dad from the bar. He's good at sports, has great sense of humor, sweet, makes life fun. I enjoy his friendship, but refuse his offers of marriage, terrified of sex. Two years later, decide to act normal. Maybe marriage will make me happy. Dad walks me down the aisle, I wear white. I cry so hard, the pastor almost stops the wedding; each step closer to sex. Jim is kind and patient, I'm angry that sex is in my world. Resentment grows. Numb the pain by drinking, go back to old tricks to make it through—fantasize about violent sex then "go away," tune out.

Snapshot 8: Tidal wave, age 23. Visiting Dad one morning, find him dead on the kitchen floor. Mom had died three months before. I run screaming crazy down the street. After his funeral, the church ladies visit. I'm rage-filled—couldn't God have waited? *Didn't He want them to be saved?* They say, "It's a sin to be angry with God." I blow up. They don't have loved ones going to hell. I want to believe they are in heaven: my heart slams shut to God, my faith collapses. Quit church, drink wildly, start swearing, have an affair, mock Christians every chance I get. One night, I scream at God to let me go, feel like I pound on His chest until I'm worn out. I decide there is no happiness in the world. Life is only pain.

Snapshot 9: The prodigal returns, age 25. Tired of eating pig slop, I turn back to church. If I ask the questions right, maybe someone has answers. Sermons on missions and witnessing help me understand church but not life. Their answers are: Come to church. Tithe. Convicted by a sermon about sin of drinking to handle the pain of sex. Stop drinking cold-turkey; face the terror of intimacy sober. Re-live abuse every time. Cry, throw up, freeze, stop him in the middle, run out of the bedroom. Keep trying, desperate to get pregnant. After nine years of marriage, receive the sentence of infertility. I quit. Spend more time partying with ball team and less with my husband, glad to be off the hook about sex. Their answers to the questions: Drink, party and get laid (the straights); Drink, party, and come on over, Baby (the lesbians). Find the split life impossible to keep up. Hate being married. Move out.

Snapshot 10: Roller-coaster ride from hell, age 31. A gal from church and my ball team rooms with me, has no one else to turn to. I'm a lousy wife, but try to be a faithful friend. She blames me for her life. Unlike Jim (who avoided me), she returns my anger with cruel taunts and crushing words. Badgers me to divorce Jim. I refuse, she threatens then attacks—bangs my head on the floor, kicks, bruises my ribs, throws me out of my house naked. Get migraines from being beaten. I keep going back. Too afraid to kick her out. Held as a near-prisoner in my home. My shame is bottomless, fear is crushing. Think of suicide constantly. Have peace only when imagining the end of pain.

Snapshot 11: Church retreat, age 32. Don't know anyone, terrified to room with strangers, but I need to escape. The speaker, Dorie van Stone, gives searing testimony about childhood sexual abuse. Her two answers seem to be: Forgive and walk with God. My heart screams against it. *I will **never** forgive my dad.* But how is she okay? She loves God and has a good life. Can I ever have that? *You don't deserve love.* When I fall apart, Melanie offers to let me talk. I snub her kindness. *You have to figure this out alone.*

Today: Desperation, age 33. "Barb, you are the most bitter, angry woman I have ever met." Like a surgeon's scalpel, truth cuts before it heals. That day her honest words sliced through my excuses and self-protection and exposed the cancer in my soul. My life was a wreck—my marriage dissolved by anger; my friendships marred with abuse and distrust; my parents gone but still spewing poison through close-held secrets; my life crashing through too-tight controls; my dreams mocking me; my body barren; my faith crumbled and helpless.

My Right to Be Angry

"Bitter and angry." I hadn't seen that before; I was stuck on desperate and destroyed. In the quiet as Melanie prayed, I realized I blamed my pain, anger, heartache, and despair on everyone else. If my abuser had never hurt me, I would be okay. **Their** anger had started mine. My bitterness was their fault. I was angry because of abuse I had suffered at their hands. My innocence had been stolen and the course of my life forever changed by someone else's sin. I had every right to be angry!

But as the blade exposed the bad, I could see the good too: I wanted more—I wanted a real life. I wanted to be known as a child of the King, but my soul was stamped **Childhood Victim of Sexual Abuse.** I wanted freedom but my heart was shackled to a 20-year-old pain I couldn't outrun, ignore, or forget. It followed me into every relationship, every conversation, every waking and sleeping moment like a dead body strapped to my back. I was sick of examining the pain, re-living it and being defined by it, but I didn't know how to change. It was like I had given the "key" to my life—the key to my happiness—to my abuser, and until he repented and changed, my life was wrecked. (He had been dead for ten years but he still controlled my life. How despairing.) But God is not that cruel. He doesn't give our key to someone else; we each hold our own key.

Staying on the Sin Team?

For the first time, I heard that the core of my problem was not abuse. Melanie didn't like my dad's actions, but she didn't approve of mine either. She treated all sin as sin. It was like my dad ran a "Sin Team" and I had joined his team in my anger and hatred. I never wanted to be like him in any way: I didn't want to hurt people through selfishness or rage. When I saw that even though I had been hurt and broken, I had sinned too, everything became clear. Anger about the abuse was a big problem, but not the source. It wasn't my dad's rage that was eating me alive; it was mine. **My** choices tied me to the past; I stayed a victim of my dad's abuse and kept his sin cycle going. I was ruining my life by my own sinful choices. The key to my happiness was in my hands, but I refused to turn it. As this truth pierced my heart, I cried, "I want to change teams. I want to join the "God Team." How do I stop being bitter and angry? What do I do?" Quietly and firmly, Melanie told me the answer: "Forgive. Forgive all those who have sinned against you."

Feeling the weight of all my sin on my heart, I got off the couch and onto my knees. I asked God to show me any area I had not forgiven. I asked Him to deal with my sin too. Over the next two hours, He brought to my mind:

    Hurts that had poisoned my soul for years;
    Memories I had forgotten;
    Words that had broken my spirit;
    Physical violence that scarred my soul and my body;
    Cruelty I had poured on friends and enemies;
    Convictions I had ignored in my rush to avoid pain.

I let go of sins, little and big, and confessed my unforgiveness toward people for their sins. As I released them, God took them away, removed the stinger from my heart, and comforted me with His grace. He cut the root of bitterness out of my soul and washed my black heart clean. Then He softened me with soothing ointment of mercy. His peace surrounded me.

I got up from the couch a changed person. It was my first taste of freedom and my first touch by God's hand. I felt lighter, joyful and hopeful about life for the first time ever. The cords of despair were cut and the shards of my old life were being swept away. At church, people asked what had happened. They said my face had changed; it looked sweeter. One woman asked if I was in love? No, but God had lifted my head from shame.[10] His goal for my life was the same as the Israelites He rescued from slavery: to

---
10 Psalm 3:3

set me free to worship Him.[11] For the first time in all my years of searching, getting out of pain seemed small in comparison. The first real answer to my questions—the first one that worked—was: Forgive.

Define Trust

Trust in the Lord with all your heart. Lean not on your own understanding.
In all your ways acknowledge Him and He will make your paths straight. (Proverbs 3:5-6)

I thought forgiveness was hard, but at our next counseling session, Melanie named another problem: before I could love God, I needed to trust Him. Crazy! Had she listened at all? I didn't trust people I could see, how could I trust a God I couldn't? I thought I was being generous by letting God come along for the ride (to bail me out when I got stuck), but I was still the boss of me. Then she explained that God works through people. Great. For the ten years I had been a Christian, I saw religious people like the church ladies as legalistic and selfish. Could I trust my unwilling husband or my evil roommate to be used by God? All the pain in my life came from people and she wanted me to trust them and call it God? Terrifying.

But I could see she trusted God and loved people without fear. She tried to change my picture of God by saying, "God is your Heavenly Father." I told her *father* wasn't a good word at all—I saw an angry tyrant who abused me and destroyed my life. She tried again, "Jesus is your big Brother."[12] I hated that too, because my brother, who was ten years older than me, had tormented me mercilessly and mocked my childish attempts to show love to my parents.

On the third try, she said, "The Holy Spirit is a Counselor." I said, "You mean, like you? Kind and patient?" She smiled and said, "Yes, even better, because He knows everything about you and loves you completely." I could accept that, because a counselor was the first person to help me get out of pain. I found an A.W. Tozer book, The Attributes of God,[13] and started meditating on the names of God. Studying each name for a few days or a week expanded my picture of God. Healer—I really needed that one. Provider—Oh yah, I had infinite needs. Shepherd—weird. My Ruler—no way. My Comforter—that one I could stand on.

I started to see God act in new ways, and worked on my prayer life. I started a Journal, where I wrote PRAYERS and the dates they were answered. It had a SORRY part, to confess my sins and failures. I wrote on this page every day, which made me wonder if I was making any progress. But I wrote something in the THANKS part too, listing things

---
11 Exodus 4:22&23
12 Romans 8:29
13 A.W. Tozer, The Attributes of God, Christian Publications, (c)1997

I was thankful for. The fourth part was called HELP, for things I needed. Melanie said to write everything, so I poured my heart out to God. Talking to God got easier.

In spite of Melanie's explanations, I didn't trust God because of His omnipresence or omniscience or sovereignty (the big words that mean God is everywhere, all the time; He sees and knows everything; and He works everything according to His good plan). I trusted Him because of little things: He wanted to hear me talk; He listened without anger; He answered my prayers; He got "small enough" for me; our relationship was based on love, not force. I built trust on these little bricks of God's love. Then He did bigger things. He answered my prayer about whether to get baptized (yes). He moved my roommate out (she got married). He got me a good job. Trusting gradually became my new habit.

Desperate Trust

I finally trusted God's goodness enough to ask Him the BIG question; the one about my marriage. It had been two years and I needed to make a decision. I begged God to let me divorce Jim. I pleaded, groveled, reasoned and whined, but God was a brick wall. Shaking in fear, I faced a choice to trust God with my life and not control Him.

One Saturday, I "had it out" with God. "Ok God, I will do this your way. I don't want to go back to Jim, but if you say, 'Go,' I will." I read in the Old Testament until Ecclesiastes, chapter 5 stopped me: *When you make a vow to God, do not delay in fulfilling it...It is better not to vow than to make a vow and not fulfill it. Do not let your mouth lead you into sin. And do not protest to the temple messenger* (or pastor's wife), *"My vow was a mistake."*[14] That clearly meant honoring my marriage vows. I wasn't happy, but I had asked and God had answered: Stay Married. Trust Me.

I phoned Jim and told him what happened. I said I was willing to give it 100% and asked if he wanted to work on our marriage. I was stunned when he said yes. He moved into my home the following Friday but I didn't tell a soul. By Sunday, Melanie had heard that we were back in the same house (small town). She hugged me and said, "God is going to bless you so much for your obedience!" I lacked her enthusiasm but I was committed to try.

Determined to Find a New Me

Melanie had agreed to help me be a godly wife, and over the next year she showed me how <u>she treated her</u> husband, our Pastor Ken. Jim and I spent a long weekend holiday

---

14 Ecclesiastes 5:4-6a

with their family. As I listened to them talk to each other, I thought it was an act because we were watching. They were kind and encouraged each other. They solved problems and laughed together. I waited for the real stuff but that was it.

God's Spirit convicted me that my words to Jim were nothing like that. I was critical and bitter, cutting and unloving. So when we got home from the trip, I made a jar called my "DRA" jar—Dirty Rotten Attitude. Every time I said something negative, Jim could raise his hand to signal my DRA. I couldn't argue or defend it, just put a dollar in the jar and change my words. Since I am a tightwad, I hated spending the money, so I quickly cleaned up my act. I have to admit that one time, I was so mad at him, I took out a $10 bill, popped it open in front of the DRA jar and said, "This is going be worth every penny," and started yelling at him. But an amazing thing happened. As I spoke kindly, Jim spoke kindly back. God graciously allowed us to adopt a baby boy, who we named Robbie. God was blessing all over.

Jim and I both worked hard on our marriage. My homework was to love him as an enemy: *Love your enemies, do good to those who hate you…bless those who curse you… pray for those who spitefully use you….*"[15] I made him great lunches so the guys at work would think he was blessed. I wrote him notes that said "I ♥ you," because I couldn't say, "I love you." I prayed for God to give him a good wife, because I couldn't pray *make me a good wife*. I fearfully walked toward sexual intimacy, praying frantically. I told myself all the while *this isn't your dad, this is Jim. Jim is kind and doesn't want to hurt you.* It helped little by little. At least I wasn't drinking, I told myself.

Desperate to be Done

I was the first sexually abused woman Melanie had counseled. She saw that I needed more help than she could offer. She only found Christian psychology books, which I devoured. Inside Out by Larry Crabb revolutionized our counseling. We studied The Wounded Heart[16] every semester for years. The pastors preached the 12-Step program (Alcoholics Anonymous) from the pulpit, with some Bible verses sprinkled on top.

Even though my biggest changes came from doing it God's way (forgiveness and trusting Him), I was drawn to the quick fixes psychology offered. I thought I was pretty much healed anyway. The worst was over, and I didn't want to work hard anymore. Wouldn't God be merciful to me now (look how obedient I had become)? Hadn't I already suffered enough? I put myself on cruise control.

---
15 Luke 6:27&28
16 Inside Out by Larry Crabb, NavPress, Colorado Springs, 1988
The Wounded Heart, by Dan Allendar, NavPress, Colorado Springs, 1990

For me, Christian psychology was like an antiseptic ointment for the pain—it offered some insight and protection, but it couldn't heal the wound. It took me a little farther in my journey but it failed to "finish the job" and take me to maturity. I found it a pretty substitute for the hard work of soul-searching and sacrifice I still needed to do. Any system that encourages you to focus on yourself and your needs rather than on God cripples you sooner or later.

Desperate to Make a Difference

I wanted to help, so after a year of counseling, Melanie and I started a ministry for sexually abused women. I did individual counseling, group counseling and phone counseling. I ended up carrying a staggering amount of responsibility. Because I had been abused and she hadn't, I was the "go-to" person at church for anyone in crisis: I felt like a magnet for hurting women. I sounded like a one-stringed guitar, playing the same song over and over—mostly about the power of forgiveness. Within a few months, our small church had over 100 women in weekly support groups.

Because I was willing to talk about sexual abuse, the hurting women admired me and brought their friends, but the other women resented, feared and criticized me. Gossip flew about my relationship with Melanie, and after two years, her husband pulled her out of the ministry, saying she and I were "too close." Without her strength and leadership, I spiraled down into the old pit of depression and anger. I couldn't carry the work alone, and the hurting women were drowning, taking me with them. No one helped me; I couldn't help anyone, least of all myself. The ministry shriveled and died of neglect and the hurting women scattered to the cold winds.

I had trusted Melanie and she abandoned me like everyone else had. I was devastated. I thought I had obeyed God. Where had I failed to love her well and support her vision? Where I had missed the signals of discontent? Had I even for a minute been selfish? I had done all I knew how to do. I couldn't function in this amount of pain. I tried to forgive, forget, confess, thank God, bless my enemy with my words, and ask her what I had done wrong, but nothing helped. For a year, I dropped off my son at church and went to a coffee shop for two hours. I had one or two good days in a month but I cried all the rest. Jim didn't know how to help me. I started praying about moving away from that church and the painful memories there. God moved even through that situation.

Desperate for God

Two years later, God's providence allowed me to visit a church in Albuquerque, New Mexico with a friend. I felt the Spirit's presence when I walked into the building. My heart soared to hear the Word of God preached with power and conviction. My friend whispered, "It's like at home we are just barely alive, being fed intravenously." I felt spiritually anorexic, starving on my diet of Christian Psychology. The Bible-based teaching gave me a taste of real food and a driving hunger to know God. I wanted God more than anything else. On the first leg of the flight home, I couldn't stop crying and finally asked God why. God said, "Because you are leaving your home. Albuquerque is your home." I started my quest to move there.

It wasn't easy for a Canadian to move to the States. I had to have a U.S. degree to get a job. I was a Canadian Chartered Accountant (C.A.), which meant little in the U.S. I prayed and studied for two years, and eventually passed an exam to become a CPA. God graciously let our house sell; I found a job in Albuquerque and rented an apartment. We were going!

In June of 1998, I tearfully left my husband and son behind to pack, and flew to Albuquerque. In addition to leaving my home, my familiar culture and all my relatives, I found life in America overwhelming. Americans were pushy and our mega-church of 12,000 adults was bigger than my hometown. We knew only one person there (and she was mad at me). We had agreed to stay one year and I was determined to tough it out, but by October, both Jim and Robbie were angry and unhappy and I was struggling to keep a positive attitude in front of them. I poured out my heart to God. *I am lonely and lost. Please help me.* Two days later, I was invited to a Bible study called Self-Confrontation[17] that changed my life.

If I would have known what I was in for that first night, I never would have gone, but God had better plans. The ten women were all hungry to grow and change. Cris, who co-wrote this book, was the teacher and during the four-month class, she became my counselor. In those tough few months, God cut out roots of selfish, childish, wrong and psychologized thinking and replaced them with dependence on the Bible alone. The Word was in my sights every minute; it challenged me and changed me. I say I began life in two new countries at once—the U. S. and the Bible.

Good Things Out of Desperation

Recently when I shared my story at a church conference, a man came up to me afterwards and said, "I feel so sorry for you. I can't imagine the ways it has affected you." I said honestly, "Yes, it has hurt immensely, but let me tell you how it has helped me too." Then he honored me by listening to understand my history and rejoice in my freedom.

---
17 Now called Step-by-Step Discipleship published by Biblical Counseling Foundation, Indio, CA © 1998

Mark chapter 5 tells a story about a woman who was sick for twelve years with an issue of blood. She had spent all her money on doctors, with no relief. She was a reject of society for all those years, unclean and unwanted, untouchable and feared, until she heard Jesus teach. She believed He had the power to heal her, and if she could just touch Him, she would be clean. She pushed through the crowd, intent on one thing—reaching Him. When she touched the hem of His garment, she received her healing. She didn't make Jesus unclean by touching Him—just the opposite. His holiness made her clean, overcoming her dirtiness.

At that moment, Jesus was in a crowd, surrounded by many people. They had also heard Him teach and followed closely enough to touch Him. But only one person was healed—the woman who had nothing to lose and everything to gain; the woman who was desperate enough to keep on going; the woman who defied convention, crowd pressure, the disciples' disapproval, shame, fear of exposure, and her history of failure to pursue her hope. Desperation took her to the end of herself and drove her to Jesus' feet to be healed.

I was a desperate woman too. Pain and grief drove me to God, but His sweet love has held me. Many Christians have a "good enough" relationship with God; I guess they don't need His touch like I did. He saved me from myself and my prisons. He heard the cries of my heart—to grow up and be strong, to lose the anger, and to help hurting women—and answered them in hundreds of gracious ways. He patiently taught me His life, leading and encouraging me. I no longer want a life without pain; I want a life with Him, no matter what the cost, no matter what the trial. I want God and God alone. Desperately.

Bottom Lines:

1. Desperation can force you off the old path, onto a new one.
2. There is always hope ahead—keep going, keep looking, keep asking.
3. God is probably not who you think He is.
4. God will break through your desperation to save you.

Discussion Questions:

1. Do you have a tape loop or voices in your mind? What do they say? Are they condemning and harsh or gentle and encouraging? Bring them to the light, either in a journal or a group discussion. Ask God whether that voice is His or the enemy's.

2. What do you really want in life? Are you desperate for God? Or more desperate for that thing?

3. If someone described you as the most _____ person they have ever met, what would they say? Ask someone. What would you like them to say? What is one way you can change?

4. Do you have a pain you can't "outrun, ignore or forget?" What is it? Write about it in a journal for 20 minutes or share in a small group for 5-10 minutes. Is anything good coming out of that?

5. Have you been bumped off the path and had your innocence stolen? How have you responded on the "Sin Team?" How have you responded on "God's Team?"

6. In what small ways do you trust God? What are some little foundational blocks you see Him building in your life? Look for these little blocks every day, and write about them in your journal.

7. Write in the PRAYER, THANKS, SORRY, and HELP parts of your journal every day. Record answers to the HELP prayers when they come.

Anything for the Poofy file? Anything you didn't get, or need more explanation about? Write in your journal, then pray—wait and watch for God's explanation.

A Word to the Traveler's Friend:

1. Listening with love is a tremendous gift you can give. God gave Barb great gifts in people who listened without trying to fix her. One friend read a sexual abuse book early on and helped her connect dots. Another told her of a childhood incident she had forgotten, when she stayed overnight at Barb's house. When Barb told her about the abuse, her actions that night made sense. One friend listened to the entire story (the first time she had told the whole thing) and cried for her. Listen to understand. Gently help connect some dots, or ask if two things are connected. The younger the abuse happened, the more she will need to be given words and word pictures (connect what they know to what they can't express), explanations and connections. When she shares her story, reaffirm your love and care for her. Tell her how brave she was to speak, and that you think she's amazing for having survived. Encourage her with kindness.

2. There may be a very good reason for your friend's anger, hatred, helplessness or depression. What in her past has contributed to these reactions? Pray for her heart change. Write down what you see, so you can remember it in the coming months.

3. Have a biblical vision for your friend. Commit to praying and/or fasting one day a week for them (you don't have to tell them). Some examples:

   I pray for my friend to endure, to be mature and complete, lacking nothing. (James 1:4)
   I pray that our friendship would be founded on God's holy agape love.
   I pray for my friend to be free from old prisons and walk in newness of Christ.
   I pray for my friend to know the height and depth of God's love for him. (Ephesians 3)
   I pray for our marriage to reflect God's love for His Bride. (Song of Solomon)

4. Remember that you will hear mountains of pain. You have to quickly take it to God, instead of carrying it on your shoulders. Forgive the abuser/perpetrator/sinner quickly and don't carry the hurt out of the room where you meet.

Worship Song: *Chasing* by Glenn Packiam[18]

---

[18] © 2005 Vertical Worship Songs (Admin. by Capitol CMG Publishing (IMI)) on album Portable Worship 4

Chapter 2
A New Road to a New Destination

Pastor Wayne and his wife Dawn were friends of mine who loved to canoe. Wayne's parents knew how their children enjoyed it, so one day they also rented a canoe and went along. Wayne's dad was 6' 2" and mom about 5' 5" (for you non-canoers, this is a crucial fact!). It takes skill to move forward, because both people have to pull at the same time with the same amount of force or they end up going in circles, like they did.

Dawn said, "Wayne, can you teach them how to do this?"

He said, "They aren't ready yet." Mom and Dad paddled in circles while Dawn urged Wayne to help them. His answer was always the same, "They're not ready yet."

After 30 minutes, his Dad finally asked, "Wayne, how do you do this?" Wayne said, "Now they're ready!"

This describes how most people respond to a need to change. We do what is familiar until frustration forces us to find a different way. For me, that time came when Jim and I were separated. My pastor suggested reading one chapter of Proverbs every day to gain wisdom. I doubted that the Bible had any answers for my problems, but I was desperate. I read pretty faithfully for months, when one day God spoke to me through the text. Proverbs 12:1 looked like this to my eyes:

Whoever **loves discipline** loves knowledge, but he who **hates correction** is **STUPID**.

A few days later, I read Proverbs 28:26 which looked like this:

He who **trusts himself** is a **FOOL**, but he who walks in wisdom is kept **safe**.

I was stunned. How could words on a page score such a direct hit?[19] Had God called me stupid? But the verses kept nagging me:

Do I love knowledge? (Yes)

---
[19] Because the Bible is *living and active, able to divide thoughts and intentions of the heart.* (Hebrews 4:12)

Do I love being corrected? (No)
Am I being stupid? (I don't think so)
Do I only trust myself? (You bet)
Do I receive wisdom from people? (No)
Do I accept correction as being God's love? (Never)

I heard God say *your problem is that you hate correction.* Well, I did think no one had the right to tell me what to do. Correction is difficult for everyone, but with an abusive history, the idea is super-charged, twisted by the abuser's hand. My dad disciplined me with screaming threats and pounding fists. How could anyone love that? "How do I do this?" I asked God. *Do it My way.* That was so different from what I wanted to do, I made up a 180° Rule: Do the opposite of what you want to. I tried hard to trust people and take input, but after months I was no different. Anger, pride, vengeance and fear of pain still crippled me. I even struggled to accept Melanie's advice without punishing her. I listened silently until the last five minutes of each session, when I poured out my despair. I left feeling more hopeless every week. Driving myself went nowhere. I was paddling on the other side of the boat, but going in circles.

God was breaking down my self-protective walls, and I didn't want Him to. By the fourth session, I was ready to fight (a bad 180°). I wasn't stupid, and Melanie didn't get it. I challenged her and justified my walls. Who was she to criticize me? If everyone else knew better than I did, why didn't somebody help me? It was a battle session. Finally, she looked me straight in the eye and said:

"Barb, if you're so right and I'm so wrong, why is your life such a mess and mine is so blessed?"

How's Your Garden Growing?

I answered with a word picture. In the garden of life, it seemed like she was given a garden tractor, and all I had was a broken spoon. I scraped in the dirt and turned up rocks, while she puttered past bunches of roses and daisies. Her relationships worked, her children loved her, the church people admired her. But I was not blessed. I labored but got nothing; no blooms, no vegetables, no fruit. My relationships were wrecked. The church people avoided me. Thirty-three years of my life/my way had left me stuck and suicidal. My 180° rules weren't working. I was sick of my broken spoon. I wanted her life and I wanted a tractor![20] She said:

---

20 People who grow up in good homes just use good tools. They can't explain why their life works and you can't guess the secret. You want to knock them off their tractors and kill them with your broken spoon!

"If you keep on doing what you've always done, you'll always get what you've always got."

I hated what I "always got," so I listened. She said I could be angry about the abuse, but it wouldn't help me get over it. I could resent her tractor but that wouldn't help me get one. I had a choice— keep digging with the spoon, or drop it and do something different.

Facing Up to My Wrongs

For years, I had asked God to make me a better Christian, but I thought He could teach me without ever telling me I was wrong. I ran away from correction into the ditch of self-loathing—self-hatred, punishment and condemnation. I didn't ask for help, so I never reached the "paddling forward" part. Criticism (as I saw it) meant I wasn't perfect, I hadn't earned love and, worst of all, someone had seen my failure. Anything I couldn't do perfectly, I didn't do.

Her quiet rebuke made me face my biggest enemy: myself. She said our Christian life starts when we admit we see God and ourselves wrongly—we are sinners and God's enemies, until we stop fighting Him and accept His gift; the substitutionary death of Jesus. That is the hardest failure to admit. Why does it seem harder to be corrected over much smaller things? As one gal said, "Going into despair is easier than facing up to yourbad."

Our sin is no surprise to God and failure isn't a dead-end for His plan. There is hope for our failures, the way out in Proverbs 12:1: admit we are wrong and receive correction from people, knowing it's often from God, then change.

Hop In

Imagine you are driving and you get sideswiped by a semi carrying a load of other people's sin. Your car swerves, rolls and lands on its roof in the ditch. You climb out of the car shaken and bruised, but instead of recognizing the car is totaled, you try to push, pull, drag and roll it home. When you are exhausted, Jesus pulls up in a brand-new red Mustang convertible and says, "Hop in!" You run over, excited to own such a gorgeous car, but Jesus smiles and says, "I'll drive."

Dragging your broken life never makes you righteous before God. Instead of trusting that car to get you to the goal, just admit it is trashed and accept the new one. The Apostle Paul said, "You foolish Galatians! ... *Did you receive the Spirit by observing the law, or by believing what you heard? ... After beginning with the Spirit,* **are you now trying to**

attain your goal by human effort? (emphasis mine)"[21] Some of us would rather drag our ruined life than let God drive.

Back on the Right Track

> **Correction: 1**. The act of correcting; **of bringing back**, from error or deviation, to a just standard, to truth, rectitude (morality), justice or propriety (decency); the correction of opinions or manners. (*All Scripture is profitable for... correction*, 2 Tim. 3:16.) **2.** Reduction of faults or errors; as the correction of a book; **3.** That which is substituted in place of what is wrong. **4.** That which is intended to cure faults; punishment; discipline; chastisement. (*Withhold not correction from the child*, Prov. 23:5). In scriptural language, whatever tends to correct the moral conduct, and bring back from error or sin, as afflictions. (*My son, despise not the chastening of the Lord nor be weary of his correction*. Prov. 3)[22] (emphasis mine)

From God's perspective, correction is a good word. It can cure faults and errors, change behavior from wrong to right and bring us back to truth, godly actions and decency. If your car got sideswiped and ended up driving in the ditch, would it be wrong to "correct" your path and get back on the road? No. Believing a lie (living in error) is like being sideswiped.

When you leave truth, you gradually head off course. What if you were driving to a town 400 miles away and steered off the road by just one degree (a deviation)? The longer you drove off-road, the more trouble you would be in—driving across traffic, through fences; up mountains or down gullies. And you would never get to the right destination! God doesn't send postcards, so He uses people to bring you back on track.

Melanie set a great example. Because she taught without punishing or rejecting, I saw correction in new ways. Instead of defending myself and building thicker walls, I could admit my sins. Did I trust God enough to let Him correct me? Could I believe He still loved me? The self-protective walls had to fall before input could get in. *Ready to learn?* I heard God ask me. When I left the session after Melanie confronted me, I started the "Barb Revolution," declaring war on my old thoughts, words and actions. It went deeper than the 180° Rule. I asked God every day:

> *How do I hear Your voice in the middle of correction?*
> *How can I accept criticism and not punish myself?*

---
21 Galatians 3:1
22 Webster's 1828 Dictionary definition of *correction*, http://1828.mshaffer.com/

Why do I have to trust? It's so much safer to protect myself.
So I'm wrong; show me how to do it right.
Is that an "old Barb" thought?
What is a different way to think about this problem?

God's Ways are Not My Ways

Hold onto instruction; guard it with your life. (Prov. 4:13)

After a few months, I had made progress taking my counselor's input. So God tested me. One day, my roommate verbally stabbed me in the back. Screaming swear words, she shamed and exposed me, cut me without mercy. I cried to God, "She said _____ and _____ and _____! She's so mean, she just wants to destroy me. It's not fair!"

His quiet answer was: *"Is it true?"* I was shocked. Who cares if it was true, it hurt! "She was mean. Her words cut me."

God gently asked the question again, *"Is it true?"*

"But God, she's not living right either."

"I know, but is it true?"

"Well, yes, it was true—but look how she said it! It wasn't loving, it didn't build me up."

Then God unfolded the lesson. I didn't realize that I only accepted correction from someone who liked me and never hurt me. I only wanted sweet words wrapped in a fuzzy pink pillow with hearts on it. My standard wasn't truth; it was painlessness. A hint of pain stopped input fast. To reword Proverbs 27:6, I wanted the *fake kisses of a lying enemy, but no wounds, even from a truthful (faithful) friend.*[23]

Truth often hurts, like a surgeon's knife, but it can also reveal and repair, bringing healing. My angry roommate was a tool in God's hands, uncovering something He wanted me to address. I didn't have to love the pain, but I couldn't run from the truth. Pastor Wayne Barber said, "Pray that God's truth will be delivered by someone who loves you. Love is an anesthetic … and soothes the sting of the cut."[24] If you reject the message because you don't like the messenger, the motive, or the delivery, you will have to repeat the trial (I call

---
23 Prov. 27:6 *The kisses of an enemy may be profuse, but faithful are the wounds of a friend.*
24 Pastor Wayne Barber, at Hoffmantown Church, sermon in 2005.

this "reruns"). Look past the poor delivery; hang on to the core of truth. Forgive the person and choose to change.

Gentle Correction

Do not rebuke a mocker or he will hate you; Rebuke a wise man and he will love you.
Instruct a wise man and he will be wiser still;
Teach a righteous man and he will add to his learning. (Prov. 9: 8-9)

Proverbs 9 defines those who can receive correction and challenges those who don't. Wise men—those who love correction—become wiser and wiser, but mockers hate it. They scoff or criticize or mouth off when they should be listening.

When you are ready to receive input, new ideas as positive instead of life-threatening, you see God's gentle course corrections all the time. You are like a pilot who constantly makes minor adjustments to allow for wind and air pockets, while making steady progress toward the destination.[25] Once you change from "I am right" to "I will receive input," you will see new ideas weave through the day naturally. Input gives you new information, helps you grow spiritually,[26] and helps believers build up each other in love. New truths deliver us from deception, confusion and bondage (John 8:32—*truth will set you free*) while giving *power, love and a sound mind* (2 Timothy 1:7). Correction becomes helpful, instead of the worst thing that can happen to you.

I'm Better than That

One day, I asked Melanie about friendships. I didn't have friends partly because I couldn't tell whether people were good or bad. Several verses in Proverbs handed me some new tools.[27] As I was leaving, her young daughter burst into the kitchen crying, "How do you tell a good person from a bad person?"

Shame flooded my soul as I ran to my car, sobbing. Satan screamed, *"You fool, asking the same question as an 8-year-old."* I felt cold condemnation crush my new knowledge. But God spoke quietly, *"Which is more foolish? To blame yourself for not learning at age 8 when no one was teaching or refusing to learn at age 33 when someone is?"* Then, into the storm of my emotions He said:

"Put your pride in your back pocket and sit on it."

---

[25] Concept from counselor Dr. Marty Goering, Albuquerque, NM, Sunday School class at Hoffmantown Church.
[26] Proverbs 27:17, like iron sharpening iron
[27] Fools, gossips, scoffers and angry people are bad friends, also sexually immoral people and liars

I had a chance to learn and I was going to refuse because I was embarrassed? True, I was asking eight-year-old questions. But I really didn't know the answers. *If my parents had been good, I would have gotten this when I was a child.* Would I miss my chance because I felt stupid, and still not know the answer in ten or twenty years? I chose to squash my pride and hang onto my new wisdom.

Feedback

A few months later, I challenged myself to ask people how they saw me. I wrote asking some friends for an honest evaluation. The answers were split in half; the women said I was kind, great to work with and considerate, but the men's responses were shocking. They saw me as hostile, stubborn and angry. At least I knew how far I had to go.

I didn't know what I didn't know, but I knew I could learn. My thoughts were changing:

> *I want to receive truth as God's love and care.*
> *I want to have a heart to respond quickly.*
> *I want to be conformed to God's image.*
> *I want to be open to relationships, even if they include correction.*
> *The hurt is only temporary, the change can be eternal.*

Humbly, I admitted Melanie was right: when I changed what I did, I changed what I got. Failures changed to surprising victories, especially in my marriage. Receiving correction affected the way I solved problems, received praise and handled my emotions. Over the next year, I saw that when I stopped listening, God used stronger voices or harder natural consequences to break my stubbornness. His truth often hurt but it also was taking me to the new life I wanted. In that year, I saw correction come in many positive ways. Here are twelve different ways I received correction that changed my life:

Teaching

Teach me, O Lord, to follow your decrees and I will keep them to the end. (Ps. 119:33)

When we are abused as children, we stop learning and growing and get stuck in childish thinking. We cover up instead of catching up. We miss basic lessons because we are busy surviving, or the lessons weren't taught in our home. We think everyone lives that way and some people get over it faster. We don't know we are ignorant, so God works through people to teach us what we need to know.

For example, because my dad drank, guests never visited our house so I didn't know how to have friends over. Melanie suggested asking someone who made me feel comfortable as a guest to teach me. My patient friend showed me how to set a table and welcome friends, how to offer a variety of food and good conversation, even how to "help" them leave when they stayed too long. At first, I was humiliated to admit I didn't know something so simple, but I listened and learned a new skill.

Are you able to learn from good teachers? You wouldn't harass a 1st grader for not knowing times tables or cursive writing. They will learn in time. Even if you feel like a kindergartener with relationships, today you have the chance to learn new things. The Holy Spirit teaches God's truths.[28] God says *Listen and learn, child. Practice every day. Keep going, don't give up, and you will pass this grade.*

Discipline

Say "No" to godless living and sinful pleasures and live in this evil world with wisdom, righteousness, and devotion to God. (Titus 2:12, New Living Bible)

In order to help me escape the violent relationship with my roommate, Melanie required me to cut off all contact for six months. She said if I talked to my roommate even once, she would not invest any more time in me. It was hard. I felt powerless against my former friend who kept tricking me, inventing problems and crying for help. But I felt stronger every time I said no or refused to give in to her threats. Melanie's stance made it easier for me to walk away from my old life. Through her ultimatum, I could **hear** the right choice for the first time. It was my first experience of being disciplined in love. I gradually regained control of my life, then at the end of the period, my roommate refused to meet with me.

The idea of discipline is to say "no" to sinful, harmful things and "do" to godly things; we separate from the world's ways, and do what is right. The goal of correction is self-discipline, so we can control our own actions. When we know good thoughts, words and actions from bad ones, we can practice the good, even when it's hard or our feelings are screaming.[29]

Correction and discipline are good things that God does out of love. ... *My son (or daughter), do not make light of the Lord's discipline, and do not lose heart when He rebukes you, because the Lord disciplines those He loves and He punishes everyone He accepts as a son.*[30] Even when we choose to sin, God shows mercy in the consequences.

---
[28] John 14:17
[29] Hebrews 5:14
[30] Hebrews 12:5-10

He has my good in mind and wants me to be like Jesus. (Rom. 8:28-9)
He wants me to grow and gives many chances to do things right.
He doesn't delight in my failures, He grieves. (Ephesians 4:29)
He loves me enough to say stop when I am doing it wrong.

When you accept correction from words, you won't have to be disciplined. But when we refuse correction, the road becomes hard and ends in destruction:

Stern discipline awaits him who leaves the path;
    he who hates correction will die. (Proverbs 15:10)
He who ignores discipline despises himself…. (Proverbs 15:32a).

I'm convinced if I would have gone back to living with my abusive roommate, I would have felt that stern discipline and suffered mental and physical harm, maybe even death. Instead, I had a period of spiritual growth and freedom.

Because my parents never disciplined me, I had no idea how to discipline my son when he headed into the terrible twos. Overnight, he wanted life his way. I asked Melanie, who showed on my open hand how hard to spank him with a wooden spoon. Ouch!! I watched her hold her children on her knee, explain what they did wrong and tell them she loved them enough to correct them. I saw her spank them until they cried (3-4 swats) and comfort them until they stopped. They prayed, asked for forgiveness, then she reaffirmed her love. She disciplined her children so they would not repeat wrong behavior. Love carried them through the temporary sting of correction.

Helping

Correction can be loving and helping, like my "pantyhose theology." Imagine you go into the bathroom at church, but you come out with your skirt accidentally tucked in your pantyhose and your glory showing. As you walk through the lobby, is it more loving for a friend to tell you, "Let me help you … your skirt is tucked in your pantyhose," or ignore it and let you walk down to the front of the church all exposed?

If my sins are hanging out for everyone to see, I want to be corrected so I can cover up and walk right. God the Holy Spirit points out sin[31] and helps us change.[32] He leads into righteousness, and shows how and where to walk, often speaking through people. When I listen to that still, small voice inside[33]—even if I don't understand—it always turns out better than ignoring it and doing it my way.

---

31 John 16:8
32 John 14:16
33 1 Kings 19:11-12

He is more gentle with me than I am with myself—because there's no condemnation for those in Christ.[34] I love that.

People have helped me in hundreds of ways. I have had many chances to admit, "I don't know how to do this, can you help me?" like finally learning to cook at age 47. I'm not a great cook, but I can feed my family and I'm not afraid of poisoning people anymore. Cris wondered why I was stubborn about some issues, but not about others, then walked with me to change and growth. I want to be a better witness of God's love and power and I'm not offended when people say, "Barb, your sin is showing."

Counseling

...a son will be given to us ...and His name will be called Wonderful Counselor, Mighty God, Eternal Father, Prince of Peace. (Isaiah 9:6)

My first positive picture of God was as a Counselor: He wanted me to have peace, joy and blessing but my sin interfered, so He corrected me. I accepted Melanie's correction because she wanted me to have a better life. God as a Counselor also meant:

> He was patient and good and fair.
> He didn't reject me or condemn me. (Rom. 8:1)
> He had solutions for my problems.
> He gave me wisdom and didn't judge me. (James 1:5)
> He walked alongside me and gave me choices.
> He wanted to communicate with me about everything.
> He wasn't an angry, punishing control freak.

Direction

And your ears will hear a word behind you, "This is the way, walk in it," whenever you turn to the right or the left. (Isaiah 30:21)

I knew all the streets and most of the houses in the small town in Manitoba where I grew up. I could walk anywhere in 30 minutes. I had never read a map; I just knew the town. But in Albuquerque, I was always lost. The freeway terrified me and I could barely drive anywhere in 30 minutes. After I met Cris, who had lived there for twenty years, I could call on my cell phone and ask, "How do I drive where I'm going?"

---
34 Romans 8:1-4

(Once she quietly said, "Lock your doors and make a U-turn.") What a difference it made, getting directions from a native. I knew I would get home safely.

I was saved when I was 19, so abuse, anger, sin and selfishness paved familiar roads in my soul. But I always felt lost. Correction showed me I was driving the wrong way and needed to take a different road. When I started trying to obey God, I knew what He wanted me to do. Whatever I *used* to do, I made a U-turn, and that was usually the right way. The Holy Spirit is like the ultimate GPS. No matter where we start, He can get us home. He knows what's up ahead and the best way to get through it.

Protection

You have been a shelter for me, a strong tower from the enemy. (Psalm 61:3)

I once worked for a chicken farm and got to see baby chicks hatching. It was fascinating as they slowly pecked their way out of the shell. One struggled so hard, I wanted to reach down and help. I had the ability. Wouldn't it be loving? The farmer said no, the chick had to break out of the egg by itself. As it pecks, its neck muscles get stronger, but if I helped, the muscles would be too weak to hold up its head and it would die.

We need to build our spiritual muscles so they won't snap in the real world. We try to manage our outside circumstances (stay inside our shell) so that we never get hurt, but God gives us inside promises that deal with our spirit. Psalm 121:7 says *the Lord will protect you from all evil*, but before we argue that He doesn't protect us from ALL danger or keep us safe from ALL harm, the next verse says *He will keep your **soul***. My spiritual life is hid with Christ, not my physical body. God protects our hearts (an inside promise) even if our bodies are attacked.[35] Truth (Ps. 40:11), discretion (Prov. 2:11) and wisdom (Prov. 4:6) also protect us. God protects His faithful ones (Prov. 2:8), the just (Ps. 37:28), those that love God and call on Him (Ps. 91:4-5). God often protects me from other people's sin and from my own bad choices.

I thought if I put my hand inside a lion cage, someone who loved me would stop me. Instead, maybe God wanted me to obey warnings, or run to Him for comfort. I wanted a formula like God's Love + Protection = Nothing Bad Happening. I doubted His love and didn't value His promise to keep my soul. But I've learned that obedience and righteousness protect me.[36] And I rejoice that nothing I do (or anyone else does to me) can ever separate me from His love.[37]

---

35 Psalm 41:2
36 Psalm 25:21
37 Romans 8:30-35

Watching

Teach me to do your will, for you are my God; May your good Spirit lead me on level ground. (Psalm 143:10)

God challenged me to be kind and patient with Jim, but I didn't know how to start until I saw a godly woman doing it. I watched Melanie love and respect her husband and felt convicted that I didn't treat Jim well. When she spoke gently, I heard God say *did you hear that? She wasn't snarky or snippy. Try that.* God changed me as I imitated her.

Once Cris and I walked through a parking lot and passed a dirty diaper on the ground. I was just turning to tell her how disgusted I was when she bent over, picked it up and threw it in the nearest trashcan, without saying a word. I was stunned, watching her example. I would have never done that, but I heard God say *why not?* I talked but did nothing; her actions spoke. It was a quiet moment of conviction and correction.

Reactions

When we moved to the US, we had to change jobs, money, weather and time zones, but I never worried about language. Other than saying "eh," I thought we all spoke English. But, one night cleaning the kitchen after a class potluck, I asked, "Is this the switch for your garberator (disposal)?" All the women burst out laughing, and one gal slid to the ground giggling helplessly. I had no idea what I said to cause that reaction. It was one of many times I had to humble myself and ask, "What is the American word for it?"

Being abused is like that. We say something that makes perfect sense to us, but people have crazy reactions to our words, so we clam up. We stay silent because we don't know what is normal. Instead of fearing awkward moments, we can learn from questioning our reactions.

At a women's Christmas luncheon, I blew up when a couple sang the song "Baby, It's Cold Outside." I was so angry, I sat on my hands and wouldn't clap, and I forced myself not to storm out of the room. The other women thought it was sweetly romantic, but I thought he was overpowering her, forcing drinks on her to wear down her resistance and not listening to her words. I realized my reaction was different and maybe wrong, so I pondered where it came from. For two weeks, I discussed the words and intent of the song with friends, watched it on YouTube and questioned myself. The couple loved each other and didn't want to be separated. They were cuddling by a fire and didn't want to go out in the cold. The song wasn't about abuse.

When I have a Level-10 reaction to a Level-2 problem, I ask myself:

>Why does this feel so big? What am I afraid of?
>How did everyone else see it?
>What old hurt is this bringing up? In what ways does this remind me of the abuse?
>Is that still happening today? How can I see this differently?
>What do I believe? Is it true? How does that need to change?

Sometimes it's a fight to stop defending my 10-reaction to people I hurt. Usually when I name the fear and describe the source, it sounds ridiculous. Then I plan a different response for the next time that situation comes up. I can control my reactions, not be controlled by them. I tell myself the new truth until it feels natural, a new good habit.

Listening

At my favorite job in Canada, I worked for a shrewd multi-millionaire businessman. He decided to build a new warehouse, but instead of copying the one he already had, he asked all the employees for input. He asked questions like:

>What do you like about the current warehouse and what problems do you see?
>What would you change if you could build a new warehouse?
>What is your biggest frustration with the current arrangement of space?
>If you had unlimited money, what would you build?

He was a powerful man who could force the entire town to operate his way. But he really wanted suggestions. He took the time to get input and suggestions and built a fantastic new building. He taught me to strive for win-win solutions. If both sides sacrifice a little, everyone gets most of what they want and is happy. I've learned to listen to people's opinions and find win-wins. Another perspective often saves me from heartache and disappointment.

Laughter

In Canada, I learned to pronounce words phonetically. So, in my first term teaching accounting in Albuquerque, I had a "Canadian" moment. The textbook listed a company named Yosemite which I called "YO-suh-might." The class erupted in laughter but I had no idea why. They teased me about it for the rest of class. I finally gave up trying to say it and called it "that company."

God often brings joy into my life through laughter. I can humble myself and avoid the pit of despair by laughing at my failures. It is easy for me because Canadians naturally poke fun at themselves first. The problem was turning that into self-hatred and condemnation. Laughter disarms anger and fear and keeps life from being so deadly serious.

At a Women of Faith conference in Dallas in front of 20,000 women, singer Kathy Troccoli was climbing the steps to the stage when she tripped and fell. While all the women gasped, she laughed so hard she could hardly get up. She acknowledged her fall with an exaggerated bow, then sang powerfully. Rather than focusing on her fall, she focused on His face, doing what she was there to do. Can we learn to get over failure as easily?[38]

Loving God

I used to defy my dad out of anger, rebellion or a desire for control, but I obeyed him out of fear of being beaten or worse. God's goal for our lives, just like the Israelites, is to bring us to a place of worship.[39] He will stop at nothing short of a loving relationship based on intimacy. He will point out anything that stands in the way of us knowing or following Him. I want to love Him better every day, so I listen for correction. The book of 1 John says I show Him love by obeying His commandments (2:3-6). I might do this by walking in the light, loving my Christian brother (2:9-11), not practicing sin (3:4-8), meeting people's needs (3:16-19) or letting His love push out my fear (4:15-19). I love God by showing gratitude for all He's done and I display His Lordship by obeying quickly. Obeying God out of gratitude and trusting His nature were good 180's, instead of fearing His power and punishment if I failed.

Deciding

After moving back in with Jim, we were at a marriage conference when a terrible blizzard blew in. Jim wanted to stay overnight but I wanted to be home with our young son. I accepted his decision and the next morning as we crept home over icy roads, I told Jim he had made the right choice. He choked up and his eyes were teary. It was the first time I had ever complimented him.

I followed his lead because, months before, I had decided to obey God and submit to my husband. Even when it was hard, I was committed to supporting him. When I changed what I had always done, I got something different—my husband's gratitude, God's approval and peace in our relationship.

---
38 When we asked her permission in 2012 to use this story, she didn't even remember it happening.
39 Exodus 4:22-23

Hollow Voices

In the beginning, in the Garden of Eden, Adam and Eve only heard God's voice. Then one terrible day, another voice, Satan's, entered the picture and Eve listened to it.[40] Today, that evil voice rings in our ears through celebrities, TV hosts, life coaches, even pastors and parents. Your spiritual enemy is always trying to trip you. The enemy laughs and says *You haven't learned anything.* Or, he focuses on your failures and disobedience, so you will stop trying. He uses everything against you. Remember, he is Satan—he lies. Lies and deceit are his native language.[41] We have to ignore his voice, reject the traps he spreads and believe the truth. All that depends on finding a true voice; God's voice in the Bible.

I wandered in an emotional desert for years because I failed to see where biblical truth and psychology differed. Colossians 2:8 warns *See to it that no one takes you captive through hollow and deceptive philosophy, which depends on human tradition and the basic principles of this world rather than on Christ.* Hollow philosophy and worldly principles taught me man was basically good,[42] I wasn't responsible for my actions[43] and I needed better self-esteem[44] to be healed.

When someone corrects you, how can you make sure that they are showing you a true mirror? No matter what the source, how much it tickles your ear or how good it sounds, one rule determines if something is right: Does it line up with the Word of God?

Also, be willing to let people give you stupid ideas, because if you get three bad ideas, maybe the fourth one will be really great. Be gracious about listening then extract any truths. Don't always wait for the perfect idea, go with the kernel of truth (ideas that agree with biblical truths).[45]

What Happened to My Friend?

You hope that your family members, parents or friends will be happy when you change, but they may be roadblocks. Often, their "twist" rises to the surface. Jealousy, envy, backbiting and strife show up, because your change has exposed their problems. When you were the emotional one or the sick one, was someone playing caretaker? As your emotional roller-coaster slows down, it leaves the caregiver confused—as if you were waltzing,

---

40 Paul Tripp discussed this concept in <u>Instruments in the Redeemers Hands</u>, P & R Publishing, Phillipsburg, NJ © 2002.
41 John 8:44
42 Carl Rogers
43 Freud
44 Maslow
45 Family Life Radio, caller Lynn, Wednesday morning, April 28, 2013.

but started dancing salsa. They don't know the beat or the steps, so it's awkward. They can feel unloved if their self-worth came from feeling like a better person than you.

If you have been controlled by a need for men's approval, be careful when you're changing direction. When we live for God, we love people but don't need their approval as much. Or they may give you bad advice. Gently explain that you have changed and won't go back to old ways. As your faith becomes more visible, you may lose friends. They may resent the "new you" and reject your changes.

Redeeming Words

In the back of the book, there is a glossary of words that may have twisted meanings. Correction is the first one. We encourage you to re-evaluate these words as you go through the book to see if your definitions line up with God's character. We call the "new words" the Language of Mercy. We hope you will become a fluent Mercy-speaker on your journey.

The Easier Way

My life turns out better when I listen to advice, so now I seek God's truth. I would still rather hear truth from someone who loves me than from someone who hurts me, but I want to grow. I have been changed through people's words and deeds, trained through His Word, challenged by songs and sermons and radio programs, rebuked by my son, and corrected through overheard conversations. God is always speaking. We just have to listen and change.

Bottom Lines:

1. You will be stuck until you can receive correction from people and the Bible.
2. Don't be a "closed system." Let someone else speak into your life.
3. It's okay to admit you are wrong. Then do something different, and do it sooner.
4. God corrects me because He loves me.

Discussion Questions:

1. How have you always seen correction?

2. What have you "always done" and what have you "always got?"

3. Are you always moving forward, making little adjustments, or do you keep ending up at the wrong place because you refuse to correct?

4. Which of the 12 ways to think about correction is easiest for you to receive? Which is hardest? Pick one way to receive input and look for it this week.

5. Name a time you had a 10-reaction to a 2-problem. Go through the questions on page 36. Examine this situation until your reaction calms down to a 1 or a 2.

Anything for the Poofy file? Write it in your journal, or discuss it with your friend.

To the Friend of the Traveler:

1. Build a strong relationship first before you start correcting. Maybe God showed you some fault of your friend, only to have you pray. He may want to use someone else to confront them. Ask questions and listen. There is not a formula. Listen to the Holy Spirit. Point your friend to God, the teacher and guide. Ask her what He has said through the Bible or sermons or other people. If you have correction to offer, be kind. As Gal. 6:1-5 says, be under control first before going to them.

2. When you tell your friend, "you're wrong," she may hear condemnation, judgment, rejection, failure, hatred. Be careful and gentle. Use non-threatening words and reassure her that you care:

   I am on your team, let me help you.
   Maybe you're not seeing this right.
   I won't expose your weakness. I want to shore it up.
   I have the same weakness and I have some victory over it.
   I want to walk alongside you. We all stumble in many ways.
   I want to help you be who God wants you to be.
   I want to understand why you do this before I expect you to change.

3. Be humble about your mistakes, problems, sins and faults. You don't have to be perfect, but you can consistently point to God. You will never be a perfect counselor, only God is. If you don't know something, admit it. Encourage her to read the Bible, pray and look for His answers.

Worship Song: *Beauty for Ashes* (Crystal Lewis)[46]

---

[46] Beauty for Ashes Album, Sony Records, © 1997, http://www.youtube.com/watch?v=DDhlTzbyFRo

Chapter 3
Tips From the Tour Guide — Beware of Scammers

There are lots of voices in the world: voices that will trick you and trap you; voices that don't love you or honor God; voices that call you names and tell you who you are. As you receive input and correction, be careful to listen to the right voice.

A Pinch of Error

Imagine you are baking a cake, your favorite recipe with fresh ingredients. The kids are watching impatiently, chatting. Then, while you are looking for non-stick spray, they try to help by stirring in their "flour;" sand. You pour the tainted batter in a pan and slide it in the oven. Soon, a delicious aroma fills the house. When the cake is finally done, iced, and sliced, everyone digs in. Can you imagine your faces after the first bite? The cake looked perfect—good cook, good recipe, good ingredients—but a spoonful of sand ruined it. Error doesn't have to be big to wreck your life. Too much salt on good food or a teaspoon of coffee in your computer can have the same result: ruin.

Unlike the case of a child dropping sand in, accidentally ruining the cake, most abuse is planned: someone stirs sand in the cake *knowing* what will happen. An abuser intentionally distorts the truth—emphasizes the good and hides the bad—distracts or sweetens the deal with a gift, or extracts cooperation with threats. He tricks you into thinking awful behavior is okay, or something you hate will soon become something you like. Relationship is promised but trust is shattered. Intimacy is offered but your body is ravaged and your soul taken.

There is some lie that hooks us, such as:

> Grown-ups all do this. (Yes, but with other grown-ups)
> This will be our special secret. (If you tell, I will punish you)
> It will be fun. (For me)
> This is how you show me love. (or how I show you love)

An abuser offers a piece of cake, grinning, "Try it, you'll like it; it's an old family recipe." Part of you thinks *this should taste great*, but another part screams, *there's something REALLY wrong with this*. If you ask why it tastes so bad, the deceiver replies, "You're too sensitive."

Not only sexual abuse, but all sin is wrapped in deception. Because there is deception in the world, we are all deceived in many ways. We are tricked, lied to, taken in, manipulated, controlled and blinded. Where does deception come from? Whether trickery, half-truths, flat-out lies, twisted facts, fairy-tale thinking, or total fantasies, it all has one source; our old enemy, Satan. He steals and destroys lives by hiding, withholding, or distorting truth.[47] Because this world belongs to him,[48] he speaks through all the people and resources he controls—words and pictures, movies, books and magazines, TV hosts, gurus, and the nightly news. He is the greatest spin-master of all time, drawing us into despair. He pushes people to stir sand in the batter.

Fooled You

One day, I was hanging around the older boys, who mostly ignored me—the baby of the block—while I tried to keep up with them. One of them stooped down, picked up a white stone, and told me it was a "sweet rock." I said I had never heard of one. They all winked and laughed, saying, "You should taste it, you'll really like it." Convinced by their words and wanting attention, I took a bite. I spit it out because it wasn't sweet, it was crusty old dog doo. The boys roared in victory as I ran home crying. They could never have *forced* me to eat dog poop but they *deceived* me into eating it.

Deception takes you to places you would never choose to go if your eyes were wide open.[49] Some attractive bait disguises the hook on the line. You bite thinking you are getting something good, but end up in the frying pan. In <u>The Enemy Within</u>, Kris Lundgaard writes:

> This is the art of deception: to make someone believe that things are other than they are, *so that he will do something he would never otherwise do*. If you want to overthrow a fortress, start by knocking out the watchman; if he can't warn the others, you will easily breach the wall and carry the day. The flesh plies deceit to knock out the watchman of your soul: *your mind…*and make you a willing servant of sin. (emphasis mine).[50]

I didn't know I was being conned until I bit into the white "rock." Like me, deceived people don't know they are deceived.[51] If you are sinned against, there is deception, like with the

---
47 Revelation 20:11
48 Matthew 4:8-9
49 Sin will take you farther than you ever thought you'd stray, keep you longer than you ever wanted to stay, and cost you more than you wanted to pay.
50 <u>The Enemy Within</u>, Kris Lundgaard, P & R Publication, Phillipsburg, NJ, © 1998, pp. 54-55
51 2 Cor. 11:3 *But I am afraid that just as Eve was deceived by the serpent's cunning, your minds may somehow be led astray from your sincere and pure devotion to Christ.*

neighbor boys. When you choose to sin—or if you respond with sin when you are sinned against—you are tricked and trapped by a lie, believing you can gain something by going against God. With all the deception that exists in the world, it's amazing we ever know truth.

Truth at the Right Time

A friend and I were having coffee when her 5-year-old daughter, Carla, spotted her "Uncle" Frank eating with some farmers.[52] She asked if she could say hi. Her mom said sure and went to pay the bill. Carla ran up to the table, where one man was telling a joke. Just as Carla said "Hi, Uncle Frank," the man gave the punch line and all the men roared in laughter. Carla's face fell, and she ran to her mom, sobbing, "I said hi to Uncle Frank, and all the men laughed at me." Her mom said that was silly and turned away.

Our lives are based on our picture of reality: what we have seen, filtered through our lenses of emotions, reactions, judgments and experiences. Author Paul Tripp says,

> We are created to be interpreters. People are meaning-makers; we have been created with the marvelous ability to think. We are always organizing, interpreting, and explaining what is going on inside us and around us …..We do not live life based on the bare facts of our existence; *we live our lives according to our interpretation of those facts* (emphasis mine).[53]

Was it true that all the men laughed? Yes. But were they laughing at her? No, Uncle Frank hadn't even heard Carla, but she thought he had made fun of her. Her perception was wrong, but she was alone trying to figure it out. She needed another voice, a true voice, to speak into the situation. I kneeled down and asked if she wanted to know what I saw. She nodded slowly, and I told her the men weren't laughing at her, they laughed at a joke. Her face lit up and she bounced out the door holding her mom's hand. That was the power in one sentence of truth spoken at the right time. Satan could have planted a lie that men always laughed at her or ruined their relationship through feelings of rejection. But after hearing the truth, the hurt lost its sting and a little girl was free to bounce into life.

That's the power the Bible can have in our life. Little Carla could not have found truth based on her thoughts. She needed an outsider to speak truth to her. Her life would have been changed for the worse if she only heard the lying voice. In the same way, our views will be distorted until we hear truth. Because the world, the flesh and the devil spin you,

---
52 In Canada, close family friends are called uncles and aunts.
53 Paul David Tripp, <u>Instruments in the Redeemer's Hands</u>, P & R Publishing, Phillipsburg, NJ © 2002, p. 42

if you don't have someone speaking truth into your life, you will be deceived. We need believers to speak truth, especially God's truth, into our world.

So what is truth? Webster's Dictionary says it is "the conformity to fact or reality; exact accordance with that which is, or has been, or shall be."[54] Finding truth is like putting on "truth glasses" to bring things into focus. God asks us to see life from His reality, His viewpoint:[55] to line up our thoughts with His thoughts; to call good what He calls good; to base our beliefs on what really was, what really is, or what really will be. Biblical truth is the cure for the blindness of deception.

Why Are There Lies?

Satan's motive for lying is revealed by the character Wormwood, the senior demon in the book The Screwtape Letters, C.S. Lewis' tale of spiritual warfare: "the only thing that matters is the extent to which you *separate* the man from the Enemy (God)."[56] Satan will always attack your relationship with God. Since the Bible says nothing can separate you from His love,[57] only lies and deception can trick you into leaving Him.[58] A pinch of error, a wrong thought, a wrong belief detaches you from God's truth, mercy and love.

> Lies make you look at God with a jaundiced eye. *God doesn't keep His promises.*
> Lies stop you from receiving God's good gifts. *You haven't earned it.*
> Lies persuade you to trust your feelings. *It's too scary, you don't have to obey.*
> Lies make you question the Bible. *It's not for today.*
> Lies prompt you to follow your desires. *You deserve it.*
> Lies excuse you from following God's commands. *It's too hard.*
> Lies reframe your history with God. *God is never there for you.*

While the enemy separates us from God, he also separates and isolates us from people. If someone says, "I love you," Satan's lying voice whispers *they don't really mean it. They wish you would go away. They only tolerate you because they have to.* Pastors, godly parents, and Christian friends—even seasoned believers—can be Satan's messengers, dividing, spreading poisonous lies or tempting us to sin. Paul even warned elders *"not (to) fall into disgrace and into the devil's trap."*[59]

---

54 Webster's 1828 Dictionary, definition of *truth*, http://1828.mshaffer.com/
55 Isaiah 55:8-9
56 The Screwtape Letters, C.S. Lewis, Touchstone/ Simon and Schuster, New York, NY, © 1961
57 Romans 8:35
58 Adam and Eve were sent away from the garden as a result of disobeying.
59 1Timothy 3:7

Satan wants us to nurse lies, keep secrets, and hide in darkness. He tries to keep us self-focused, hanging onto our favorite lie, our favorite bad feeling.[60] *You'll never get out of this pain. You'll never be free. You'll always be broken.* He tells you that you are the only person who feels that way. He is a schemer who can play you between two opposing thoughts. On one hand you believe *you'll never get it, you're hopeless*, at the same time believing *you aren't trying hard enough*. Or you believe *I will never be happy until* (it) *happens* (usually something out of your control), but mostly you believe *it will never happen*.

Voices in My Head

After God brought the Woman to the Man in the Garden of Eden (Gen. 1), He had to tell them their purpose. (Animals have natural instincts, but people need input to know why they were created.) He blessed them and gave them instructions: *"Be fruitful and increase in number; fill the earth and subdue it ..."* Life was perfect until a different voice—the lying voice—spoke into their world. The serpent caught Eve by spinning a tale about God and the fruit, wrapping doubt around God's instructions with the words, *"Did* God really say ...?"[61] Eve was deceived; she believed his words were true.[62] Listening to the voice was deadly: both the man and the woman fell for Satan's temptation, disobeyed God, ate the forbidden fruit, invited death into the world, and let sin reign.

God created you with a purpose, and the personality and abilities to accomplish it, but at some point a lying voice entered your world and twisted God's instructions. God, the Good Father, speaks only truth, but Satan is a father too—the father of lies.[63] He guts truth and stuffs it with lies. When one lie hooks you, he puts it on repeat. Are you shocked that I think everyone hears voices in their head? All the thoughts in my head when I first met with Melanie were familiar lies. Some came from my abuser, some from my family, some were my own thoughts, but some were from the evil one.[64]

Ice Jams and Dynamite

During Canadian winters, lakes and rivers freeze so hard that 18-wheel trucks can drive on them. When the ice melts in the spring, water from the warmer south flows up to the still-frozen northern rivers, causing huge ice jams. That leads to massive, destructive flooding.[65] Dynamite is used to break up the jams and keep the water channels open. Truth may feel

---
60 Speaker and author Jan Silvious in a conference at Hoffmantown Church, 2011
61 Genesis 3:1
62 2 Cor. 11:3, discussed in Instruments in the Redeemer's Hands, Paul Tripp, P & R Publishing, Phillipsburg, NJ © 2002 63 John 8:42-47- v. 44: *There is no truth in (the devil). When he lies, he speaks his native language, for he is a liar and the father of lies.*
64 Acts 5:3- *Paul said to Ananias, 'How is it that Satan has so filled your heart.....?'*
65 Google "1997 Red River Flood" for a good example of this concept

like an explosion, and often it hurts before it heals (Prov. 27:6). But lies hurt longer, because they keep you frozen in deception while ice water floods your soul. God breaks up our ice jams to prevent soul-destroying floods.

He revealed my worst ice jam when I least expected it, sitting beside a shimmering lake at family camp, praising God and rejoicing in the gift of our newly adopted son. My marriage was the best it had ever been and I had hope for the future when God's quiet voice told me a painful truth; everything I had ever accomplished had been fueled by anger—my career, my sports victories, my marriage and my ministry. I felt the blast of dynamite.

For the next few months, I saw ice jams everywhere. Anger had always been a successful tool for me. I thought I controlled anger, but it controlled me. God wanted more from me. As a Christian, I should reflect His character—be like Jesus and live a life of love. What has fueled your life? Fear? Insecurity? People-pleasing? Pride?

Whether it's your sin or sin done to you, sin hardens hearts like ice clogs rivers. Anger is a sure-fire way to be hard-hearted. Hebrews 3:13 warns what happens when you turn away from truth toward sin: *But encourage one another daily ... so that none of you may be hardened by sin's deceitfulness.* You lose your sensitivity to God by believing lies for long.

Get ready, because these next parts may feel like dynamite on your ice jams. You don't need to be defensive—you've been deceived, like we all have. Let's look at some of the ways deception has blinded your eyes, hardened your heart and separated you from God. Remember, truth hurts before it heals. But it can also free you from the icy grip of the past.

Foundational Lies

If you are like me, many of your foundational beliefs about God, love, relationships and sexuality were birthed in the pain, anger and despair of abuse. I call these foundational lies—core beliefs that control and direct you even today. They came from bad seeds planted by deceitful abusers or evil authority figures; beliefs based on lies about God, you, people, and life. People showed you a carnival mirror image of yourself—distorted and bent—and called it truth. *Foundational lies* hide deep in your soul, playing out for years, unquestioned. They are so familiar, they're invisible.

We believe lies we want to be true:
    He loved me; he didn't know how to show it.
    He was drunk so he didn't know what he was doing.

We believe lies we don't want to examine:
    It was my fault. I shouldn't have_____(gone in the room, etc.).
    I was protecting my sister/mother.

We believe lies because we don't want to pry open the pain:
    If I start crying I will never stop.
    I could never survive looking at the abuse.

We believe lies because we listen to Satan's voice:
    This will comfort me (going away, cutting, drinking, sex, etc.)
    I'm bad, black inside, slimy, a bad seed, damaged goods.
    I'm only good for being used.
    I have no voice.
    Life should be easy and fair. Pain is the enemy.

These lies can "soften the blow" of sexual abuse or family trauma. The most effective lies hold a kernel of truth. We are deceived when we latch onto the fragment of truth, never inspecting the rest of the story. Then it rules our lives.

Black Dots

Abuse is like a black dot painted on the canvas of your life. It was a specific incident at a specific time and place with a specific person that paints a black mark on your soul. Satan spreads that black spot, diluted, far beyond that point. He blackens events and people that are *like* the abuse/abuser in some way then spreads it to *unrelated* people and places. He wants to turn your whole world gray, so you will re-live the pain of abuse again and again. Your vision gets stained by the lie: everything is dark—*I'm dark, you're dark, life is dark.*

One of my black dots was the lie that I was abused because I wore a nightgown. So as a child, I rejected them. By age 16, I rejected dresses and skirts. By age 24, I rejected my femininity and wore suit pants and jackets with ties. One day, Melanie challenged me, "If you hate men so much, why do you dress like one?" I said, "I don't dress like a man; I just won't dress like a woman." Do you see how that black dot grew? For me, freedom means wearing dresses and skirts to work and cute pajamas to sleep in.

I often see this dark haze spread over people's lives. One girl was raped in the backseat of a car, and ten years later, she was still afraid to drive. Another woman was abused in a barn and hated being in the country. A mature person can shrink the ground and erase the black stains.

Quirks and Other Odd Reactions

Deception is also revealed through "quirks." I blamed weird reactions on "my quirky personality." I first noticed this when two men blocked the door to my office. Not on purpose, they just happened to be in between me and the door, blocking my escape. I slammed down files, yelled that I quit and stormed out.

Days later when I calmed down, I asked myself what I had felt? Trapped and targeted. But that was not true of those men, so it was an abnormal reaction. What about the situation set me off? Was there a time in the past that was similar? Yes, when I was four, the baby-sitter's drunken husband and son closed a door and threatened me with a knife. My reaction came from past terrors. But my co-workers were not bad men. I apologized to them and asked them not to block the door. I told myself I was not trapped and shamed myself into not reacting. Years later, I worked through it better. I named the old fears, forgave the bad men, asked God's forgiveness for my rage, and told myself more truths. I found freedom by walking through it with God, not avoiding scary situations.

I've had quirky reactions about receiving gifts, having company in my home, friends drinking, my son's knife collection, people not answering emails and more, because of some connection to past abuse, showing up sideways. Can you see why Jeremiah 17:9 says our heart is deceitful and sick? We can't trust it, partly because it's filled with old poisons and needs to be washed. (Eph. 5:26)

Blowing Up

When a black dot spreads, it may leak out in "10-reactions to 2-problems," like I mentioned in Chapter 2. One example for me was the dentist. I was such an anxious patient that I took Valium to make it through cleanings. After decades of avoiding and fearing dentists, I decided to examine the truth about it. Like a detective, I asked why and when was I afraid? Did I hate the whole thing or parts of it? I realized I hated when I didn't know what was happening, so I asked them to explain everything. Then I pondered what specific thing made my skin crawl? What took it from being okay to blowing up? My heart raced when he put his hands in my mouth. I changed to a woman dentist and lost that reaction.

Over-reactions are like true mirrors revealing what's in the heart. Valium had deadened my responses but couldn't free me from the past. God often recreates a scene of pain or hurt or failure so He can walk through it with us. When we hit a familiar reaction, He exposes black dots and washes away their stains. Today, I can go to the dentist without fear or Valium, because I didn't settle for a temporary fix. When I looked at the dentist through the lens of truth, identified my fears, renewed my thinking, and changed what I could, my reactions became normal.

Rules

Black dots can also become rules, another way of hardening our hearts. I was hurt when I was controlled, so I vowed never to lose control again.[66] When I first met Cris, I had lists of unspoken rules I lived by and enforced with people. Just a few of dozens:

> You have to ask permission before asking questions.
> Don't criticize me. Say only positive things.
> Don't touch me or hug me.
> Don't talk about sex.
> You may never surprise me.
> You have to warn me about any possible upset or danger or stress.

We make rules about relationships: *It's my way or no way; People have to like me; I have to drive; I can control my life if I* (stay on the couch, don't have friends, etc.). We keep rules about sex and our bodies, trying to protect ourselves from the past or the scary unknown. We become rigid and inflexible, locked in old ways, unwilling to take risks. Or we trust a rule beyond all reason to protect us from being used and abused again. Rules are our sacred, untouchable Precious.[67]

Childish Thinking

When I was a child, I talked like a child, I thought like a child, I reasoned like a child. When I became a man, I put childish ways behind me. (1 Corinthians 13:11)

Here's a black dot I made into a rule: I didn't understand why I was abused so, with 8-year-old wisdom, I tried to figure it out. Because I blocked out most of it, I only remembered my abuser's eye color; brown. I decided brown eyes caused it. As I got older, that black-dot belief grew into a rule: I will not date brown-eyed men—they are all mean, untrustworthy, and dangerous. My childish explanation of abuse tainted my life and determined who I would date and eventually who I married.[68] I had built a wall based on a lie. And, I had made myself vulnerable to blue-eyed men who were bad.

---
[66] Pastor Erik Christensen, "Control is an illusion." Hoffmantown Church, Albuquerque, NM, January 2012
[67] Precious is the Ring of Power, from <u>The Lord of the Rings</u> trilogy, J.R. Tolkein, Houghton Mifflin Co, New York NY ©1954
[68] Jim has blue eyes – God's mercy to me.

I had connected two random thoughts: brown eyes = abuse. I felt silly when my counselor talked me through this foundational lie at age 50. *Is it true that all brown-eyed men are evil and abusive?* Well, no. *Are there any good brown-eyed men?* Yes, there are. *Do blue eyes really make a man good?* No, goodness comes from the heart. Then my counselor spoke truth that broke ruling lies; alcohol was the real master in our home; my abuser loved himself and his desires more than me. When I spoke out what I believed, I saw how childish it was. Once it was brought to the light, the lies scattered like cockroaches. The truth was:

> There was a man who was my father.
> He was angry and dangerous.
> When he drank, he became more cruel and abusive.
> He had brown eyes.
> He overpowered me physically.
> He attacked me sexually.
> Not all men are like he was.

We all have made childish decisions about the world and the abuse that need to be re-examined.

Don't Believe Everything You Think[69]

Our thinking can be like a mess of wires jammed into a jar. Thoughts are connected that don't belong together—jammed, twisted and crossed, wires wrapped around each other. As we examine one small area of beliefs or thoughts or feelings, it pulls up whatever is connected to that, no matter how whacko and random it seems.

Imagine growing up in a war-torn country, where you learned to survive bullets and battles. Enemy planes were the worst. When they appeared, everyone had to hide fast. Then the bombs would fall, blasting into lives and limbs. Then, imagine a soldier adopts you and takes you to a new home in America. You can play on the streets with a full tummy and a safe house, without the terrors of war. But what happens when an airplane flies overhead? Your instincts would scream, "Run, RUN!" as if your life depends on hiding. That was true back there *but it is not true now*. This plane carries passengers, not bombs. Its purpose is positive, not deadly, but your reaction is a jolt of emotion. Now imagine a friend's reaction to planes. In your world, planes are connected to bombs and pain and death, while she just sees a quiet bird in a clear sky.

My home life was like a war zone, and the connections I made and the ways I survived abuse have twisted me. We usually can't see crossed wires until they are pulled apart. The

---
[69] Seen on a bumper sticker.

first December I knew Cris, I kept saying how much I hated Christmas. The next year she asked me why, but I didn't know. The third year I said it, she started probing for details. That's when I remembered my abuse had started on Christmas Eve. Going backwards, the wires that had been fused together were Christmas-hatred-dread-depression-faking it-get through it-escape-abuse. I had felt that way for fifty years and never questioned it. But it sounded so odd to her, she looked for connections. When I realized there used to be a valid reason for this hatred, a reason now gone, I started changing my thoughts and my words. I let the past go by forgiving more and making good new family memories.

Nothing Really Happened

It's easier to deny pain if you're not confronted with it, so we are very skilled at pretending. Every time we hit a painful place, we run away. We erase and rewrite history to fit a story, re-inventing characters as "loving mother," "unavailable dad," "confused uncle." We keep secrets and pretend the abuse didn't affect us. We make excuses for other people. We overcompensate or overwork to hide the pain. Instead of looking at truth, we deflect[70] and distract and live in denial.

I've talked to women who are tormented by their doubts: *Did it really happen? Maybe I'm making it up. What if it's not true? It's just a nightmare; how can I accuse someone because of a dream?* Talk it out with your discipleship partner or a counselor. When you combine a dream with some quirks, rules, black dots and over-reactions, it sounds more plausible, like it really happened. If it's the only thing that makes all the puzzle pieces fit, it probably did happen.

Protective Walls

In counseling, when Cris asked me to do homework that contradicted a foundational inner belief (that had been hidden to us both), I responded badly: I blew up, fell apart, cried, or agreed but refused to do it. I thought I was being totally logical, but she said I was irrational, immovable, angry and aggressively self-protective. Gentle persuasion didn't work; words had no power. I was normally easy-going, but when I was pushed, I was a brick wall. After hitting these walls many times, Cris started examining them. She came to believe they were "fortresses" or "strongholds:" a wall of protection built around a strong lie or a sinful response to old hurts.[71] I didn't see my self-protective games until the lie was identified, confessed and defeated. Here are a few examples:

---
[70] I call this "emotional volleyball." You never catch the ball in volleyball, you just redirect it. I see healing more like "hot potato:" you hold it only as long as you need to, not one second more.
[71] From Ephesians 4:27- *Do not give the devil a foothold by letting anger go on overnight.*

> **Don't trust anyone**
> **I will never** be like them
> **I will never** be a sexual being
> **I will never** be out of control again
> **I will never** say no to my kids
> **I will never** let a man/woman tell me what to do
> I would **rather die** than_____.

The charismatic church calls these powerful blockages *inner vows*. When we make a vow, it is permanent and binding in the spiritual realm, even if we forget it or change our minds. A vow made during the abuse will rear its ugly head during times of stress or hurt. It took deep soul-searching, intense prayer and fasting, God-given insight, confession, deeper application of biblical truths and deliberately breaking the vow through forgiveness and repentance to break through these walls.[72]

When do you say "never"? What do you refuse to do or say or think about? When do you get stubborn and irrational? Might be a wall. Prayerfully ask Jesus to reveal what strong lie the wall is protecting, then ask Him to help you tear it down so you can walk in freedom. The problem is that all the tricks we used to survive are the same tricks that now keep us from growing and having a good, normal life. It's time to leave them behind, and live a new way.

Deception Revealed

Search me, oh God and know my heart; test me and know my anxious thoughts. See if there be any offensive way in me, and lead me in the way everlasting. (Psalm 139:23-24)

Black dots, quirks, over-reactions, rules, walls, childish thinking, foundational lies, wires-jammed-in-a-jar, and denial are all warning signs; ways we can see our deception coming out. Satan uses them for evil: he condemns us for these reactions and keeps us in despair so we resist change, but God can use them for good; to reveal our blindness. As I look through a new pair of truth glasses, He reveals the sin/my sin, because He loves me and wants me freed from it. *How am I blind, deaf or deceived? What lie do I believe?* Truth corrects Satan's distortion. He can't keep hurting us if we reject his lies.

When we justify our sin (*I yelled because I was hurt*), minimize (*I only yelled once*), or blame-shift (*you yelled first*), Satan grins. He wins every time we cover truth with

---
[72] I could not move forward until I got to my knees and repented of my old belief, the old self-protective lie that I thought was superior to believing and living life based on God's truth.

sanitized lies. He wants us to stay chained so he can easily influence us. When you start changing and growing, Satan will toss in old lies to trip you up again. He makes us **forget** what we should **remember** (God's past victories and works on our behalf) and **remember** what we should **forget** (our past sin and the self-life). I have had to go back and relearn important things two and three times because I got sidetracked by false voices.

Fighting the Tangle of Lies

I used to describe my life like being smothered by a thick dark fog, blinded and muffled. I never saw anything coming; people hit me through the fog, leaving me beaten and confused. Then I moved to a jungle, my sight blocked by tangles of roots, vines, tall trees and hanging leaves. It took all my strength to cut through one mess and move on to the next one. The Bible was the machete I used to slice through the tangle of lies; one truth at a time freed me from the jungle. Now I live in an open, colorful meadow. I see flowers and grass and feel the warm sunshine on my face.

Because deceit lurks in the world and in our hearts,[73] truth doesn't start with us. Disbelief blinds us but the Bible opens our eyes. How do we know if something is truth or a lie? When you don't know what to believe, let the Bible tell you. Every thought, old or new, should be evaluated by the pure truth of the Bible. "Open your Bible" is your new bottom line.

The Bible is God's book, His words spoken to men who took dictation. It is the primary way He speaks to us. The Bible describes God, Satan, bad people, the past, and the future. It explains our new identity: how we are chosen, loved, adopted, redeemed, forgiven, and sealed for eternity.[74] It gives directions for life; how to think, speak, love, live, suffer, change, mature, and die. It **teaches** like an instruction manual, good from bad, right from wrong (2 Tim. 3:16). It **rebukes** by warning us about error, disobedience, rebellion, and consequences for disobedience; it exposes sin in our hearts and reveals motives. It **corrects** like a true mirror, reminding us of the right way to live by God's standards. It **trains in righteousness** by outlining how to practice living right, like a coach drilling new skills. The Word reveals truth so we can adjust our beliefs to His reality.

My son, if you accept my words and store up my commands within you, turn your ear to wisdom… if you call out for insight and cry aloud for understanding, if you look for it as for silver and search for it as for hidden treasure, then you will understand the fear of the Lord and find the knowledge of God. (Prov. 2:1-6)

---

73 Jeremiah 17:9
74 Ephesians chapter 1

Knowing and Growing

Pastor Dutch Sheets said truth comes in "seed form; whether or not it bears fruit depends on what you do with it."[75] You hear a truth and mull it over; challenge it, chew on it, ponder it. Then one day it bursts into reality and becomes **your** truth, not just **a** truth. For years I held a twisted belief about God: *God doesn't care about me*. I believed whole-heartedly if God had really loved me, He would have stopped the abuse. Since He didn't stop it, He didn't care: God + abuse = neglect. I knew *about* God's love but had not experienced it.

Then one day, I read 1 Peter 5:7: *Cast all your anxiety on Him because He cares for you.* That verse created a discord in my soul. My belief and the Bible were opposites, so they couldn't both be right at the same time. I had to decide which was true:

> my feelings or His Word;
> my belief or the Bible's declaration;
> my thoughts or His thoughts;
> my experience or His truth.

Would I believe with tear-stained cheeks that God didn't care for me or would I accept the truth of His love and bounce back into life? As I pondered the verse, I realized the truth was that God always cared for me. I had been blind to the ways He showed me love every day. My abuser didn't care for me. He was bad, but that didn't change God's love for me. I was blaming the wrong person.[76] I had taken all the bad people and their bad choices (in a world controlled by Satan) and piled them on God's plate. The day I understood that God loved **me**, not just everyone, it blossomed into **my** truth. I ran to Melanie crying, "God loves me, He loves ME!" She laughed and agreed. Ever since that truth became my truth, I have not doubted God's love and I've seen it every day in small sure ways. Later, I read more truths, like Isaiah 49:15: *'Can a woman forget her nursing child, and not have compassion on (her) son? They may forget, yet I will not forget you,' says your God.*

Experiences	vs.	Biblical Truth
Interpretations	vs.	Unchangeable, Eternal
Feelings	vs.	Faith, Belief

Can you believe that God is true and right but your beliefs may not be? The world says your thoughts, your wants, feelings, and desires are more important than God's

---

[75] <u>Intercessory Prayer</u>, Dutch Sheets, Regal Books, Ventura, CA, © 1996, p. 163
[76] Jill Briscoe, *Our Father* talk, Passionate Pursuit Conference, Tampa, FL, 2005

directions. But when doubt, despair, or distrust turn you away from God, you embrace deception and bring sin and suffering on yourself. The Bible warns: *(Don't have) a sinful, unbelieving heart that turns away from the living God.*[77] If your picture of God has been distorted by pain, I'm not surprised you don't trust Him. How can you believe in a God who is indifferent, absent, powerless, or distant? I wouldn't either. But God is not like that.

Searching For Truth

Truth is one of the names of Jesus in John 14:6: "*I am the Way, the Truth, and the Life.*" He is the Word of God "with skin on."[78] Because He is the source of truth (it's impossible for Him to lie[79]), God always "tells you true."[80] The Holy Spirit continually leads you to truth.[81] The closer you draw to God, the more truth you will hear. If the Bible and old beliefs (old nature, old ways) clash, the problem is not with the Word, it's with us. Find twisted connections and cut them, don't stay tangled in the jungle of the past. God will help you look at truth about problems and about yourself, then truth about the abuse. He gently and patiently helps you be a detective with yourself:

> What are the **facts** of the situation today? (Separate from the feelings.)
> What emotion do I feel?
> When is the **first** time I remember feeling this?
> How did this remind me of the past? Of the abuse?
> It was true then, but is it true today, in this situation?
> Is this a normal reaction or an overreaction? (Ask others)
> Is this a pattern? When else do I react like this? How often?
> What does the Bible say about this thought/belief/action?
> Do I believe what the Bible says? If that is true, what does that mean?
> How would I live if that were really true? What difference would it make?
> Who do I need to forgive? For what?

When you hear a different truth, do you listen to understand and change? Do you automatically think "NOT"? Remember Chapter 2's lesson? Be teachable, receive input from people. The living Word[82] inside you (the Holy Spirit) can apply truth to your life in new ways. He can make it *your* truth, instead of *a* truth.

---

77 Hebrews 3:12-13
78 John 1:1, 14
79 Hebrews 6:18
80 As my Polish Grandma often told me in broken English, "I tell you true, Barbara."
81 John 16:13
82 Hebrews 4:12

The Bible is a Conversation

Speaker Anne Graham Lotz teaches our favorite simple Bible study method, called "The 3 Questions (What does the section say? What does it mean? What does it mean in my life? Then practice doing it)."[83] When you find a verse that feeds you a new truth, commit it to memory, so you can think about it any time night or day. Then think about how that verse changes your relationship with God, or your relationship with people.

When you are faced with a choice, start by searching your Bible. Run to the Word daily to learn its principles, promises, and precepts. It is the answer book, our "go to" for living the Christian life. Challenge your beliefs, bring thoughts into the light, ask godly, wise people, and listen to the Spirit. Admit what verses you have been cherry-picking or rejecting.

As you open your Bible and listen to the Spirit, lies are pushed out in the open. Trust is forged in your heart as you learn truths about you, truths about God, and how they work in your life. A verse speaks to you, answers a prayer or gives directions in a crisis. One small truth laid on another soon replaces your faulty foundation with a strong new one. Write all these truth gems in your Journal, then read and meditate on them often, until you believe them and accept them. I struggled to keep new truths, getting them, losing them, getting them again. But don't give up! Someday they will stick and stay. Remember, you are on a journey. Keep going; you are going to get there!

Speaking Hard Truth

The more difficult the truth is to hear, the more gently it should be delivered. Jim and I were on vacation with Pastor Ken and Melanie when Ken received an urgent call from the church. We were nervous as he left and his face was ashen when he returned. He sat down, took Melanie's hands, and looked her in the eyes. He quietly told her he had very bad news. Then he said it was bad news about a friend. She took a few deep breaths; he said that her friend had died in a car accident. Then he held her as she cried.

I watched wide-eyed. I remembered calling my sister with similar news when she was 8-months pregnant with her first baby. She said hello and I said, "Hi, Mom is dead." No warning, no gentleness. The difference was shocking. Ever since, I have taken a few minutes during class to teach my students how to deliver bad news. I want to spare people what I put my sister through.

---

83 www.annegrahamlotz.org/resources/topic/all-bible-studies/learning-hear-his-voice; free video explaining the method and www.annegrahamlotz.org/resourses/topic/all-bible-studies/group-bible-studies/ for on-line Bible studies.

Walking With Truth

Healing grows when you accept that you *are* on this path and you *can't* change the past. You can't help that you were "bumped" onto the path of pain because a person chose to disobey God and turn to abuse; that forced you to live a new reality and make impossible choices. You had no tools, no truth, and no power to get off the path. No one brought you to Jesus. You didn't hear truth about the abuse while it was happening, only lying voices. You held wrong thoughts and beliefs. You did not know what to do or how to fix it. Then you stayed on that path because you made some bad choices. You responded to sin by sinning too.

With the Word of God leading and the Holy Spirit teaching, you can find the way off the path of pain. You can choose a new path. You can silence the lying voice. You can shred lies and honestly face some tough facts, knowing you will never be alone. You can change your future. Does it give you hope to know that you can find the real truth in the pages of the Bible? And that you can learn to tell lies from truth?

Let the past sleep, but let it sleep on the bosom of Christ, and go out into the irresistible future with Him.[84] (Oswald Chambers)

Bottom Lines:

1. Just a pinch of error can ruin your life.
2. Deceived people don't know they are deceived.
3. Open your Bible; trust it as the Truth.
4. Voices in your head come from different sources.

Discussion Questions:

1. Was there a deliberate lie connected with your abuse? Or was there a lie hidden behind something that was mostly true? What lie hooked you into being involved?

2. Have you heard the lying voice, or the lies on p. 46-47? How have they separated you from God?

3. Can you think of a time when truth was given to you at a crucial time like little Carla? What difference did it make? How has the Bible or this book given you truth that helped you understand yourself, the world, the abuse or God?

---
84 Oswald Chambers, <u>My Utmost for His Highest</u>, Barbour and Company, Westwood, NJ: 1935, p. 49

4. Black dots, quirks, rules, over-reactions, denial, wires-jammed-in-a-jar thinking—can you give an example of each of these? Journal about them, and answer the questions on p. 55.

5. Did you hear anything in this chapter that might be a foundational lie for you? Ask others if they believe it too. If it's not a "true truth," start tearing down that wall.

6. From p. 54-55, what causes you to "turn away from the living God"? Feelings, doubt, history, sinful desires?

To the Friend of the Traveler:

1. You can see the world outside the hurt and the carnival mirrors. Gently remind her it is still there, and that's where she is headed. Remember the insights she mines from lessons, especially the encouraging ones, and remind her of them.

2. Listen to her story of abuse or pain, then give her another perspective. Hold up a true mirror so she can see the abuse through different eyes. Don't say, "I know exactly how you feel." Say, "If that happened to me, I would feel (or think)_____." Tell her what God thought about it. Lead her to her loving Father, and speak His truths as always true.

3. She may have blind spots the size of buildings. Don't try to tackle them all at once—one may feel too fast for her. You may give her sound biblical direction, and she will balk, cry and whine about how hard it is. Pray or maybe back up and let her think about it. You may need to be gently persistent in asking her to change. You may need to accept her choice to stay where she is. God can change her; maybe it's not His time yet.

4. She will test you frequently: drop a hint of the past (Barb said, "My family was dysfunctional.") to see if you ask more about it, or not return phone calls, or pick a fight. She may lose her temper, silently asking, "Will you still love me if I show you the real me?" She may test you with a tiny sexual temptation, to see if you will fall. Plan a quiet response when you feel like she's testing you. Remind her that only God is perfectly faithful; in relationships we have to forgive and be patient, and trust God in the other person. Pray for her healing, send a card, or wait for an opportunity. Ask God if you did anything wrong; if so confess and ask for her forgiveness quickly.

5. You do not exist solely to help your friend through this trial. Maintain your world apart from her sorrows. Don't neglect yourself, your family, your job or your ministries to

care for her. Only God can be there for the needy 24/7. Quietly share your joys and testify of God's goodness to you. Show her how to know and receive God's caring provision.

Worship Song: *Refiner's Fire* by Vineyard[85]

---

[85] http://www.lyricsmode.com/lyrics/b/brian_doerksen/#share. Cris' suggestion for this chapter is Carman's video *Raising the Standard*, song Revival in the Land. Sparrow Home video. Copyright 1989, Some-O-Dat Music.

Chapter 4
Get on The Train

One snowy day, Cris stood by the train tracks on the main street in Geneva, Switzerland, trying to figure out how to take a trolley to a quilt shop in the suburbs. Because she didn't speak German, it was hard to figure out how to get a ticket, what coins the machine took, and which line went there. Then she had to find the right boarding platform, and see if the trains stopped for a while or dashed off. She watched trams pass and people getting on and off for an hour. Finally, she decided to get on the next train, and if it was wrong, she would get off at the next stop, cross the platform, and come back. She boarded a train, which turned out to be the right one. If she hadn't decided to get on, she could have spent the day gathering information and watching people, but never left the platform. It took a decision to move, a choice to get on board and a willingness to make another choice, if needed, that got her to her goal.

Are you in a similar place? One where you want to love God with all your heart, mind, soul, and strength, but haven't started your journey to freedom yet because you're not sure where to go? Are you still watching and gathering information? Can we help you choose well and get on the train?

The Great Gift of Choice

Inside the soul of every person is a will, like a rudder that steers your life. Your life will land where your will steers it. If the rudder floats free, you drift with the current. If the rudder is stuck to one side, you go in circles. If it heads the wrong way, you will land in enemy territory.

Children are mostly steered by their circumstances—parents and teachers, school, church, home, finances. But in normal families, they have small choices: what to wear, what to eat, what to play with. They learn by words or by example how to make decisions. They learn how to spend their time and money, how to respond to failure, how to treat people and what is valuable and important. Some of these lessons are good and useful, others confusing or destructive.

Enter the abuse, which forced us to act in ways we didn't freely choose. Abuse attacked our ability to direct our own will or make choices separate from other people's choices. We were duped, forced, overruled, or manipulated. Even if there were a few choices, they were usually lose/lose: if you tell, your dad will go to jail or your mom will die or your dog will be killed. But if you don't tell, your soul kept being destroyed, and the abuser was happy and wanted more.

As a teenager, I didn't know I had a will, or that it had been overtaken as a child. For years, I lived torn between being bold or scared; one moment confident and determined, the next terrified and powerless. At home, everything centered on my dad—keeping him happy, distracted, and away from my mom. That meant having no contrary voice, no different opinions, no other plans. If I challenged him, I was overpowered and paid for it. I learned to be a mouse, shaking and hiding. "Barbara" the person shut down as soon as Dad came home. My will was absorbed into his will.

But at school or in sports, I was a lion. I played hard and loved life. I was an honor student on student council and a team captain. At school, my will was engaged. I was confident, cocky, and powerful. No one overpowered me. I saw the goal, went for it, and got it. "Hit the ball to me so I can show my stuff!" I flourished in the freedom I had. Why did my will sometimes work and sometimes not, like a faulty starter on a car that sputters one day and turns over the next? Was it just my surroundings or was there a problem with my will?

Every Change Starts with a Choice[86]

Our will shows itself through our thoughts, words, actions, and emotions. *Will* is defined as a decision; it is a choice about which action to take or what object to pursue:

1. That faculty of the mind by which *we determine either to do or forbear* (avoid) an action…*exercise in deciding*…which we shall embrace or pursue. The will is directed or influenced by judgment…**(R)eason** compares different objects; the **judgment** determines which is preferable, and **the will** decides which to pursue. In other words, we reason with respect to thevalue or importance of things, we then judge which is to be preferred and we will take the most valuable.

2. Choice; determination. "It is my will to prosecute the trespasser."[87]

Barb's translation: You compare two (or more) things, you think what you prefer, you judge based on your values, and choose one to pursue, which becomes an action.

---
86 Bishop Dale C. Bronner, sermon at Legacy Church, Albuquerque, NM, 2011
87 <u>Webster 1828 Dictionary</u>: *will*. The modern definition of the word is "used to express desire, choice, willingness, consent …" (Dictionary.com) *Will* used to be about decision instead of desire.

Let's look at how my will worked at the moment my dad started attacking my mom. I reasoned about his level of sobriety; I decided if I could handle him or not and the outcome I preferred, then I chose either to fight or avoid him. I always chose to protect my mom from being hit even though I would get it. In that horrible situation, my will was crushed. Really, I made only one choice—to survive. I was forced to endure the abuse, but I could stop feeling it, so I checked out. Those weren't bad choices then, but as a grown-up, I've had to rethink all those decisions.

Fast forward to today: a boss yells and I jump; a child pouts and I crumble; a friend feels hurt and I twist myself into a pretzel to please them; my husband is unhappy and I lie down and die. Many years after the abuse ended, I still struggle to confront someone who sins against me; to stand up to angry men and stand for godly actions; to speak up when I disagree with someone; and to allow my body to feel anything. That is the staying power of decisions. My ongoing challenge is to see the choices I have today that weren't available then and steer the rudder of my will to a different place.

Weak-Willed Women

What happens when we lose control of our will? 2 Timothy 3:2–7 warns us about bad men and what happens when we become their targets:

> *(They) are proud, abusive, disobedient, boastful, ungrateful, unholy, unloving, brutal, conceited, rash, and treacherous...They are the kind who worm their way into homes and **gain control over weak-willed women**, who are loaded down with sins and swayed by all kinds of evil desires, always learning but never able to acknowledge the truth.* (emphasis mine)

A woman with a weak will:

Is controlled by other people:
    Allows bad men into her home and life, not realizing they are bad
    Doesn't avoid bad people, confront them, or reject their control
    Doesn't stand up for God's ways
    Rejects responsibility for her own life and choices
    Looks to others for rescue or waits for people to change

Is weighed down by sins and moved by sinful desires (her own and other people's):
    Complaining, wallowing in bitterness or self-pity
    Blaming others and circumstances for the problems

Wanting to play God, following fantasies or desires
Staying in guilt over sins, unable to get to repentance and forgiveness
Thinking shame has the last word
Drinking or other escape behaviors (that don't get her out of the situation)
Lying to cover up
Forgetting the call to love and serve other people

Is trying to learn but unable, because she doesn't see truth:
About herself, God, the other person, the domination of sin, what needs to change
About biblical commands to avoid bad company and walk in the light
About her responsibility for her own actions, thoughts, and words
About her changed identity as a believer in Christ
About her purpose and uniqueness

Loses control because someone evil takes over:
Loses her moral compass, her moral foundation
Stays trapped by keeping her will disengaged
Wears a victim badge, forgetting the victory Christ offers
Is adrift and lost

Satan uses bad men to do bad things and persuades the woman to participate: she is captured because her will is not engaged to do godly things. Then she chooses to stay in the bad situation. God doesn't remove the evil man from this woman's life (although He can), but He gives her the choice to leave and the power to act, and He grieves when she doesn't. The devil can freely destroy her life[88] because her will is in neutral. After Paul describes these bad men, he says bluntly in v. 5: *Have nothing to do with such men—just stay away.*

Unless you make different choices today, you will stay frozen on that platform, living based on choices you made during the abuse, and drifting under the control of someone else's will. You can act or do something even when you don't want to. That's not being overpowered, it's making a choice. When your life is bad, you can stay where you are or turn the rudder and head in a new direction.

In 1 Cor 7:37a, Paul described *the man who has settled the matter in his own mind, not under compulsion but having control over his own will ...*[89] That's maturity, settling the matter in my own mind, deciding how I will honor God and doing what my conscience says is right, even if it's hard or if others disagree. An old saying goes, 'A man convinced *against his will* is of

---
[88] John 10:10- Satan is the thief
[89] This verse refers to the question, "Should I get married or not?" but it can apply to any decision.

the same opinion still.'[90] Without a firm grip on our will, we will be helpless—if we believe our "chooser" was unplugged or erased by the abuse. Even if it was destroyed by coercion, intimidation, bullying, harassment, brainwashing, or cruelty, today your "chooser" still works. It may be limp like spaghetti, but God wants it to be strong like steel.

Grant Me a Willing Spirit

My former pastor, Wayne Barber, taught that at salvation, we receive two spirits; both God's Holy Spirit of power and our new spirit inside which is willing to obey God. The Holy Spirit works on both sides, explaining God's will to us and softening our hearts to respond to Him.

*I will give you a new heart and put a new spirit (*small s = your spirit) *in you; I will remove from you your heart of stone and give you a heart of flesh. And I will put my Spirit* (capital S = His Spirit) *in you and move you to follow my decrees and be careful to keep my laws.*[91]

Psalm 51:12 says *restore to me the joy of your salvation and grant me a willing spirit to sustain me.* Do you want to do God's will? My goal is not to force you into change—I hope you want to unwrap a new way of living. I hope you will be open to new thoughts and new actions, deeper levels of trust and obedience. Are you willing? Or willing to become willing?

The First Choice

In Joshua 24, Joshua pointed to God's faithfulness in bringing the nation of Israel out of slavery into the Promised Land. Then he asked them to make a decision:

> *Now fear the Lord and serve Him with all faithfulness. Throw away the gods your forefathers worshipped ... in Egypt, and serve the Lord. But if serving the Lord seems undesirable to you, then choose for yourselves this day whom you will serve, whether the gods your forefathers served ... or the gods of the Amorites, the land you live in now. But as for me and my household, we will serve the Lord.* (Joshua 24:14-15)

Here's the Barb translation: throw away the old gods you used to serve—the gods of fear, abuse, hatred, sexual perversion, lying, revenge; idols of healing, perfection and painlessness—and serve the Lord. Joshua said to make a choice and live with it. Decide by

---
90 Sir Walter Raleigh
91 Ezekiel 36:26-27

your will, not by default. Throw away foreign gods and yield your heart to the Lord…or not. Then accept the consequences.

Torn in Two

Just before the warning about weak-willed women, Paul explains the source of evil. Paul tells God's servant to gently instruct those who oppose him, *"in hope that … they will come to their senses and escape from the trap of the devil, who has taken them captive to do his will."*[92] Remember, our battles are not against flesh and blood (other people) but against spiritual forces of evil (evil spirits working through people).[93]

Imagine that in the midst of a war, a secret communication from the enemy commander falls into your hands. That is the premise of the book <u>The Screwtape Letters</u>. The enemy commander, one of Satan's demons, writes to a junior demon, teaching him how to destroy a Christian's life. He explains how to get the Man (the demon's assignment) to rebel against the Enemy (God). He explains Man's will (remember it's all opposite, from the demon's point of view):

> To us (demons), a human is primarily food; our aim is the absorption of its will into ours. … But the obedience which the Enemy (God) demands of men is quite a different thing. One must face the fact that all the talk about His love for men, and His service being perfect freedom, is not … merely propaganda, but an appalling truth. He really *does* want to fill the universe with a lot of loathsome little replicas of Himself—creatures whoselife … will be qualitatively like His own, *not because He absorbed them but because their wills freely conform to His*. We want cattle that can finally become food; He wants servants who can finally become sons. We want to suck in, He wants to give out. We are empty and would be filled; He is full and flows over. Our war aim is a world in which Our Father Below has drawn all other beings into himself; the Enemy wants a world full of beings united to Him but still distinct. Merely to override a human will…would be… useless. He cannot ravish. He can only woo.[94] (emphasis mine)

I Was a P.O.W.

Did you hear the bad news? God has a plan for your life, but so does Satan. The devil also wants your heart. His "war aim"—the bottom line on a battlefield—is to ruin you; conquer

---
92 2 Timothy 2:25-26
93 Ephesians 6:12
94 <u>The Screwtape Letters</u>, C.S. Lewis, Touchstone/ Simon and Schuster, New York, NY, © 1961, p. 41

and absorb. Doesn't that sound like abuse where you were conquered and absorbed? Your enemy wants your will erased or overtaken, so you stay trapped in sin and gripped by your past. Like in *The Matrix* movie, the system wants to enslave you, then use you up and destroy you. As Neo said, 'The problem is choice.' When he chose to keep fighting for freedom and world peace, even if it meant his death, it blew the computer's circuits and rebooted the whole world system.[95] His choices threw a wrench into the entire computer system, because the control program didn't allow for them.

> God *enables* man to accomplish His will. Satan *uses* man to accomplish his will.
> God *wants* us to choose His ways willingly. Satan *traps* us into doing his will blindly.
> God *invites* us to be part of a team. Satan *forces* our cooperation.
> God gives *information and knowledge*. Satan *hides* lies in half-truths.
> God *reveals* guidelines and commands. Satan *rebels* against rules and relies on *self-rule*.
> God *blesses* us for obedience, even if it's small. Satan *mocks* us for feeble attempts.
> God *forewarns* us about consequences for choices. Satan *downplays* and *discounts* them.
> God *disciplines* firmly but lovingly. Satan encourages *defiance*, then *punishes* daily.
> God *cleanses* us from sin. Satan *condemns* for less than perfection.
> God gives us *choices*. Satan *takes away our freedom*.

Sadly, anyone can be a tool in Satan's hand. Satan's cunning made Eve eat the apple,[96] Amnon rape Tamar, Judas betray Jesus and the Pharisees crucify Him. Abusers do as they please and serve the gods of alcohol, drugs, power, pleasure, and sex. Anyone who rages, manipulates, slanders, guilt-trips, or punishes is trying to control you and steal your choices.

C.S Lewis said, 'Each day we are becoming a creature of splendid glory or one of unthinkable horror.'[97] It all depends on your choices. Even if you didn't have any say back then, you do now. The abuser was used by Satan, but will you continue to serve him with your decisions? Or will you make different choices?

What Choices Do You Have?

When I missed a shot in tennis because I didn't move my feet, my coach would yell, "Don't just DO something, stand there!" The mixed-up line always got a laugh, but also a reaction: I had to move. Here are some choices in your actions when confronting evil:

1. When Abigail was confronted with the threat that her household was about to be destroyed by David's angry response to her foolish drunken husband, she took action.

---
95 *The Matrix*, Warner Brothers, © 2006
96 2 Corinthians 11:3
97 C.S. Lewis, <u>A Heart for God</u>

She humbly begged David to reconsider, even though her life was at risk. **Abigail stood firm and spoke**. She reasoned with her opponent, trying to calm him down and remind him his life was in God's hands. (1 Samuel 25)

2. When Joseph was tempted by Potiphar's wife, he took off. He rejected her sexual advances and left the house (naked) to avoid sin. **Joseph ran**. Even though he was falsely accused of rape and thrown into prison, he acted in a godly way. (Genesis 39)

3. When giant Goliath mocked God's people, David proclaimed his faith in a big God. David remembered God's faithfulness, got prepared, then used what he had available (stones) to defeat the giant. **David fought**. (1 Samuel 17)

4. When believers attacked the Apostle Paul's past, he admitted both his religious history and his murderous, sinful actions. Then, he **put the past behind him** and looked ahead at what God had planned for him. **Paul walked forward**. (Philippians 3:13-14)

I used to feel like the sum total of all the abuses that happened. Today, I believe even if my circumstances are bad, and the people around me are evil, my will is the bigger issue. My choices are more crucial than my circumstances. If I can't control my surroundings, I can choose my actions and reactions, my words, thoughts and decisions. I won't just stand there when I can do something.

Warning! There is no formula for knowing which action to choose; you have to depend on the Holy Spirit to lead you in each situation.

Rethink Failures

My mom was not a Christian, but she taught me some important truths. One of them was, "Always get up one more time than you fall down." We will fall, fail, and falter. But failures can turn into successes if we learn from them, get up, and try something different. Based on Galatians 6:9, my pastor taught, "It's always too soon to quit."[98] Melanie drew an upward coil to explain Christian growth, with a dark side and a light side. "You want to go from success to success, always in the light," she said, "but life is more like moving along a **coil**. Sometimes in light and sometimes in darkness, but gradually moving higher. Darkness doesn't mean you are back at ground zero. Soon you will come into the light again. The key is to keep going and not stop on the dark side." We can learn faster, and get to the light sooner. I had always thought God dropped me (when I sinned), so I sat down in the dark, waiting until He found me again.

---
98 Galatians 6:9—*Don't grow weary in well-doing.*

One bad day, I was at my desk crying because life was so hard. My boss said I was looking at failure all wrong; that it meant starting over at the beginning, like the game Chutes and Ladders, sliding back to square one. He said really every step took me higher. If I had climbed up five steps but fallen back three, I was still two steps ahead. That made sense to my accounting brain. Focus on progress instead of failures. Fight back to life.

Why Don't You Choose?

Does your "I can't" come from frustration when you can't do something perfectly? Writer Barbara Crafton ponders this in the Bible story of Jesus and the children:

> "Let the children come," (Jesus) said, "and don't shoo them away. You must become like them …to enter the household of God." We usually think of their innocence…or their vulnerability. But…we must add children's endless curiosity, their boundless drive to know things they do not yet know, and to try to do things they cannot yet do.
>
> The frustration of being unable to master a task is bitter. It takes a brave person to persevere in the face of it. Toddlers are that brave—they climb steps as high as their hips, struggle mightily to push across the floor a chair that weighs as much as they do. **Their drive to learn is greater than their frustration, and it carries them.** (my highlight)
>
> When does a child lose that desire to learn? When does the size or frustration of a task overwhelm the drive to know? When does it become too hard? When does it turn into "I'd rather not know," instead of "Why?"[99]

Do you remember when you stopped wanting to learn? When did a task first seem overwhelming? I learned so little about real life growing up that I have started at zero in almost every area. I was bad at things like cooking, making friends, loving strangers, and handling bullies, until I practiced. When I first learned to ski, even easy green runs felt risky. Now I take blue runs with ease. 'The first time is always the hardest,' Cris says, 'but it gets easier.' I believe that anything worth doing well is worth doing badly at first. What can you start doing badly? God accepts baby steps, and says if you are faithful in little things, you will someday be faithful in bigger things too.[100]

The Flylady says that to have a clean house and a life that runs smoothly, start by washing

---
99 Barbara Crafton, *Almost Daily eMo* from the Geranium Farm, copyright 2001-2010.
100 Luke 16:10

the dishes and shining your sink every night before you go to bed.[101] It's a little thing, but she encourages "establishing little habits that string together into simple routines to help your day run on automatic pilot." Changing a lifetime of thoughts, emotions, actions, or habits is discouraging, overwhelming, confusing, and frustrating. Small changes and small steps will lead to bigger ones.

People Traps

Decisions are often driven by people's reactions. Fear of disapproval or shame or punishment is a strong motivator to give them what they want: obedience, good-girl behavior, silent cooperation with wrong, etc. Rejection, withdrawing, a lifted eyebrow, an angry outburst, a slap, or a beating taught us to make sure others were happy with our decisions. We learned to be marionettes on someone else's stage. They pulled the strings and we complied. This is the "*fear of man (that) proves to be a snare.*"[102]

One day I was telling Melanie how my husband/boss/friends/church were all doing it wrong. If they would just do it right, my life would be good. Melanie stopped me mid-thought and said, "Barb, once *you* do it right, then you can tell *others* how to do it right." She meant stop trying to change others (who you cannot change); change yourself (who you can). I told her I had my hands full with my own actions. She smiled and said, "That's the point." I heard speaker Florence Littauer admit that she tried for years to change her husband, Fred, but he was a slow learner. One day, she decided she couldn't change Fred, so she would change herself. Everyone laughed when she said, "And I am a fast learner!"

I Just Don't

One day at camp, I was in trouble for putting honey on the outhouse seat (I was Bold Barb away from home). I didn't understand a sign in the director's office: "Not to decide is to decide." She explained that if I put off making a decision, my choices can disappear. For example, if a sale ends Thursday, but I wait until Friday, *time* made the decision for me. By waiting and doing nothing, I "decided" not to take the sale price. My choices are limited because of circumstances or other people's choices. My "decision" is the only possibility that remains, if there is one.

No choice IS a choice. Not to decide for God is to decide for the enemy of your soul. Do you want to give more control of your life to your enemy? Or let someone else decide for you? Get off the platform by choosing. Hebrews 5:14 says you train yourself to know

---

101 aka: Marla Cilley at http://www.flylady.net/d/getting-started/31-beginner-babysteps/
102 Proverbs 29:25, which ends with *but whoever trusts in the Lord will be safe.*

good from evil by consistently obeying God's directions. Stubbornness keeps you locked in pain, but obedience can help you avoid years of consequences. Want to graduate from the School of Hard Knocks? Want to leave the platform of indecision behind? Bend your knee; submit your will to the Lord, then act.

I Don't Feel Like It

"The difference between perseverance and obstinacy is that one comes from a strong will, and the other from a strong won't."[103] Which is stronger, your will or your won't? Are you the kind who will finish something despite every obstacle? Could someone call you a bulldog as a compliment for hanging on? Or are you more like a mule, digging your heels into the ground and refusing to move?

How often are you expected to do things you don't want to do? Can you do something even when it's hard? Giving Christmas presents to people who hate you; honoring someone at work when you think they are undeserving; cleaning; finding receipts for your tax return? These things may be difficult, or seem impossible, but they all have to be done. Have you felt the sense of relief when the taxes are mailed? The hard conversation behind you? The award dinner over? When you do what is right, God blesses you, and you grow in maturity.

I Can't Trust God

Two people board a plane bound for Australia. The woman has flown many times, takes a book to read, doesn't even listen to the safety announcements, and sleeps for most of the flight, arriving rested and confident. But an elderly man on his first flight is panicked. He frantically reads the safety instructions, asks the flight attendant about every bump and noise, white-knuckles it all the way. They both land in Australia, but who enjoyed the flight?[104] Trusting God is like trusting the pilot to get you there safely, so you can relax and enjoy the trip.[105]

You can choose to get on a tour bus without knowing the guide, but the longer you are on the tour, the deeper your relationship will be. He knows the road and will lead you through interesting places that can change your worldview. Trust develops when you follow his directions and enjoy new experiences. Over time, you develop a good history based on his predictable directions.[106] He may have protected you from disappointment

---

103 Henry Ward Beecher
104 Daniel Schumann, Counselor, Biblical Discipleship seminar, Hoffmantown, Albuquerque, NM, summer 2011
105 Proverbs 3:5-6 *Trust in the Lord with all your heart, do not lean on your own understanding.*
106 *He that putteth his trust in the Lord shall be safe.* Proverbs 29

or rescued you from a problem. He doesn't backstab or criticize. He isn't run by emotions or impulses. His word is good. Your mind rests on his integrity, trueness, and justice.[107] His integrity gives you confidence. God alone is good.[108]

"Jump, Barb, trust Me," God whispers. I say I will, but I don't let go until I can feel the ground beneath my feet. He wants me to jump into the air, trusting that He will catch me. Our words say, "God, I will trust and follow," but our actions shout, "I'm in charge." It's like buying a ticket for a 30-day tour, boarding the bus, but getting off an hour later.

Isaiah 30:19-21 says: *O people of Zion, who live in Jerusalem, you will weep no more. How gracious he will be when you cry for help! As soon as he hears, he will answer you...Whether you turn to the right or the left, your ears will hear a voice behind you, saying, 'This is the way; walk in it.'*

Sometimes it feels like you are driving from L.A. to New York when God says, "Turn right at St. Louis." Seriously, Lord? Change direction in the middle of the trip? But if you choose to turn, you will see Him working and experience His presence in new ways. Your faith will grow, and soon you will experience the joy that comes from obedience.

The Problem with Promises

I used to believe that when God promised an abundant life, it meant my **outside** life (my circumstances). Abuse didn't fit into my picture of a good life, so I doubted God's love and rebelled against His commands. But God's promises are mostly **inside** promises. He changes us so we can walk through the circumstances. He fills us with the fruit of the Spirit; love, joy, peace, patience, goodness, kindness, humility, faithfulness, and self- control. If we expect inside promises to be outside fixes, we will be angry when it doesn't work. For example:

> God doesn't promise peaceful circumstances, He promises peace: *inner calm* in the storm.
> God doesn't promise a life without pain and suffering, but *comforts* us in the midst of it.
> God doesn't promise life without problems, but offers *wisdom* in the problem.
> God doesn't promise life without hardships, but promises *strength* to endure.

We interpret joy to mean that our circumstances will be joyful; we will have loving parents, be esteemed by others, treated fairly, and will be blessed beyond measure. But when you experience joy in your heart, when you know and believe that God is good, wise and

---

107 Webster's 1828 Dictionary definition of *trust*, http://1828.mshaffer.com/
108 Matthew 19:17

sovereign, you can confidently move through difficult circumstances. You don't have to work at having joy—because Christ is in you, joy is in you! Your job now is to let what is inside you flow out.

God will work all things out for your good and His glory. And you are not the exception. (He will bless you too). One woman's daughter was getting married back East in Spring, where the weather is unpredictable. The morning was beautiful, but the wind whipped the bride's veil around later, getting in the car. With weak faith, the mom said she prayed selfishly, "God, can you make the day clear for us?" When they got to the church ten minutes later, it was like Oz; calm, clear, blue, perfect. She was grateful for the answered prayer and felt like a loved child. In spite of her little faith, God blessed her abundantly. He changed the outside situation, but more importantly, He grew her trust and changed her prayers.

Draw Near to God

You can know God's will for your life by getting to know Him: the God who reveals Himself as One who loves, woos us to relationship, and waits to be loved in response. Jesus taught us to invite God's will through prayer: "*Your kingdom come, Your will be done on earth as it is in heaven*"[109]—that is, perfectly, completely, and continuously.

Cris knows me really well. She knows my value system, my character, and most of my responses. If someone pretended to be me and said, "You should go get drunk," she would reject it, because I would never say that. Jesus said, '*My sheep know My voice.*'[110] You may not have seen it, but God has proven His faithfulness to you hundreds of times. God's desires and plans for you are good, pleasing, and perfect.[111] Learn to recognize God's voice by reading and memorizing the Bible. Spend time hanging out in His presence (pray, meditate on Scripture, rest before Him), listen to the counsel of godly people and fellowship with His people (in church, Bible studies, discipling).

> Did a friend stand with you against an enemy? God defends when Satan accuses us.[112]
> Did a relative help you in difficulty? God is our refuge, an ever-present help in trouble.[113]
> Did your co-worker work for you when you were sick? God covers our sin.[114]
> Does your pet love you unconditionally? Nothing can ever separate us from God's love.[115]

---
109 Matthew 6:10
110 John 10:27
111 Romans 12:2
112 Romans 8:33-34
113 Psalm 46:1
114 Psalm 32:1
115 Romans 8:38

It All Boils Down to Choices

Every day, we have thousands of choices about how to live. Even in trials, He always "provides a **righteous way out** so that you can stand (a powerful verse to memorize)."[116] Temptations are normal (common to man) but our faithful God will not let you be tempted beyond what you can bear. We can choose:

> to act or to be paralyzed
> to believe new truths or old lies
> to accept authority and submit to God or reject it and rebel
> to worship God or else a person, your feelings, or your fantasies
> to forgive or hold onto a grievance; to let go or plan revenge
> to give in to temptation or to deny it
> to say kind words or to tear someone down in anger
> to draw back in fear or to walk forward in faith

I counseled a gal who had been raped, then rebelled for many years. She railed at her situation, but when she understood about her will, she snapped, "Choices, choices, choices, it all boils down to choices!" Then she took charge of her will and changed her life by submitting to God. Rising above the trauma, she found freedom from her past, eventually leading a women's Bible study using her sweet, strong faith.

When Actions Aren't Enough

Engaging your will is a fierce battle, which begins with behavior change and controlling your thoughts. But lasting change only comes from heart change. Oswald Chambers explains:

> The reason the battle is lost is that I fight it first in the external world. Get alone with God, do battle before Him. *I must first get the thing settled between God and me, once and for all, in the secret places of my soul,*[117] *where no one else can interfere.* Then I can go ahead, knowing with certainty that the battle is won. Until this is done, I lose every time. The battle may take a minute or a year; that will depend on me, not on God. Lose it there, and calamity, disaster, and defeat before the world are as sure as the laws of God.

---

116 1 Corinthians 10:13
117 I think these include past hurts, inner vows, foundational lies, motives, and other hidden things.

> In dealing with other people, our stance should always be to *drive them toward making a decision of their will. That is how surrendering to God begins*…When God brings us to a major turning point—a crossroads—from that point we either go toward a more lazy, slow, and useless Christian life, or we become more and more on fire, giving our utmost for His highest—our best for His glory. (all emphases mine)[118]

Remember the Future

The Jews are the only group of people in history who were still a nation after being exiled from their homeland for 1700 years. But every year, at the end of Yom Kippur (the Day of Atonement), they proclaimed, "Next year in Jerusalem!" They were saying, "I'm not there now, but I know where God wants me to end up. I may not like where I am, but God promised me that I will live in the Promised Land, and I will keep looking to that future."[119] The challenge was to act on their faith—did they believe God would keep His promises or not? "Next year in Jerusalem" means many things:

- It suggests being on the cusp but not yet having arrived.
- It holds a sense of possibility that is rich and alive.
- It looks forward to the Messiah's coming.
- It represents the final peace of complete spiritual redemption.
- It represents the possibility of total intimacy with God.
- The prophecy that Israel will soon find peace and Jerusalem will remain a haven for Diaspora (outcast) Jews who still live under oppression.
- Looking to the future offers the completeness[120] that feels beyond reach in our shattered daily lives.[121]
- It offers potential for revolutionary change—things don't have to be the way they are, and oppressive regimes can change.[122]

Imagine God's future for you: where could you be on this date next year? What is your Jerusalem? An abundant life? Peace that passes understanding? Supernatural wisdom about things you couldn't know? Hope for the future? Restored relationships? Trusting in God's mercy and grace? Knowing God's purpose for your life? Take time to Journal. Heading toward the future means leaving the platform you are standing on now. Instead of dwelling

---

118 Oswald Chambers, My Utmost for His Highest, Barbour and Company, Westwood, NJ: 1935
119 Hebrew4Christians.com/Holidays/Fall_Holidays/Yom_Kippur/yom_kippur.html
120 *shlelmut*: also wholeness, healing. Hebrew4Christians.com Hebrew glossary
121 http://www.myjewishlearning.com/holidays/Jewish_Holidays/Passover/The_Seder/Conducting_a_Seder/After_the_Meal/Next_Year_in_Jerusalem.shtml
122 Ibid, citing both the miracles of creation and the exodus from Egypt, but this also applies to our lives.

on the despair of the past, decide to head out in a different direction. You **can** change your life—not the past, but all your tomorrows. Trust me, God has an incredible life planned for you in the Land of Grace.

Does it give you hope to know that your life can be based on your choices, instead of a bad person's? Does it give you hope to know that you can change your choices right now, without waiting for something or someone? Following God's directions will change your life.

Anything for the Poofy File? If you haven't already, write your Big question.

Bottom Lines:

1. You have a choice. Get on a train headed anywhere, away from where you are.
2. Take responsibility for your own choices.
3. Follow God because you choose to obey, not because you are overpowered.
4. Four choices: Run Away, Fight, Stand Firm, or Focus on the Future.
5. Anything worth doing well is worth doing badly at first.

Questions to Discuss:

1. Have you been a weak-willed woman? Are there times when you were held captive by Satan to do his will? Or times when you let a bad man or woman take over your life?

2. What keeps you from making choices? Have you ever blamed someone for making bad choices that you went along with?

3. Did you have real choices growing up or during the abuse? What were some of the lose/lose choices you had?

4. What have you been unwilling to do poorly?

5. What would you like your future to look like? Pray and make plans to travel there.

To the Friend of the Traveler:

1. Your friend is capable of doing much more than they think they can. As you listen, help identify "frozen" places and the reason for being stuck (It's helpful to write these down, because they will come up again and again). Together, come up with a change

based on the Bible. Encourage their baby steps. Be patient with failures. Remind them of truths when familiar fears crop up.

2. It takes an incredible amount of mental, physical, emotional energy to fight old habits. Support your friend by praying for them and praising changes. Remember, they're climbing a mountain.

3. After a while, if they still don't engage their will, ask them if they don't know what to do or are they unwilling to do it? If the first, go back to the Bible to find direction and/or talk to a godly discipler, counselor, or pastor for help. If the second, find what's keeping them frozen. Remind them of the pain of staying in old patterns and the joy that's waiting for them.

Worship Song: *It's a New Day* by Hillsong London[123]

---

[123] Tim Michael, /www.youtube.com/watch?v=4mCdDetLp-U Album *Jesus Is*, Integrity Music, © 2006

Chapter 5
What Drives You?

The whole second year I was separated from Jim, I felt torn in two by the war in my heart. I toyed with moving forward; part of me screamed *divorce him*, but part still wanted to reconcile. I fought with Melanie about divorce, trying to convince her that I had already blown it by marrying Jim; why make the same mistake twice? I lay awake nights begging God to set me free, reminding Him how young and banged up I had been. Yet for all my excuses, I couldn't make a decision and I couldn't stop the fire raging in my soul. So one Saturday morning, I grabbed a cup of coffee and my Bible and sat down at the kitchen table to find a way to put out the flames.

Have you been there? Was there a time in your life when you felt torn between two opposite directions? Mine was: leave my husband or go back to my marriage. What was yours?

This chapter will be a bit different than the previous ones. It is more "theological." Rather than jumping in the car and racing down the road, we will take it to the garage to prepare for the trip. But we will do more than just get gas, rotate the tires, change the oil, check the belts, or get a tune-up. This chapter will be a heart check.

New Engine

Imagine that you inherited a 20-year-old Toyota, an old car with odd quirks. Some days it runs smoothly, sometimes it won't even start. The mechanic says the engine is beyond repair and you shouldn't spend any more money fixing it. You limp it along until one day you hear about a Master Mechanic who can fix it permanently. When you pick it up, you realize he didn't fix the old engine; he unhooked it—making it powerless—and installed a new engine in the trunk. The new engine is amazingly powerful, smooth and reliable. It runs on a completely new power source: air. Just think, no more car repairs, and no more lines at the pump!

At first, it's awkward learning to work the new engine. It doesn't respond like you are used to. One day, in frustration, you disconnect the new engine and hook up the old one, thinking *just for today. It's easier to shift the old way. I can't handle learning to drive a new way.* The car doesn't have as much zip but it gets you there. You like feeling in control, so you install a toggle switch on the dashboard that lets you choose which engine runs the car. If you want to show off your power, you use the new engine. For everyday stuff, you switch to the old one. *Why waste the new engine on such mundane things?* Soon you toggle back and forth depending on the situation.

C.S. Lewis said Christians are "hybrids," with two powerful engines inside.[124] Our heart has dual motors: two natures that operate in the spiritual realm. Before salvation, you have one engine. After salvation, you can choose by the toggle switch (a.k.a. your will) which engine runs the car. You can drive from place to place using either engine, but you will have vastly different amounts of power and dependability.

Working Against Each Other

Every person is born with one engine—the old nature—but Christians have a second engine: a divine nature like Christ's. The two engines aren't neutral powers; they continually fight within us. That morning, sipping coffee and searching through my Bible, my two natures were at war, pulling my heart in opposite directions. My new nature wanted to do good (commit to my marriage). But my old nature fought me: it wanted my sinful will to dominate (divorce Jim and walk away from God). This inner battle is described throughout the Bible:

For the sinful nature desires **what is contrary** *to the Spirit, and the Spirit (desires) what is contrary to the sinful nature. They are* **in conflict** *with each other, so that you do not do what you want.* (Galatians 5:17)

When I want to do good, evil is right there with me. For in my **inner being** *I delight in God's law, but* **another law (is) at work in the members of my being, waging war** *against the law of my mind and making me a prisoner of the* **law of sin**... (Romans 7:21-23)

It happens so regularly, it's predictable. The moment I decide to do good, sin is there to trip me up. I truly delight in God's commands, but it's pretty obvious that not all of me joins in that delight. Parts of me **covertly rebel**, *and just when I least expect it, they* **take charge***. I've tried everything and nothing helps. I'm at the end of my rope.* (Romans 7:21-24, the MSG)

"Really, Barb, so what if I have two engines? Does it matter?" Oh, yes. Unless you recognize the battle, you will be puzzled by your choices. Like me, you will believe what is wrong with you is because of what happened to you. You think you can fix yourself, your marriage or circumstances, your friends, your heart or your life if you just work **really** hard. Like me, you couldn't be more wrong.

---
124 The Screwtape Letters, C.S. Lewis, Touchstone/ Simon and Schuster, New York, NY, © 1961

Mirror, Mirror on the Floor

If you don't understand the two engines/natures, you might see your heart very differently. For a long time, I described my heart like a mirror shattered into hundreds of pieces by abuse. I tried to put it back together; combing through the pieces, finding a few that fit. The edges cut, but I kept on, accepting the pain and trying to repair the mirror. Over the years, I glued enough pieces together to have a small heart. But success at best was a jagged, broken reflection, marked by abuse. Friend, is that the abundant life God promises?[125] No. Do you yearn for more? I did.

Broken Heart

I thought I was wrecked because of what happened to me—if the abuse hadn't happened; if I wasn't married; if my family had been normal—then I would be all right. I thought I was a victim of life: my problems came from something outside my control. I was broken and needed to be fixed, so I kept struggling to glue the mirror back together. I tried to fix myself by recovering my lost child, repairing my self-esteem, and digging deep into my wounded heart. But the Bible says my problem was not outside of me; it was inside. Why couldn't I just repair my heart like fixing a broken engine or a shattered mirror? Because the heart is *terminally ill*. I was trying to fix the unfixable. Jeremiah 17:9 says, "The heart is *deceitful* above all things, and:

> *beyond cure,*
> > *hopelessly dark,*
> > > *desperately wicked,*
> > > > *incurably sick.* "[126]

Listen carefully, my friend. It doesn't say "an abused person's heart" or "a depressed person's heart." There are no qualifiers. Every heart is the same; desperately, incurably sick and—even worse—totally deceitful. That sick, broken heart is the heart I had *before anything bad happened, even before the abuse. I am not messed up because I was abused. I am messed up because I was born that way.* It's like I was born with a defective heart that needed a transplant (that was me originally). Later, I had a heart attack (that was abuse against me). A heart attack only compounded my need for a new heart. I was broken, but I was *"broke before I was broke."* Abuse intensified the mess and turbo-charged my sin nature. Would you want to fix your heart from the heart attack but ignore the original defects? That's what I did by trying to fix my old nature.

---
125 John 10:10
126 Jeremiah 17:9 from different versions—NIV; The Message; KJV; HCSB; ESV; Amplified

How much energy have you expended trying to fix the unfixable? Want off the hamster wheel? Want off the merry-go-round that makes you sick with the spinning? Realize the battle between hearts is not because of your abuse. It's not because of your past, your parents or your present circumstances; it exists because you are a spirit-being clothed in flesh. Former pastor Mark Driscoll of Mars Hill Church said, "You were born in a battle."[127]

The Problem of Sin

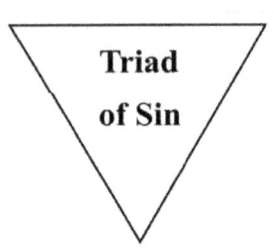

When you describe the defective heart (the old engine), there's bad news and worse news. The bad news is that the old nature is naturally sinful, with nothing good in it. It has desires of its own that reject godly goals. It is a bigger liar than the greatest liar you have ever known. The old heart lives for self—it's all about ME: what I want, how and when I want it. Every time we act out of the old nature, it comes out in sin. Sin means missing the mark of God's perfection. We sin when we fail to obey God's standards either deliberately or from ignorance—when we cross a moral line; defy God's commands; plan evil or wickedness; give in to old desires; go back to rebellion or self-rule; pervert God's purity or focus on self instead of God.[128] The Bible calls the old nature *the flesh, the sin nature, sin living in me, the old self, the old man.*

Every choice you make is a toggle to an engine, old or new. The desperate wickedness of the old heart doesn't stay tucked inside: the raging battle within shows outside, when sinful desires spill through our actions. This sinful progression that starts in the heart is described in James 1:14-15: *But each one is tempted when, by* **his own evil desire***, he is dragged away and enticed. Then, after desire has conceived, it* **gives birth to sin***; and sin, when it is fully-grown,* **gives birth to death***.*

Evil desire: I want more money any way I can get it
→ Conception—*I could fudge my expense report*
  → Birth of sin—*I put in personal expenses on my expense report*
    → Birth of your death—*I get fired for stealing, am separated from God's heart*

Then the news gets worse: because the soul's default is the flesh (the old nature), if you're not driving forward, you are driving backwards. If you don't walk by the Spirit, you WILL operate out of the flesh. Romans 8:8 says *those who live in the flesh*

---

127 Mark Driscoll, Vodcast, Gospel of Luke part 49, Luke 11:14-28: Jesus vs. Satan, 10/11/10
128 Sin lives in the will. Vine's Complete Expository Dictionary, p. 576 (266 b.) Gr. *hamartia* - is seated in

cannot please God. Galatians 5:17 (MSG) says: *These two ways of life are antithetical (opposites), so that you cannot live at times one way and at times another way according to how you feel...* It says 'cannot,' but we do it all the time; toggle between old engine and new. Sadly, most Christians I meet don't know how to toggle to the new engine, out of their flesh.

God's Solution — A New Heart

We can never fix the old engine (the sin nature), but God the Master Mechanic has solved the problem several ways. First, Christ the sinless Son of God died on our behalf. He took all our sin and God's wrath onto Himself on the cross, which disconnected the old engine. Then He transplanted His divine nature into us (the new engine). Greek scholar Kenneth Wuest explains this dramatic change from Romans 6:

> These two things are the result of a major surgical operation which God performs in the inner being of every sinner He saves; breaking the power of indwelling sin (v. 2—*are dead to sin*) and imparting the divine nature (v. 4—*walk in newness of life*). The sinful nature, although cut off, is not gone. Verse 6...*our old self (sin nature) was crucified with him so that the body of sin might be rendered powerless* (brought to nothing, destroyed),[129] *that we should no longer be slaves to sin*. We are dead to the sinful nature, separated as death separates soul from body. The separation between the believer and the sin nature is a permanent one.[130]

Finally, here is some good news! "*Our old way of life was nailed to the cross with Christ, a decisive end to that sin-miserable life, (so we are) no longer at sin's ever beck and call!*"[131] The flesh remains but no longer controls us. The new driving force is the divine nature: Christ within us, holy, perfect and righteous. "*The Spirit of life in Christ, like a strong wind, has magnificently cleared the air, freeing you from a fated lifetime of brutal tyranny at the hands of sin and death.*"[132] The brutal tyranny of your life is not sexual abuse or your past: it is sin, all sin—your old nature acting out sinful desires: sins you have done and will do; and your sinful responses to sins that were done to you.

The Bible offers only one cure for an incurably sick heart: a total heart replacement. '*I will give you a **new heart** and put a **new spirit** in you; I will remove from you your heart of stone and **give you a heart of flesh*** (Ezekiel 36:26).' By His grace, He sweeps all the

---

129 Rendered powerless (NIV); brought to nothing (ESV); destroyed (KJV).
130 <u>Word Studies in the Greek New Testament</u>, Volume 1, Romans, by Kenneth Wuest, page 93-94
131 Romans 6:6, The Message version
132 Romans 8:2, The Message version

broken pieces of your heart into the trash and gives you a new, whole, perfect heart as a gift: a miniature of His heart to keep. This transplant fixes both heart problems at once. So here's more good news: you can stop trying to fix your broken heart. Open your hands and accept the priceless gift He's given you.

What Reveals Which Engine is Driving?

So how can you know which engine powers the car? The battle *within* always becomes the battle *without*: our words, actions and attitudes reveal the heart that is driving. The sin nature responds to temptation (pulling us toward sin like a magnet) or testing (rejecting God and running toward self-rule). We see the split in two lists from Galatians chapter 5. The first list describes actions that are flesh-driven. The second list describes our fruit when we operate in the Spirit.

List 1: The Old Man—the acts of the sinful nature are obvious (Galatians 5:19-20):

Sexual immorality, impurity and debauchery; idolatry and witchcraft; hatred, discord, jealousy, fits of rage, selfish ambition, dissentions, factions, and envy; drunkenness, orgies, and the like.

List 2: The New Man—the fruit of the Spirit is (Galatians 5:22-23):

Love, joy, peace, patience, kindness, goodness, faithfulness, gentleness, and self-control.

As ugly as List 1 is, it is *who we all are* apart from Christ. There are four main ways the natural human heart acts out in sins.[133] (After each part, I've inserted part of my story from Chapter 1 that showed my sinful heart driving.)

The first area of sin is *sexual immorality, impurity and debauchery*,[134] which relates to **counterfeit love**. We want love, but immorality gives a lustful twist: hook-ups, casual sex, friends with benefits, sexting, masturbation, fantasizing, threesomes, pornography, pedophilia and prostitution. Uncontrolled passion displays the heart's sinful bent.

> *I go back to old tricks to make it through—fantasize about violent sex and then "go away," tune out.*
> *I quit church, drink wildly, start cursing, have an affair, mock Christians every chance I get.*

---
133 Pastor Wayne Barber on Galatians 5, Hoffmantown Church, Living Grace sermon series
134 Debauchery is unrestrained self-indulgent behavior.

The second area of sin is **counterfeit worship**, which shows up in idolatry and witchcraft; we worship created things, people or objects rather than the Creator.[135] John Calvin said, "Our hearts are idol factories."[136] We will worship anything other than God.

> *My whole goal in life was to get out of pain.*
> *If only Jim would do things my way. If only he would love me....*

One way to reveal the object of your worship is to identify "if only's." Thoughts of "if only I had ..." or "if only they did ..." can reveal what you think will make you happy. What do you *want*? What do you *need*? What do you spend your time, money and energy trying to get? When desires control your life, they become idols, something you *must* have. "Demand is closing a fist around a desire."[137] When you demand something, you expect that other people will help you get it and resent them if they don't. We blame God for our failures and go back to self-rule: I worshipped having my own way, and expected Jim to cooperate with that.

The third area where we sin is **counterfeit relationships**. We crave relationships, but we destroy them through *hatred, discord* (fighting and strife), *jealousy, fits of rage, selfish ambition, dissensions, factions* (taking sides), *and envy*. Have you yelled at your husband or kids to do something right? Have you gossiped about someone you don't like to win the favor of someone you do? Have you pitched a fit or slammed the door when things didn't go your way? We demand, manipulate, and control to get what we want and get mad when it is withheld, all from selfish motives. I often say, "It's not who you are when you get what you want, it is who you are when you *don't* get what you want."*[138]* One person controlling another isn't a real relationship. There is no pure love for people in our natural heart; only self-love or lust. To quote Pastor Skip Heitzig: "'I love you' may mean 'I love the way you make me feel.'"[139]

> *... no matter how much I had asked Jim to change, he wouldn't listen.*
> *I treated him the same way my parents treated each other ... all anger*
> *or sarcasm. I yelled at him, demanding that he lead ... then mocked his*
> *choices. I berated him for simple mistakes, then called him lazy when he*
> *stopped trying. When I tore into him, he lied to me, then avoided me.*

The fourth area of sin is **counterfeit pleasures**. We desire pleasure but over-indulge in *drunkenness, orgies, and the like* (think frat party). If one drink feels good, five will feel

---
135 Romans 1:25
136 Paul David Tripp, <u>Instruments in the Redeemer's Hand</u>, P & R Publishing, Phillipsburg, NJ © 2002 p. 86
137 Ibid.
138 Good advice when you're dating someone!
139 Calvary Chapel ABQ, sermon series in 2000.

better. The last lover didn't do it, so hook a better one. If one piece of pie tastes great, the whole pie will be better. We take a pleasurable experience and morph it into a lifestyle seeking good feelings or pain relief.

> *I had offered Jim the biggest sacrifice I could give. When I drank enough to numb the pain in my body and my heart, I could have sex with him. (For me, pleasure meant not feeling anything.)*

We all find ourselves on the wrong list somewhere. When wrong love, wrong worship, wrong relationships or wrong pleasures drive us, we cry out *how can I be godly*? If you're shocked at the things you do on this list, you're probably not on the battlefield yet. Being a Christian doesn't mean you won't do sinful things; Christians have a way out—we can choose to toggle to the second list, the Spirit-powered engine. The battle begins when you *turn away* from your sins. Then every day—sometimes minute-by-minute—face the battle within.

Forcing Myself to Be a Christian

What I want to do, I do not do, but what I hate I do.
When I want to do good, evil is right there with me.
What a wretched man I am! Who will rescue me from this body of death?
(Romans 7:15,21,24)

Does your internal battle feel harder than anyone else's? Until I understood the battle, I tried to obey Him in my own strength. I didn't understand my new power source (the new engine), so I tried to be godly by making myself. I didn't understand that the flesh's hatred for the spirit kicks up when I try to draw closer to God.[140] God had given me a new heart, but that didn't take away the frustration, anger, hurt and despair of trying to be good and failing.

I used to do Christianity like this: imagine you really want a cookie. It calls you by name. You can imagine how good it will taste, how sweet it will be. You know you shouldn't eat it, so you walk away and turn on the TV. You resolve to not eat it, but you can still hear its voice. You call a friend and ask her to hold you accountable. And still the cookie calls. You hear the excuses; you think you would eat less at dinner if you had the cookie now. You won't eat as much because you won't be so hungry. The battle rages:

I want a cookie. I need a cookie. (like hitting the gas pedal of my flesh engine)

---
140 Kris Lundgaard, The Enemy Within, P & R Publication, Phillipsburg, NJ, © 1998, page 47

I shouldn't eat the cookie. (putting my other foot on the brake pedal of my flesh engine)
My wheels are screaming and smoke is coming off my tires. (I am miserable)

The Key to Freedom

The Holy Spirit takes up permanent residence to aid us in the battle against sin and our effort to live a Christian life.[141]

I agree with speaker John Lynch, who says in his video *TrueFaced*: 'The way to have victory over the sin nature is not trying harder, it is *surrendering to God*.'[142] The secret of Christianity is summed up in James 4:7: Submit. The key to freedom is to stop trying harder to overcome your sin; let Christ overcome you. Then out of that relationship, new actions will flow.[143] Out of His power and grace, you find new strength to do what's right. Then, you call out to God:

"Lord, I want that cookie but I want You more. You never withhold any good thing from me. I want to glorify You even when I eat. (I shift the flesh engine into neutral and engage my Spirit engine). Can I eat the cookie? (I hear a quiet No.) Lord, I bend my will to Yours. Thank You for Your care. You are the bread of life. Your love will fill me. I will turn my eyes upon Jesus and look full in His wonderful face, and the things of this earth (even a cookie) will grow strangely dim, in the light of His glory and grace."

I use *cookie* as a silly example, but you can substitute any desire or sin that controls you. Turning away from a controlling sin is good, and it helps you resist temptation. You can avoid difficult places or ask a friend to hold you accountable. You can push through it, even "do it afraid." But the best way to walk in the Spirit is to '*deny your selfish compulsions and live freely, motivated by God's Spirit.*'[144] He will direct you; will you follow?

Romans 6:13 warns *Do not let sin reign ... so that you obey its evil desires.* **Do not offer the parts of your body to sin**, *as instruments of wickedness but rather* **offer yourselves to God** *as those who have been brought from death to life; and offer ... your body as instruments of righteousness.* Actions are an either/or choice: either obey your evil desires (let your body be a tool of your wicked heart) or obey God (use your body to express God's righteous heart). Either feed your flesh and make it stronger, or feed your spirit. Either follow your flesh or follow Christ. Starting in Albuquerque, you either walk toward Mexico or toward Alaska.

---

141 Word Studies in the Greek New Testament, Volume 1, Romans, by Kenneth Wuest, p. 94
142 John Lynch, See *TrueFaced* video by John Lynch www.youtube.com/watch?v=Rfy03PEVUhQ&feature=related (based on the book by the same name).
143 John 15:5- He is the vine, you are a branch.
144 Galatians 5:16-18, The Message version

Drawn By the Spirit

Galatians 5:18 says "... *if you are led by the Spirit, you are not under the law.*" Led is the operative word. *Led* means following, not leading. *"The grace of God ... teaches us to say no to ungodliness and worldly passions (old nature), and to live self-controlled, upright and godly lives in this present age."*[145] The Spirit leads as we run to God: read the Bible as a road map, look for directions and travel tips, listen to Him as the Guide; take God's highway—His roads, His speed, His method of traveling.

You have a choice to drive under the power of the old nature–sick, sputtering, severely wicked–or the new one–supernaturally strong and reliable. Jesus said, *"If anyone would come after Me, he must deny himself and take up his cross and follow Me."* (Luke 9:23) Does it say "fix yourself"? Build up your self-esteem? Heal yourself? Understand the problem? Talk a lot? No, it says "*deny yourself* and follow Me, daily." Does it give a time frame: when you feel like it, when you feel loved or your self-esteem is high enough, when you don't feel so hopeless? Again, no. Pastor Chuck Smith said, "The only way to deal with the flesh is to starve it to death."[146] You don't build walls, negotiate, hide, run away, blame others, pout, or power up. You consistently disconnect the old engine and choose to toggle to the new one.

Toggling Back and Forth

So what does this choice of actions mean to you? Here are some examples:

Your friend hurts you with her words:
    The flesh says *I can't forgive, I can't let go, I'll never get over this.*
    Flesh wants to retaliate, punish, withdraw, pout, gossip, ignore, condemn.
    The Spirit says *Christ paid all debts and bore the agony of every sin on the cross.*
    The spirit within you honors God by forgiving, considering her needs, walking toward.

Your child embarrasses you in front of your friends:
    The flesh yells *someone must PAY!*
    Flesh controls with anger, humiliation, punishment.
    The Spirit whispers *to God alone belongs vengeance.*
    The spirit within you displays God by teaching, patiently training in righteousness.

---
145 Titus 2:11-12
146 Sermon by Pastor Chuck Smith at Calvary Chapel Costa Mesa

You are drawn towards lustful deeds:
> The flesh thinks *I deserve this; I'm not hurting anybody; God understands.*
> Flesh dwells on, reviews, nurses and increases the thoughts and desires.
> The Spirit whispers *your body is a dwelling place for a holy God.*
> The spirit within you submits to God; you take your thoughts captive to obey Christ.

How Do You Tell?

Examine the Galatians lists and give yourself a *fruit inspection*: compared to the lists, what fruit is growing? Anger, jealousy, bitterness, revenge, sexual sin and wrong worship reveal a heart rooted in the sinful nature. Holiness, humility, gentleness or compassion reveal a new heart working. Matthew 7:1-5 says *examine yourself and take the blinding log of sin out of your own eye first.* Here's an example: imagine you are standing in a long line at Walmart. The customer three people ahead needs a manager's help, then the next person writes out a check rather than swiping a card. How do you react? If you are frustrated and impatient, you may be "worshipping" a short line. In essence, you think *I am here and the line should part like the Red Sea to let me pass. I shouldn't have to wait.*[147]

God uses normal daily circumstances to reveal your heart: in this situation, a heart that wants ease, no hassles, to be first, or to have life go its way. Here's your fruit inspection: Start by asking the Holy Spirit for insight. *Which list am I on? Are my actions from the flesh? What is my heart drawn to? Which action in the second Galatians list can I practice?* Love wants others to be blessed more. Patience waits and waits. Kindness is happy for the good service all the customers get. Goodness isn't easily angered.

We need to examine our fruit, but here's a caution: because the heart is deceitful, our self-image is distorted, protected by denial and self-justification. If you only examine yourself, it's like taking your picture in a carnival's funny mirror. We will not always judge our own actions rightly, so we need the Body (the church and Christian friends) to tell us if our actions are fleshly or spirit-led. You can extend your own fruit inspection by asking others: *Do you see my reaction anywhere on the bad Galatians list? Have I hurt or offended you or others with my actions or words?*

The good news in Matthew 7:5 is that after you have checked your own fruit (taken the log out of your eye), *you can see clearly* to help others take the speck (of sin) out of their eye. You may be able to see what fruit other people are growing, and which heart drives them. We can't judge people's hearts—only God can do that—but we can examine their actions, including words and deeds.

---
[147] Thanks to Daniel Schumann, Biblical Counselor, pastor at Sullivan's Island Baptist Church, for this concept.

Ouch!

God may reveal which heart is in control through our reactions, whether painful, emotional, or too strong.[148] Father Fortane, a Catholic priest in the 1600s, said if you feel pain in a situation, it may reveal a part of your sinful heart that is still alive. When you have died to self, you won't feel pain. Pain can reveal a place not surrendered to God: one that holds secret agendas, demands, desires or expectations. Pain can be a symptom of the battle, showing a driving flesh that hasn't been crucified.

Pain should turn us back to the Bible: as King David said, *"It was good for me to be afflicted so that I might learn Your decrees."*[149] Brought before God, pain changes to sorrow (grief for our sin), confession becomes repentance, and confusion finds wisdom and direction. Rather than trust your feelings, God wants you to test them:

> Why am I hurt? Why am I offended? Why am I feeling_____?
> Am I hurt because my reputation was attacked? Because I didn't look good?
> Because the words were not true, or too true?
> What did I want or desire? Has a need morphed into a demand?
> How was I disappointed? What were my expectations? Was I being selfish?
> What is my "must have?" Am I holding onto something as an idol?

When my goals are the opposite of God's, how do I change? As soon as I realize the old engine is driving, instead of turning to even more fleshly reactions, I flip the toggle switch. Switching to the right engine, I humbly admit *Yes, I am all that. My heart is sinful, but it just shows my need for a Savior, the One who is right here with me.* I run to His love and forgiveness. I can repent in a heartbeat and let God work something new in me, even if it feels awkward. Sometimes it's hard saying no to my way. Sometimes it feels like a sacrifice; something I give to the Lord even when it's painful. But when you consistently nourish the spirit and starve the flesh, the part that "wants what it wants" shrivels and dies.

The old man has to die so you can live the new life. Your part in the battle is to be a "minuteman;" make a choice—sometimes every minute of every day—to drive God's way, not your way.

The Road to Maturity

Daily tests and trials will uncover junk in our hearts. James 1:2-5 tells why: *Consider it*

---

148 Romans 12:21
149 Psalm 119:71

pure joy whenever you face trials of many kinds because you know that the testing of your faith develops perseverance. Perseverance must finish its work so that you may be mature and complete, not lacking anything. Perseverance means keep going and don't quit in the middle of a trial: you do the right thing even when you don't see results, you don't understand, or when people mock you. This builds spiritual muscles. The flesh is weak,[150] so God matures us by testing (to see whether we will give into the flesh's temptations) and trying (to see if we will follow our desires or submit to God's plans). Day by day, we should look more like Jesus, with radical trust, perfect fellowship and joyful obedience. Keep doing what the Bible says to in the day-to-day things, in the little things that are big to God.[151]

The law of sowing and reaping should motivate us: *A man reaps what he sows. The one who sows to please his sinful nature ... will reap destruction; the one who sows to please the Spirit ... will reap eternal life. Then the reward for persevering: Let us not grow weary in doing well, for at the proper time, we will reap a (good) harvest if we do not give up.* (Galatians 6:7-9)

Growing Good Fruit

We compare our actions to the Galatians lists, to see which engine is driving. When the new engine/new heart (Christ in us) is driving, we display sweet fruit; *love, joy, peace, patience, kindness, goodness, faithfulness, gentleness, and self-control.*

The **source** of all good fruit is **love**. This is **real intimacy**: openness, acceptance, caring for others, meeting their legitimate needs. The second part is joy and peace that come from laying things and people aside to **worship** rightly; God alone. The third part marks our **relationships** when we are powered by the Spirit. In godly relationships, there is patience instead of fighting, kindness instead of control, goodness instead of **perversion**, faithfulness that leads to trust and vulnerability, gentleness toward weakness and failures: people working together as a team, practicing daily forgiveness.

The final part is self-control, which is what we need in our **pleasures**. Can you honor God with your body and stay celibate until marriage? Can you eat a meal without having any wine? Can you deny yourself unhealthy foods? Can you watch one TV show instead of an entire evening? Can you hang up on a gossiper?

Big Flesh or Big Spirit?

When I choose to obey God when nothing inside me wants to obey, it's obeying out of **duty**. My flesh is big and strong because I've catered to my thoughts, my desires, and

---
150 Matt. 26:41
151 Luke 16:10

nourished my self-centeredness. I have to drag my will to obey so my flesh doesn't win. The flesh dies hard when I keep feeding it.

DUTY: FLESH   >   spirit

I do something because I have to, to look good, keep the law, or gain favor with God, because of peer pressure. *I do it for* God, like a slave obeying his master. God trains us like a 3-year-old, "You don't know what is best but I do, so obey." There is no joy or sweetness, just my will doing the right thing. It is a starting place, but it still comes out of the old heart. Eventually, I do the right thing again and again, choosing to obey God because of **debt**. 1 Corinthians 6:20 says y*ou were bought at a price* (Jesus' blood). *Therefore honor God with your body*. I obey because of what He did for me. Seems fair. Flesh shrinks and spirit grows, so they are about the same size, roughly equal in strength.

DEBT: FLESH   =   SPIRIT

The battle within is less bloody: it is just as easy to submit to the flesh as it is to the spirit. This is like a 23-year-old saying, "Because God did it for me, I should do it for others. I will obey." I do it *because* of God, out of obligation, as my reasonable service. Again, my actions may look right but my heart may not. I am neither hot nor cold: just lukewarm, with a "whatever" attitude.

Getting the Heart Right

Finally, as I habitually do the right thing over and over—and I know and trust God more—I obey Him out of delight. I don't have to drag my will, because I want to obey Him. My relationship is a good Father to a loved child. I rest near Him and receive His sweet favor, which I pour out to others. As I look to Jesus, my jealous Savior, my spirit rises. I'm delighted to say "yes, Lord" because I know how well He will be honored by my obedience. My motive is love: God's love lives within so I want to love and serve others. Christ gives me the ability to obey: *He does it through me*.

DELIGHT: flesh   <   SPIRIT

The spirit is stronger because I have starved the flesh. Living out of the spirit is joy. My actions are right, but it's not just behavior change; it's heart change. I die to myself so Christ lives in me; then I walk in gratitude and love. God wants the old life crucified and powerless, the new life shining out of a right heart. This is like a 43-year-old, an adult with mature character. When you engage your will, choose righteous deeds and learn to operate in the new nature, remember, God looks not only at what we do, but *why* we do it.[152] He sees our motivation and desires, idols and goals. He looks at our innermost being.[153]

Back to My Coffee, My Bible and My Battle

Do you see the battle that raged in my heart that Saturday morning? I said if God clearly told me to stay, I would, no matter what I wanted. I opened to the Old Testament (where it said God allowed divorce—I tried to stack the deck). I read Ecclesiastes 5:5: *It is better not to vow than to make a vow and not fulfill it. Do not let your mouth lead you into sin. And do not protest to the temple messenger, "My vow was a mistake."* My flesh wanted a divorce, but Christ called me to trust Him in my marriage. At that moment, I chose to deny my demanding flesh and trust God where He was leading. I dragged my will to obey, and chose His way over mine: I followed Him back to my marriage. It started with duty; it wasn't easy, it wasn't perfect, but in 2013 we celebrated 37 years of marriage (I say "37 with a burp"). The first 12 years were flesh-driven and miserable but the past 25 have been Christ-led and amazing. Not always blissful or easy, but wondrous as God has transformed two fleshly sinners into a couple who loves God and loves others, as we walk toward delight.

Why a New Heart?

Why does God give us new hearts and His Spirit to live inside? God explains in Ezekiel 36:22-23: '*It is not for your sake, O house of Israel, that I am going to do these things, but for the sake of My holy name, which you have profaned among the nations ... (T)he nations will know that I am the Lord ... when I show Myself holy through you before their eyes.*' When the new heart powers us, our lives "pink up" so people see His holiness in us. The world is shocked when they see the new engine's power.

One more piece of good news. The gospels tell many stories of Jesus teaching His disciples to act right; *follow Me ...pray like this ...fast ...don't worry*. But after they saw the Resurrected Christ, and received the Holy Spirit, they changed the world. Start every day in relationship with Him, then let your actions flow out of that. His presence will give you more power than you have ever known.
We have this treasure in earthen vessels, that the excellency of the power may be of God and not of us (2 Cor. 4:7).

Yes, Lord, You get all the glory.

---
152 1 Corinthians 13:1-3
153 1 Samuel 16:7

Bottom Lines:

1. You were "broke before you were broke."
2. You are a spiritual hybrid— double-souled.
3. You are in a battle every day, sometimes every minute of every day.
4. God uses circumstances to reveal what drives your heart.

Discussion Questions:

1. How would you respond to standing in a slow line at Walmart?

2. What are the warning signs that you are driving with the old engine (Physical signs, thought patterns, over-reactions, failures, lack of power, hurting people)? Keep track of these in a daily log.

3. Pick a normal situation in your life (being late, dealing with stubborn children, cleaning up after your family, etc.) How do you usually respond? Which list is this response on? What could you start to practice from the second Galatians list? Work on one thing or situation at a time.

4. Where do you live your Christian life most often: in Debt, Duty or Delight? What does that look like? Are there any areas where you have gotten to Delight? What has helped you get there? How can you apply that to other areas of your life?

5. Does it give you hope to know that every Christian struggles with old engine/new engine choices?

6. Are you excited that you have a toggle switch, one that you control?

To the Friend of the Traveler:

1. Be humble and honest with your fellow traveler. Share some of your struggles with your flesh. What are your battles? Show that the flesh-spirit struggle is part of every Christian's journey, not just those who have experienced abuse.

2. Talk about the concept of Duty, Debt and Delight. Where do you each see yourselves? How does your relationship with God need to deepen to get to the next level in some area?

3. Don't tackle every area where you see her driving with the old engine. Pick one she wants to work on. Make a plan, help her see how the old sinful heart shows up in her thoughts, words and actions.

4. Sin is a part of every person's life. Don't be shocked by her sin, and don't be judgmental. God can forgive any sin. Sin and forgiveness should always be tightly connected, without space in between for self-condemnation to slip in. Encourage her to ask for forgiveness for sins quickly.

Song: *Come Thou Fount* (Old Hymn)

Come, thou Fount of every blessing,
Tune my heart to sing thy grace.
Streams of mercy, never ceasing,
Call for songs of loudest praise.
Teach me some melodious sonnet,
Sung by flaming tongues above.
Praise the mount! I'm fixed upon it,
Mount of thy redeeming love.

Here I raise mine Ebenezer
Hither by thy help I'm come
And I hope, by thy good pleasure
Safely to arrive at home
Jesus sought me when a stranger
Wandering from the fold of God
He, to rescue me from danger,
Interposed his precious blood.

O to grace how great a debtor
Daily I'm constrained to be!
Let thy goodness, like a fetter,
Bind my wandering heart to thee.
Prone to wander, Lord, I feel it,
Prone to leave the God I love.
Here's my heart, O take and seal it,
Seal it for thy courts above.

Chapter 6
Gifts for the Journey

From the fullness of His grace we have all received one blessing after another. (John 1:16)

In the last chapter, we explored failures caused by the flesh; the sinful nature that all Christians fight. God overcomes it by implanting His divine nature through a new spirit and a new heart. When I fail, I comfort myself by saying *this is exactly who I am without Jesus. Here's the plumb line that marks "before" and "after." So just keep running to Him.* Let's look at another cause of failure; not receiving the blessings God has given.

As Cris and I were writing this section, our small group fell under strong spiritual attack for two months, with trials, discouragement, depression and sickness. After praying about it, Cris asked if she could anoint us with oil for protection and as dedication to God (something her charismatic church practices). We were not of that "flavor," so it was unfamiliar to us, but we let her. While she gently anointed our heads and tearfully prayed over us one at a time, most of us (including me) wrestled with her gift. One gal said she couldn't even hear the words Cris prayed over her. Another kept thinking, "Just listen, accept the words in love." One gal was relieved she had missed it. She said she felt like throwing up just hearing about it. It was just a quiet prayer, so why was it so hard for us to receive?

Closed Fists

After pondering it all week, I landed in Matthew 7:9-11: *Which of you, if his son asks for bread, will give him a stone? Or if he asks for a fish, will give him a snake? If you, who are evil, know how to give good gifts to your children, how much more will your heavenly Father give good gifts to those who ask Him?* As a child, I did not receive good gifts from my parents: I asked for mercy and got mocked. I asked for love and got lust. I asked for protection and got punished. Instead of good gifts, I got stones: my Christmas "gift" was my father's abuse. So how eager do you think I was to receive gifts? Or to receive anything from anybody? I decided very young there were no free gifts; they always came with price tags or strings attached. Because I knew only evil gift-givers, I refused all gifts. I felt like I had no right to exist, and no right to ask for anything. Then my heart closed, and I stopped asking.

Even as a Christian, I was so focused on all I had lost, I barely noticed the new life I had been given. Matt. 7:7-8 says *everyone who asks receives*—and I had bravely been asking, seeking and knocking—but my hands were still empty. Why? If it felt like a gift, I rejected it and kept working on my own. One day, when I read in the Bible: "*His divine power has given us everything we need for life and godliness,*"[154] I was suspicious, not joyful. *So what's the catch? How much will that cost me? If God had given me everything,* I thought, *He would take it all away too.*

Like me, do you struggle to ask for or receive gifts? Are you afraid of gifts or gift-givers? Or the strings attached? Like me, do you think you don't have a right to ask for anything? Perhaps you want to receive from people but your heart clenches when they come near. Perhaps it's scary to be vulnerable or needy. Or you feel obligated to give back something of equal value. So how do you move from rejecting to receiving?

What's in a Gift?

A gift is "a present; anything given or bestowed; anything which is voluntarily transferred by one person to another without compensation; a donation." But, the second definition was the one I knew well: "a bribe; anything given to corrupt the judgment. *Neither take a gift (a bribe); for it ...blinds the eyes of the wise. (Deut.16)*"[155] That was my childish viewpoint; I never saw gifts–I saw bribes and obligations. The cost was high; they had taken my body, my soul and my life.

My "feelers" and "thinkers" were not right, because the enemy had tainted them. To receive Cris' prayer as a gift of love, I had to see it as a good gift instead of something scary or undeserved. Just because it was a surprise didn't mean it was bad; it was an unexpected blessing, an offering from her caring heart. I had to trust her enough to believe she had no secret motives or obligations, no strings attached or traps set. And I had to tackle my bad feelings about gifts and bring them to light, reframing her prayer as a gift from God working through Cris' hands.

A Red Rose Means Love

It may be a challenge to retrain yourself to receive gifts as good. It feels like this: imagine you are dating a guy but you begin to feel like something isn't right. When you break up with him, he starts stalking you. You see a pattern: each time, *a single red rose* is delivered to your door just before he attacks you. This goes on for months before he is finally arrested

---

154 2 Peter 1:3 Greek tense is perfect participle passive—something that happened in the past (at the moment of salvation) whose finished results are reflected in the present.
155 Webster's 1828 Dictionary, http://1828.mshaffer.com/*gift*

and imprisoned. Later, you begin dating a really terrific guy. One day, he decides to show his love by sending you *one red rose*. How would you respond to the florist at the door? Would your feelings be right? Probably not. Would they be understandable? Oh, yes. But to keep that great guy, you would have to **admit** your feelings have been twisted and **relearn** what a red rose means; **reconnect** it with good things like love and sweetness and thoughtfulness, then **accept** it as a gift of love, letting it fill your heart. A *red rose moment* is that moment at the door when your old feelings fight a new truth.

God Gives Us Good Gifts

Ephesians 1 exalts God "*who has blessed us with every spiritual blessing.*" Blessing means an action at salvation[156] "where God acts for our good as He sees what we need most ...." and gives it to us.[157] Here are just a few gifts He knew we needed:

Eternal Life—The gift of God is *eternal life* in Christ Jesus our Lord.[158] Have you received it?

Relief and Rest—'Come to Me, all you who are weary and burdened, and I *will give you rest. Take* My yoke upon you and learn from Me, for I am gentle and humble in heart, and you will find rest for your souls. For My yoke is easy and my burden is light.'[159] Are you walking under it?

Replacement for Fear—For *God did not give us* a spirit of fear, but of power, love and a sound mind.[160] His perfect love casts out fear.[161] Do you have power, love and a sound mind?

Peace—"Peace I leave with you; *My peace I give you*. I do not give to you as the world gives. Do not let your hearts be troubled and do not be afraid."[162] Do you live in peace, without fear?

Comfort—Even though I walk through the valley of the shadow of death, I will fear no evil, for you are with me; your rod and your staff they *comfort* me.[163] Comfort others with the *comfort that you yourselves have received*.[164] Have you accepted His comfort?

---
156 Greek tense is aorist participle active, a one-time action.
157 <u>The Complete Word Study New Testament</u>, Spiros Zodhiates, AMG International, © 1991 #2127
158 Romans 6:23
159 Matthew 11:28-30
160 2 Timothy 1:7
161 1 John 4:18
162 John 14:27
163 Psalm 23:4
164 2 Corinthians 1:4

A Generous Portion—'Instead of their shame, my people will *receive a double portion*, and instead of disgrace they will rejoice in *their inheritance*; they will *inherit* a *double portion* in their land, and everlasting joy will be theirs.'[165] Do you have joy and a "double portion" life?

When you read that list, do you think:

> Don't have 'em. Never seen 'em. God hasn't given me anything.
> What's the catch? How much do I have to pay for this?
> Nice-sounding words but it's just an empty promise.
> Yah, whatever… blah, blah, blah.
> Who would want that? Give me something I really need.

Do those gifts seem out of reach, or even ridiculous? 1 Corinthians 2:14 says, *the natural man does not receive the things of the Spirit of God, for they are foolishness to him; nor can he know them because they are spiritually discerned*. God gives gifts liberally, but this verse says if you are living on the "old man" side of the flesh/spirit conflict, you will reject them; it feels foolish to receive them. God's gifts don't make sense to the natural man because they aren't dependent on our actions, our abilities or our faith. And Satan gets involved. In the Garden, he suggested to Eve that God was withholding what she needed.[166] Sadly, she didn't believe God was a perfect provider, but she did believe the devil's lie. The devil can't stop God from giving good gifts but he can deceive you into rejecting them.[167] He blinds you to their presence or lies about the gifts, calling them purchases you can't afford.

God gives gifts solely because of your position in Christ. When you say "yes" to God, it's like saying "I do" on your wedding day. Being the King's Bride grants you all His wealth, status and privilege. Your new Husband loves to lavish good gifts on you, blessing you with what you need and more. What would it mean if you refused His generous, loving, thoughtful gestures to provide for yourself? Many gifts have been given to you; are you enjoying them or are they sitting on your table wrapped in pretty bows?

Go back and read the list of blessings as if they were life-giving and precious: Lay aside your doubt, fear or cynicism and open your hands to accept God's gifts. *He wants to give me good gifts. I believe they are for me too.* Is this a red rose moment for you?

---

165 Isaiah 61:7
166 Genesis 3:5, because God had set one rule: don't eat the fruit from that tree. Satan interpreted God, "He doesn't want you to know the difference between good and evil."
167 1 Timothy 4:1-4

You Are a Loved Child

Yet to all who received Him, to those who believed in His name, He gave the right to become children of God. (John 1:11)[168]

During Cris' prayer, my friend Kathleen also struggled to receive her gift. When she prayed about why, God reminded her of the story of the prodigal son in Luke 15: *When the younger son said, "Father, give me my share of the estate," he divided the property between them.* Both sons received their inheritance. The younger brother wasted his on sinful living, but the elder brother didn't enjoy his gift at all. He bitterly accused his father, *"Look! All these years I've been slaving for you and never disobeyed your orders. Yet you never gave me even a young goat so I could celebrate with my friends."* (v. 29) The father's answer in v. 31 is a gentle rebuke: *"My son, you are always with me, and everything I have is yours."* The relationship was more important than the inheritance, and the elder son had both but didn't enjoy either one.

You have received *Him*—the Father. He doesn't only want you to do things for Him; He wants to grow in relationship with you, so you will know Him. You don't just obey rules, you receive His love and return it. He saves you from your self-righteousness, so you can enjoy the things He worked to give you. Do you live like a child of the King?

Are you like the elder brother living by his own strength? We are used to obeying orders and slaving for God, performing for love. We take gifts only if we do well, deserve them, appreciate them enough, and are willing to pay the cost (loyalty, sacrifice, etc.). Becoming a Christian means better performance and dutiful obedience: *Now I can be holier for God.* Obedience under grace should bring joy, but without the relationship, resentment grows. Don't forget, if you are in Christ, you are an heir of God and a co-heir with Christ.[169] You are no longer a slave; you're a child, His beloved child.[170] You are like a spiritual trust baby because Christ has provided you with a limitless inheritance. Are you living off His generous provision?

His Love—Constant and Generous

God sends love gifts in a constant stream like radio waves, but if my heart is not tuned to His station, I only hear static. If there is a problem between God and me (like whether or not I feel His love) it is *my* problem, not His; *my* thinking is wrong. If I want to receive His gifts, I have to change frequencies and listen.

---

168 *Receiving* is your one-time action at salvation. Greek tense is aorist indicative active.
169 Romans 8:17
170 John 1:12

The main Greek word for love is *agape*, which only refers to God's perfect, unchangeable love. His love is based on His character, not on our good deeds. He shows His goodness by loving. Nothing you do can make God love you any more or any less. "(Love's) benevolence is shown by what *the one who loves* (God) deems needed by the one loved (us)."[171] Being in Christ means you are loved lavishly, beyond measure. Do you live as a precious child, basking in God's love?

I see this like our church's Christmas Eve tradition. At the end of the service, all the lights were turned off so we sat in total darkness. When one small candle was lit, our eyes were drawn to it. We did not notice the darkness; we only saw light. In the same way, when God looks at you, He doesn't see darkness. He only sees His light; the Holy Spirit filling you. He sees you, dear one, through eyes of love. Because you are in Christ, you look just like His Son; perfect, clean, holy, righteous (all-good) and beautiful in the spiritual realm. Do you love being loved by Him?

Adopted—You Belong

Here's a real-life word picture: my son is adopted. He is legitimately our son, deeply loved and favored from when he was placed in my arms, nine days old. We loved him, accepted and provided for him and taught him. He has the rights and privileges of being in our family but doesn't live as a loved boy. Instead, he has wrestled with being adopted most of his life. The adoption was a life-changing event he didn't want, and he deeply feels his birth mother's rejection. He has mostly not felt our love and it seems to us that his heart iscovered with a concrete slab.

He has held his losses so tightly he has missed the grace we've given. He willingly accepts things from us (money, a car, vacations, dinners out), but not his place as our son. He still dreams about going back and undoing the past, reshaping the circumstances of his birth; replacing me with his birth mom and being surrounded by another family. As long as he dwells on the pain of rejection, he will live in anger and hurt. He has not done what we hoped—built his life based on his loving family; broken the concrete barrier; thankfully received our love and grace; released the pain of the past, forgiven his mom and accepted his privileges as God's blessings.

Don't you grieve for my son? Isn't it sad when a child doesn't fully receive all the love he has been shown? But for much of my life, I didn't live as a loved woman either. Concrete covered my heart as long as I focused on the pain of abuse. I didn't receive God's restorative love and unearned favor. Oh, I had heard about it, sung about it, even taught about it, but I

---

[171] The Complete Word Study New Testament, Spiros Zodhiates, AMG International, © 1991, #26

didn't believe it in my heart. My vision was so colored by my hurt, rather than seeing my core identity as a child of God, I only saw myself as abused. I didn't receive His love, His care or His resources. (The good news is that my son is changing. He is happier to spend time with us, we've had some good conversations, and he has admitted he was messed up and needed time to sort it out.)

You too can choose every day which family to live from. You can live from Adam's family (feeding the flesh); or live as a child of your old family (whatever rules and lies controlled it), or you can live from Christ's family (being led by the Spirit). You don't have this battle just because you were abused. Every Christian, abused or not, fights this battle of faith.

You Were Chosen

Have you ever waited to be chosen for a team? Relief washes over you when you're called. All through school, I was called to choose the teams. In my senior year, I saw beyond the game and looked at the people. One day while picking teams for field hockey, I deliberately called the girls who were always chosen last. They were stunned and the other captain was thrilled because she knew she was going to win.

My team played hard and laughed hard. We lost the game, but I won the girls' hearts. Being in Christ means being unchangeably chosen. God has called you: "Come be on my team." He chose you, but not because you are so great. He chooses broken-hearted and weak, fearful and sickly ones.[172] He builds His team with His plan in mind; He shines most brightly when rebuilding broken lives. God is *for* you. God is for *you*!

Redeemed—Rescued and Set Free

For He has rescued us from the dominion of darkness and brought us into the kingdom of the Son He loves, in whom we have redemption, the forgiveness of sins. (Col. 1:13-14)

Before God could bring us into His family, He had to first bring us out of the darkness and bondage created by our sin. The biblical word for that is *redemption*. Redeem means "to purchase back; to ransom; to liberate or rescue from captivity or bondage, or from any obligation or liability to suffer ... by paying an equivalent."[173] It's like Cris' cat. He had been trapped and caged, with no future, no hope until she paid for his freedom, adopted him and named him Purrks. When he ran away and ended up in the shelter again, she redeemed him again.

---

[172] 1 Peter 2:4-10
[173] Webster's 1828 Dictionary, http://1828.mshaffer.com/*redeem*

Jesus redeemed us like that; He bought us for a price (His shed blood and His death in our place). He rescued us and delivered us from sin's control, liberating us from captivity. Being in Christ means your ransom price has been paid and you are free to walk away from your cage. You are no longer a P.O.W. in Satan's camp. All your hidden thoughts, paid for. All those shameful actions, paid for. All those unclean motives, paid for. Your debt has all been paid and you owe nothing. You are free to bounce into life with that truth ringing in your ears. It's not because you qualify; just believe and receive.

Hebrews 9:15 says *Christ is the mediator of a new covenant, that those who are called may receive the promised eternal inheritance–now that He has died as a ransom to set them free from the sins committed under the first covenant*. Jesus died to set you free from sin's power, so you could have peace with God.[174] The Greek word for "receive" means that Christ died in the past so that we can receive our inheritance now.[175] There is some uncertainty in the word—not if Christ gave it to us but *if we will receive it*. This means we have a choice; whether to receive or refuse our inheritance and freedom from past sins.

The Israelites suffered in Egypt, but after 400 years of back-breaking slavery, it was TIME. God stepped into their story and miraculously carried them to freedom. If you are reading this book, God has stepped into your story. He is here, ready to deliver you:[176] you are no longer a slave—to the past, pain, emotions, to sin[177] or to this world. Are you ready to move to new life?

How Much is This Ticket Worth?

Jim and I had a tough day stuck at a train station in Paris (national holiday, cafes closed, trains shut down, no one understood our Canadian French). We finally decided to leave and head to Switzerland. We walked from car to car in the packed train and finally found a seat, but we didn't know if our Euro-pass allowed us to sit there. When the conductor came, he looked at our passports, smiled and moved on. We had hours of anxiety because we did not know what we held; our premium tickets meant we could go anywhere and sit in any seat. How can you live in fear when you hold priceless tickets in God's kingdom?

Many Christians are on the train but don't know the value of their tickets in Christ. As Jim and I walked through the train, we saw people standing next to their suitcases. After several

---

174 Romans 5:8-11
175 Aorist subjunctive active tense- an action completed in the past that will have results in the future. Subjunctive mood, active voice.
176 Galatians 5:1
177 Romans 6:6-7

hundred miles, their feet swelled, their knees buckled, and they complained about the hard journey. This is like people who do Christianity in their own strength: pride makes the trip hard. Some travelers sat on their suitcases. They knew it was a long trip, but they trusted their suitcases to hold them up. Our own efforts are no match for a comfortable padded seat. Jim and I kept walking until we found what we owned: rest. Rest in Christ is ours, but we have to sit down there.

The Perfect Gift

Praise be to the God and Father ...who has blessed us... with every spiritual blessing in Christ. For He chose us in Him before the creation of the world to be holy and blameless in His sight. (Eph. 1:3-4)

We are redeemed as part of an amazing gift exchange. God saw our incurably sinful hearts and ruined lives and, with compassion, poured out love and favor on us. Jesus took on ALL sin—sins you did and sins done to you—when He died on the cross. On a spiritual level, you traded places with Jesus. He paid the penalty for all your sins, then He gave you His righteousness (His perfect holiness and sinlessness).[178] This exchange made you spotlessly clean: perfect, holy and blameless before God. You are now the opposite of sin-stained and shameful. You are not tainted or ruined or damaged or broken; not a victim or second-class or worthless anymore. You are not beyond help or beyond hope. Trust me, you got the better end of the deal.

Romans 3:23-24 says it beautifully: *for all have sinned and fall short of the glory of God, and are justified freely by his grace through redemption that came by Christ Jesus.* The Message version says it this way:

Since we've compiled this long and sorry record as sinners and proved that we are utterly incapable of living the glorious lives God wills for us, God did it for us. Out of sheer generosity He put us in right standing with Himself. A pure gift. He got us out of the mess we're in and restored us to where He always wanted us to be. And He did it by means of Jesus Christ.

Because of grace, we are justified. Because Christ is in me, I am as holy as He is. In Christ, I am blameless—just as if I have never sinned; just as if I always obeyed.[179] Too often we read that verse as if it says *He has blessed us with every spiritual blessing in Christ...except me.* You are not excluded, my friend. If you are in Christ, all the promises are yours too.

---

[178] 2 Corinthians 5:21, Strong's #1342- innocent, holy, just, meet, right
[179] Elyse Fitzpatrick, <u>Counsel from the Cross</u> webcast, October 27th, 2012 (based on the book by the same title).

Grace

All this love and goodness comes from God's generous grace. Grace is more than just God's good favor and blessings. Webster's 1828 Dictionary says *grace* is:

1. The free unmerited love and favor of God, the spring and source of all the benefits men receive from him. *By grace we are saved, not by our own works* (I call this saving grace);[180]
2. A favorable influence of God; divine influence (of the Holy Spirit) in renewing the heart and restraining from sin (our new power source—grace for living);[181]
3. The application of Christ's righteousness to the sinner.[182]

Grace is multi-faceted. His grace is "a favor done (to us) without expectation of return."[183] It is how His indwelling Spirit treats us, renewing and recharging our hearts, teaching us to live holy lives and empowering us daily.[184] By grace, Jesus' righteousness is transferred to our spiritual bank account when we believe; faith means we receive it. Grace is our joyful filter for life's events; a positive perception of how well God treats us. Grace is how God sees His children–with favor. (Read: I am His favorite!) He cares, provides, blesses, while knowing and accepting us. His grace means we don't have to do things perfectly. But too often, rather than living under grace, we die under law.

Have you played Hide and Seek but were not quite hidden when the count was done?
    Law says, "Ha! You're it!" Grace says, 'Go hide, I'll give you another chance."
Have you ever been pulled over for speeding?
    Law says, "Guilty! Pay!" Grace says, "You're guilty but here's a warning, not a fine."
Have you ever blown it with a friend and gone to ask for forgiveness?
    Law says, "You will pay me forever." Grace says, "You are free. Let's start over."

When you don't live under grace, it's like you believe in peaches—you know how they look and smell—but you've never taken a bite when one was given to you. You don't know the burst of sweetness in your mouth or the sticky juice running down your hand. *Taste and see that the Lord is good.*

A Precious Key — Forgiveness

Everyone who believes in Him receives forgiveness of sins through His name. (Acts 10:4)

---

180 Ephesians 2:5
181 1 Corinthians 15:10
182 Webster's 1828 Dictionary, http://1828.mshaffer.com/*grace*
183 The Complete Word Study New Testament, Spiros Zodhiates, AMG International, © 1991, #5485
184 Titus 2:11-12

Forgiveness is so important there's a chapter about it later in the book. So here, let's talk about one corner of forgiveness. Being in Christ means we are forgiven people. *When you were dead in your sins and in ... your sinful nature, God made you alive with Christ. He forgave us all our sins, having canceled the written code ... that was against us and that stood opposed to us. He took it away, nailing it to the cross.*[185] By taking away our list of sins—ways we violated the law—and nailing it to the cross with Jesus, God gave us a priceless gift: forgiveness. Being forgiven by God means:

> You do not owe the wages of sin. (Romans 6:23)
> You are free from condemnation. (Romans 8:1)
> You don't have to do penance. (1 John 1:9)
> You can run to the throne of grace and find mercy, not judgment. (Hebrews 4:16)
> You are no longer under the law but under grace. (Romans 6:15)
> You are no longer dead in your transgressions but alive in Christ. (Ephesians 2:5)

Christ's death paid for our original sin nature (disconnecting the old engine). Then, 1 John 1:9 applies to our daily sins: *If we confess our sins, He is faithful and just and will forgive us our sins and purify us from all unrighteousness.*[186] I believe Christians who are unable to forgive others haven't received their forgiveness. They don't fully understand their gift, so they live like they are going to get a bill for their sins. If they do forgive, they're stingy about it. But once you have experienced the freedom and joy that come from being forgiven, you can give it away generously. Want to know the joy of salvation again? Confess your sins and accept His promised forgiveness.

Black Dots Start with a Hook

Even though I lived forgiven, I didn't know how to get rid of ongoing shame and guilt. If you are anything like me, Satan has hammered you hard here. I have found that many who were sexually abused have a "hook" Satan pulls on. If there was something "offside" during the abuse—some small thing you did to contribute to it happening—Satan heaps all the blame for the abuse on you.

For example, one girl was distressed because she went into the barn when her parents had forbidden it, and was raped there. Even though she was maybe only 2% to blame for the abuse (in my opinion), Satan made her feel 100% guilty because she disobeyed her parents. She was 100% responsible for her disobedience, but barely responsible for what happened to her. Have you beaten yourself up for years because you had a small part to play in the

---

[185] Colossians 2:13-14
[186] 1 John 1:7 "*the blood of Jesus... purifies us from **all** sin.*" 'All' means *every* (Greek *pas*)--the sin that leads to death, which is rejecting God's provision.

abuse? Perhaps you went for a forbidden car ride to that illegal party, or took that tempting ice cream. Perhaps you believe if you had not worn a dress or not been on the playground that day, the abuse would have been averted. That sounds like a black dot spreading.

Then consider your reactions to the abuse. Mine led to some pretty shady and rebellious choices, piling on shame and blame that haunted me for years. Maybe you reacted by sleeping around or turning to homosexuality; getting into drugs, dropping out of school or running away from home; having a baby out of marriage or an abortion or two, punishing all people who were like your abuser. Shame and guilt for bad choices chain you to the past and drag it into the present.

Stain of Sin

Let's go deeper. Let's look at the real reason we won't receive God's gifts. In the Garden of Eden, Adam and Eve were naked and not ashamed. But when they sinned, they felt shame. They reacted to the shame by covering up, hiding and running away from God. When I sin or fail or do something wrong, my sinful inner flesh is revealed and I feel shame. My instincts are to cover up, hide myself and run away from people. It's not just the embarrassment of failing or been seen as stupid or "less-than." I feel a flash of shame from head to toe; a firestorm that burns out all sense of God or righteousness or grace. I don't feel *I did that wrong*, I feel *I AM wrong. I am bad and will never be good. If you really knew me, you would hate me.* Shame overwhelms me, then grows and spreads. I bury my secrets, veil my actions, cover my inadequacies, and build walls to keep others out.

Unlike most people, God revealed my shame late in my journey to freedom. I had seen the play *Les Miserables* many times, so I wasn't prepared for my reaction to Fontine's song in the movie. As she hopelessly prostituted herself to earn money for her child, the familiar emotions from the final year of abuse swept over me. As her shame mounted, my anger grew. When she sang, *'Can't they see they're making love to one already dead,'* I exploded. My defenses were stripped away and the fortress wall crashed down. I faced the monster of shame for the first time.

Like her, I was trapped in a hopeless situation. Like her, I found a solution that stole my soul, one that flooded me with shame. Shame that my father had done such evil things to me. Shame that I was unloved and used and meant nothing to him. Shame that I sold my soul for some control over what happened. Shame that I had cooperated with him. Shame that I stopped fighting. Shame that I was broken, our family was broken and I couldn't fix anything. Shame that others would see the terrible things I had experienced and done. Shame that I was damaged goods.

Shame is a spiritual problem. Everything about shame has Satan all over it. He sends shame and disgrace your way, and your flesh agrees with his words. When you believe it and embrace it, Satan's got you: you accept the handcuffs, or go back into the prison cell. You get silent so it won't be exposed. Shame starts your self-destruct switch. Abusers push shame on you to control or intimidate you. People give you their shame, or use your shame against you to keep you in a box. Shame cripples you and ruins your life. Do you see that everything I felt shame for were things my abuser did? He gave me all that shame and I agreed that it was mine. So why did I receive the blame? Because I believed I was bad; I knew I had done bad things, so when my sins were exposed, my flesh resounded with his condemnation.

Stain Remover

...fixing our eyes on Jesus...For the joy set before Him, He endured the cross, scorning its shame... (Hebrews 12:2)

Shame won't go away on its own; it must be refused. Instead of convincing yourself and others that you are okay, you are not broken—in spiritual terms, you don't have a sinful flesh—the antidote is to reject shame, like Jesus did. Christ scorned shame, rejected it, despised it, and didn't allow it to gain entrance. Because He was sinless, there was no sinful flesh inside that vibrated with Satan's accusation. Because we have taken part in the amazing gift exchange, we can also scorn shame. We can reject it, refuse it, not let it define who we are. Admit that your old nature is sinful and black, but your new nature is holy, sinless and perfect like Christ. Receive His gracious forgiveness. Pull out the hook, toggle to the spirit and walk in His love.

This is how we handle shame: I am in the dressing room getting ready for my wedding. I have my dress on, putting on the last touch of make-up, when I drop the mascara wand and get a big black smear on my dress. I scrub the spot for a long time, but for me the beautiful dress is ruined. Even if everyone says the stain is gone, I will be so self-conscious and so focused on it, it will steal my joy from the ceremony and the happy day. So I cope. I hold my flowers up too high to cover the stain. I will imagine everyone looks at it as they talk to me. I may imagine that my new husband doesn't want to be married anymore because of my ugly dress. But God says, "What stain??" Then He gives me a perfect and beautiful new dress anyway (the one I couldn't afford) so I can live in freedom and joy, walking forward as a loved woman. But I have to receive it.

Run to God instead of away from Him. Let Him reject shame for you, then you refuse it. Instead of beating yourself up, accept His proclamation about you—you are loved and precious to Him. You were forgiven and you are being purified. *I am new in Christ, and I am becoming new* (who God has declared me to be). I think God wants us to live knowing *because I am in Christ I have no shame. Who will declare me guilty? God has declared me innocent. I'm a mess, but I'm a loved mess.* His righteousness destroys shame. Do you trust that He doesn't want you to live in a stained dress?

Imagine God gave you a brand-new red Mustang convertible that's sitting in your driveway, locked and unused. You know you didn't earn it and don't deserve it. Of course you don't deserve it, it was a gift. What gives more pleasure to God: when you excitedly drive that car or when you refuse until you deserve it? Won't you enjoy your gift and show it off? *Stop trying to earn what you already own.*

The Holy Spirit

A dear friend who had always wanted to be married visited me. Her face was full of joy as she waved her left hand and the glint of a diamond caught my eye. We rejoiced that she was going be a bride. Her heart was full as she looked toward her future. As Christians, we too are engaged. We are the Bride, our Groom is coming, and we rejoice knowing there will be a marriage celebration.[187] The Holy Spirit's presence is a diamond that sparkles in our spirit, a deposit on a promise—we will get a rich inheritance in heaven.

Repent and be baptized, every one of you, in the name of Jesus Christ so that your sins may be forgiven. And you will receive the gift of the Holy Spirit. (Acts 2:38)

The Holy Spirit lives in believers, helping, teaching, leading, drawing us to God. "Spirit is the element in man which gives him the ability to think of God."[188] He is the Counselor,[189] the Giver of life,[190] the Spirit of Truth,[191] who reminds us of what Christ said.[192] The Holy Spirit is a gift, but He also gives gifts so we can work in "the family business." These spiritual gifts are: teaching, evangelism, words of knowledge, faith, gifts of healing, working of miracles, prophecies, discerning of spirits, different tongues and interpretation of tongues.[193] The different gifts profit the whole Body (the church) so we can work together to honor God.

---

187 Revelation 19:6-8
188 The Complete Word Study New Testament, Spiros Zodhiates, "The vertical window," - "the soul is man's horizontal window making him conscious of his environment." AMG International, ©1991, #4151
189 John 14:26
190 John 6:63
191 John 17: 13-16
192 John 17:25
193 1 Corinthians 12:1-11

Early in our counseling, Cris asked me if I had received the gift of the Holy Spirit. Jesus was my Lord and Savior, but I felt repulsed by the idea of letting the Holy Spirit *enter* me.[194] She said that in the Old Testament, priests were set apart for service with oil poured on their head, as a symbol of the Holy Spirit. That made sense. Opening my heart, I asked God to pour out His love for me like oil. When she prayed for me, I felt a warm glow like liquid love flowing from my head down. I felt God's approval, His generosity and tenderness, and I cried with gratitude that my hurts and fears didn't keep His kindness from touching me. There was nothing to be afraid of.

Receiving Mercy

Hebrews 4:16 describes how to receive God's good gifts:

> *Let us then approach…*

Who do you imagine you approach when you are tempted or weak or have sinned and failed? Do you approach an angry, sullen fist-pounding God or a gentle Father? A throne of harsh judgment or a throne of favor you don't deserve? Then how close will you draw near? That shows how close your relationship is with God.

> *the throne of grace…*

Run toward Jesus, your High Priest, with hurt and sorrow instead of running to the world. Looking to the world for soul healing or unconditional love is like hitting a drive-thru expecting healthy food. They don't sell good food, they sell convenience. In Christ, we receive abundant grace according to His riches; sweet kindness shows the generosity of the Giver. Christ lived and died in this world: He knows life's cruelty and sympathizes with our weaknesses.[195] God looks on us with mercy, compassion and understanding. His grace is "absolute freeness of the loving kindness… to men, finding its only motive in the bounty and free-heartedness of the Giver."[196] When you entered His kingdom (at salvation), God extended His grace to you like a treasure.[197]

> *with confidence….*

The NASB says "come boldly;" openly, frankly, confidently. Travis Cotrell's song *Mercy Seat* says, "Come runnin':"

---

194 Sadly, this fear is a common result of sexual abuse. We want NOTHING to enter us, anywhere (for starters, needles, catheters, dentist drills and OB/GYN exams).
195 Hebrews 4:15
196 <u>The Complete Word Study New Testament</u>, Spiros Zodhiates, AMG International, © 1991 #5485
197 Here, the Greek tense is aorist indicative active- God did it one time; the grace given at salvation.

> Where Jesus is calling, He said His grace would cover me.
> His blood will flow freely, it will provide the healing.
> I'm runnin' to the mercy seat, I'm runnin' to the mercy seat.[198]

Do you crawl, whimper, whine, drag or slink toward the Father as a poor stepchild begging for crumbs? Do you stomp in expecting a disapproving lecture? We can enter the throne room boldly because we know *who He is* and *whose we are*. We are beloved children who belong in His family, and the throne room is our home. Walk in with assurance and gratitude for your relationship. Go daily, go without question.

> *so that we may receive mercy*

Mercy is when God withholds something bad you deserve. I struggled to receive God's mercy because I knew I had done wrong. I was a victim, but also a sinner. I expected to be treated as my sin deserved; judgment and pushing away. Why would I run to the Righteous One expecting good things from His hand? I might get mercy, but it would come with a dreaded IOU; punishment, paybacks and rejection (which is not mercy). I didn't expect the steady compassion and kindness He gave.

> *and find grace to help us in our time of need.*

We find grace and help instead of a deserved punishment for wrong-doing.[199] Fresh, clean, life-giving grace to help in our time of need. Your Good Father wants to surprise you with joy or provide something you need for victory in the trial ahead. When you need help, God will always give it to you, but it won't always be what you expect.

What About God's Anger?

Isaiah 54:7-8 used to frighten me: *"for a brief moment I abandoned you, but with deep compassion I will bring you back. In a surge of anger I hid my face from you for a moment, but with everlasting kindness I will have compassion on you," says the Lord.* I have felt abandonment and surges of anger. But one day it hit me that we live post-cross, where God's wrath was perfectly satisfied by Christ. Now we live in verses 9-10: *Though the mountains be shaken and the hills be removed, yet My unfailing love for you will not be shaken, nor My covenant of peace be removed.* We have God's deep compassion with everlasting love, from an eternal covenant of peace that will never be shaken. Instead of hiding His face in anger, He tenderly gathers us to Himself. What confidence that gives us.

---

198 *Mercy Seat*, Travis Cottrell Live CD, Capitol Christian Music Group © 2009
199 Romans 8:1

Mercy is Manna

Throughout the Old Testament, God's chosen people the Israelites also struggled to receive what they were given. At one low point, they had been delivered from Egypt and were headed to the Promised Land, but they stalled out in the desert. The people grumbled and complained because they were hungry. They dreamed about the food they had in Egypt but forgot it was a side dish of slavery. Still, the Lord provided:

'I will rain down bread from heaven for you. The people are to go out each day and gather enough for that day. In this way I will test them and see whether they will follow My instructions.' (Exodus 16:4

God gave them food, but it came with a test. If they obeyed, they would eat miraculous manna. If they disobeyed, they would be hungry (if they didn't gather or have maggot-filled manna (if they gathered more than one day's worth. Every day God pours His mercies on you: *Your mercies are new every morning; great is Your faithfulness.*[200] Every day you can choose; go and gather mercy for the day or complain about what you don't have. If you don't go, you either don't believe God's promise, you choose not to do your part or you choose not to receive. The gifts are held out to you; come close and take them from His hand. Open them and use them in your day-to-day life.

Praying for More

Ask, and you shall receive, that your joy may be full. (John 16:24)

This chapter looks at a few of the gifts God gives His children. On the first page, I quoted from Matthew 7, saying that I didn't have things because I hadn't received them. Another reason you don't have is because you haven't asked. (James 4:2 There is no limit to the gifts we can ask for in prayer. We can ask for anything from a good parking space to a good performance evaluation. God wants to love you and bless you with what you need. Maybe you just need to ask for it.

Scarred Lakebed

I am the Lord your God, who brought you out of Egypt.
Open wide your mouth and I will fill it. (Psalm 81:10)

After struggling to receive Cris' gift, I prayed for God to give me everything He has for me. I opened my heart and asked Him to pour His gifts on me. He gave me this picture:

---
[200] Lamentations 3:23, written by Jeremiah, the weeping prophet who knew heartache, sorrow and pain.

My wasted life was like an old, dry lakebed, scarred and useless. It was treacherous to walk through the after-effects of sin; burning trash, ticking bombs ready to explode, old bomb craters, traps and broken glass littered the bottom. I tried to cover the craters with boards of protection and concrete, but the job was too big for me. Then God took over. *Where sin abounds, grace abounds more*,[201] so His living water of grace flowed into my ugly life, filling in the craters and potholes and covering all the scars. Soon, a beautiful lake concealed the damage and reflected the Son. Flowers and meadow grass grew by the lake's edge, because life flowed through the fresh water.

He didn't repair the damage or make the lakebed perfectly smooth and level. He overcame it with His living water, covering the scars by His grace. Now, I have a new purpose as a lake that reflects His image. Will you receive His living water? Will you be open to receive all that God has given you? When you accept grace, and walk in it every day, all the changes we talk about in this book can happen. His life flows through you and you grow real fruit; love, joy, peace, patience, goodness, kindness, gentleness, faithfulness and self-control. More precious gifts for your journey.

Does it give you hope to know that God has given you dozens of good gifts, to help you live life? Does it give you hope that He won't stop giving gifts for the rest of your life? Does it give you hope to realize that His gifts are based on His loving character, and not on your actions?

Anything for the Poofy file? Anything you don't understand or want answers to?

Bottom Lines:

1. Open your hands to receive all that God has given you.
2. Stop trying to earn what you already own.
3. Live as a spiritual trust baby, living off your Father's rich provision.
4. Run boldly to the throne of grace.

Discussion Questions:

1. Have you handed God your shame and accepted His double portion: your inheritance, and joy?

2. Have you let God comfort you back to life?

---

201 Romans 5:20

3. Have you applied His peace to your troubled and fearful heart?

4. Are you working under an easy yoke and a light burden? Matthew 11:28-30

5. Are you rejoicing in your future inheritance or still living in the disgrace of your past?

6. Can you name the greatest life-changing event of your life as being adopted by the King or is it being abused?

To the Friend of the Traveler:

1. If there's an area where you "hit the wall" time after time, pray about whether it's an area of shame from the abuse, and when and how to address it. Convey God's love and grace to her. Tell her His vision of her—perfect, sinless, pure and righteous. Help her to refuse the shame.

2. Give your friend a special gift and see how she reacts. Talk about it. Try to find out her attitude toward gifts, if she has to deserve them or return gifts equally.

3. Name the spiritual gifts she has been given and the character of the Gift-Giver. Find a place to practice your gifts.

4. Talk about what makes it easier for you both to receive from God, and examine the thoughts and attitudes that block receiving.

5. Have communion together. Come to the table empty-handed: open your heart to receive life-giving grace and resurrection power. Make a plan to live in grace every day, and walk as a loved child of the King.

Worship Song- *I Receive* by Israel Houghton & New Breed[202]

---

[202] Israel Houghton & New Breed, from the album *The Power of One*, Integrity Music © 2009 http://www.youtube.com/watch?v=ILT61ZZvrVc

Chapter 7
Engine Trouble

Follow your heart. What are you feeling? How do you feel about that? How often have you heard or said that? David may be the "King of Emotions" because of his honesty in the Psalms, but women are definitely the Queens. Women and their emotions; what can I say? Strong, stormy, debilitating, delightful, confusing, controlling? Joy of life? Taste of death? All of these and more, sometimes in a 10-minute period. Let's look at some godly ways to deal with our emotions.

Pressure Cooker

I grew up in a home ruled by emotions. If the adults were angry, they slammed doors, fought, swore, kicked the dog and broke things. I saw how to act out my feelings, but as a child I wasn't allowed to. Like most children of alcoholics, I learned warped family rules: Don't Talk—Don't Feel—Don't Think. My feelings were shut down so young, I didn't know them—except lost, confused, and frustrated. I was a stuffer who sometimes blew. Mad at my dad; stuff. Hurt by a friend; stuff. Lied to by a boss; stuff. If I was a teddy bear, I was definitely puffy. But as I grew with God, I questioned whether stuffing was all that good. I knew I was more emotionally dead than other people, but what was I supposed to do with thirty years of feelings? Letting them out was too scary and I had no tools to handle them, so I mostly ignored them. One of my friends said it best: "If I could get a divorce from myself, I would."

When I got older, I had "two-second-delay" emotions, when I watched people's reactions and copied them. If they laughed, I laughed. If they cried, I cried. I mimicked a lot and pretended more. Most of the emotions I showed were not my own—except anger. Anger I knew! I often had "time bombs," when something happened that set off an explosion in my soul (I never knew what). I would "snap out" of paralyzing anger or fear two days or two months later and realize no one was speaking to me. What had I said or done? How did I function during that "frozen" time? How could I ever make real progress if another bomb could go off any time? I felt like a victim of myself. Drowning in a tidal wave of emotions hardly felt like forward progress, but onward I marched.

Warning!

Maybe you don't stuff anything; feelings fly out of you right and left, so much that people call you a drama queen, or bi-polar. Your emotions seem to control you: they are in charge and you feel helpless against them. You could call them "super-charged." You often explode with "10-reactions to 2-offenses," you are often paralyzed by emotions, or you have hurt people and destroyed friendships with emotion-fueled fights. Sound familiar? It's hard being around them, but it's exhausting being one.

Like all created things in the world, emotions can be good or bad. They are a warning sign; an indicator of something going on in the heart. They are a tool that God uses—like a "check engine" light on the dashboard—to bring problems to your attention. If your engine light comes on, you need to pull over fast and look under the hood to see why it's flashing. If you don't find the trouble and fix it, your engine will be ruined. Here are someways we handle a check engine light without taking the time to pop the hood:

1. Apply masking tape. Most Christians wear permanent masks, hiding their feelings and living by fake ones. Once in church, I heard a woman sobbing behind me, but when I turned to ask if she was all right, she smiled, assured me she was fine and left. My heart broke for her. Did she believe you shame God if you have problems? God was revealing some hurt, but instead of looking under the hood and accepting the help God provided (me), she covered up the problem. We put on our "church face" and flatten our emotions when we don't want people to know we're hurting, we are afraid no one cares or wants to help,[203] or we think we dishonor God.

2. Hit it with a hammer. We don't want to look at the light, so we just smash it. There, problem solved—light's gone. *I can handle that; I don't have any emotional problems.* That takes care of the visible reminder, but what about the problem under the hood? An internal crack builds until the whole engine seizes. This can be a nervous breakdown or a spectacular blow-up.

3. Worship the light. Like ancient wooden idols, feelings are women's goddesses, the center of our universe. Feelings, not God, must be obeyed at all costs, so we delay obedience until we can "manage" them. We indulge them, and justify emotionally-driven choices: *I feel this way, so I'm right to act this way.* Our feelings must be expressed, accepted, fully understood and valued by others.

Follow Your Feelings?

Current wisdom says follow your heart; act the way you feel. The Bible says just the

---

[203] John Lynch. See *TrueFaced* video by John Lynch www.youtube.com/watch?v=Rfy03PEVUhQ&feature=related (based on the book by the same name).

opposite; feelings follow actions. Let's look at this principle in Genesis 4. When Cain's offering (action/choice) was refused (because he gave a grain offering, not a lamb), he was exceedingly angry, upset, sad and depressed. *The Lord said, "Why are you angry and why is your face downcast?"* Then the teaching: *"If you do what is right* (action), *will not your countenance be lifted up* (emotion)?[204] *But if you do not do what is right, sin crouches at your door; it desires to have you, but you must master it."* Sin did master him because he killed his brother Abel. Good choices bring "elation, cheerfulness, dignity, a raising of character."[205] But wrong choices give sin an entrance: we will be downcast (angry, depressed, sullen, self-focused) and, in the end, dominated by the sin.

Another Battle

It is not reason that is taking away my faith: on the contrary, my faith is based on reason. It is my imagination and emotions (taking away my faith). The battle is between faith and reason on one side, and emotion and imagination on the other. (C.S. Lewis)[206]

Remember the big battle of Galatians 5, sinful desires vs. the spirit?[207] Just like actions, thoughts and words, either the flesh engine or the spirit engine can drive your emotions. The battle in this chapter is not whether you *have* feelings; it's how you choose to *act* on them. Emotions are God-given, but they need to be God-guided too. Flesh-driven emotions cause nothing but problems on the journey. Women who are godly in many ways can stumble over their emotions and be taken out of the race. In counseling, the main excuse I hear for disobeying God is "I must follow my feelings." Emotions are a spice of life. But treated like the main dish, they can ruin your life, your testimony, and your relationships.

Here is the Galatians 5 list again, but with the *emotions* that connect to sinful actions:
Lust, greed, sexual pride, sensuality (sexual impurity, debauchery, orgies);
Wrong desire for power or control; idol worship (worshipping any created thing or person above the Creator, including yourself);
The high of a mood-altering substance or influence (alcohol, drugs, witchcraft, cutting);
Hatred, discord, dissentions (love to fight), factions (taking sides), fear of man;
Anger, fits of rage, selfishness, self-focus, entitlement, defensive;
Relief, comfort or escapism through drunkenness, purging, masturbating, or sleeping;
Guilt, regret, grief; and the like …(the list is endless) (Galatians 5:19-22)

---
204 Genesis 4:6-7, NASB
205 Strong's Concordance, Hebrew #7613- the definition of "be lifted up."
206 Mere Christianity, C.S. Lewis, page 124.
207 Remember the world, the devil and the flesh are allies, all three trying to take us down.

Author Jan Silvious talks about a "favorite bad feeling."[208] I too have a dangerous emotion: when I feel wronged, I sense a "rising" inside, and I feel fighting mad to defend myself. My reason is swallowed up by fury and pain; emotions and imagination drag me toward the flesh ("what if...?" "She thinks I ..."). I reject truth, retaliate or return evil for evil. Every time I go with my dangerous emotion, I leave a wake of broken people behind. Over time, I have learned not to trust it or act on it. *The heart is deceitful above all things* (Jer. 17:9, fraudulent, cannot be trusted;[209] frail, feeble; crooked and polluted)[210]. Because of this I say, "*Follow your heart?* **No**. *Follow His heart?* **Yes**."

I think your brain shuts down when your emotions kick in. If you act out of old-nature emotions, your first reaction will show your old heart. But your second one can be grace-based—loving God, rejecting the sin nature, refusing the temptation, obeying and choosing right actions. I had never heard a sermon on godly emotions, but when I prayed about a biblical example, God led me to Matthew 26.

Feel Like Jesus

Jesus felt the full range of emotions: He wept at his friend Lazarus' death, zealously cleansed the temple (zeal is *godly* passionate anger), laughed with children, and comforted mourners. But He never let His emotions control Him or block His obedience to the Father's will. Let's look at the severest trial in His life, the Garden of Gethsemane (Matt. 26:36-44), to see how He handled powerful emotions. Before He faced this distress, called "the Passion," He didn't isolate Himself. He brought three disciples with Him and **asked them** to pray: *"Could you not keep watch with me for one hour?"* Jesus leaned on them, even though they fell asleep. Do you handle your pain alone, then share with others once you have victory? I urge you again; don't make this journey alone, no matter how much you want to. Invite one person to do this book with you, and two lives can be changed. Even Jesus didn't want to be alone.

1. Jesus **admitted** how He felt. *"My soul is overwhelmed with sorrow to the point of death."* He assessed the feelings with full honesty: He didn't pretend about His pain. He was overwhelmed by a storm of emotions, but He never let them take over.
2. Jesus **asked** God to intervene—remove the cup, change the circumstances, and work in the situation with power. *"Father, if it is possible, may this cup be taken from me."*

---

208 <u>Big Girls Don't Whine</u>, Jan Silvious, W Publishing Group (div of Thomas Nelson), Nashville, TN, © 2003
209 <u>Webster's 1828 Dictionary</u> definition of *deceitful*, http://1828.mshaffer.com/
210 <u>Strong's Complete Concordance</u>, Thomas Nelson Publishers, Nashville, TN, © 1996 #605 and 6121 (from 6117): to lie in wait, to seize by the heel, to trip up or restrain. This is what our natural, sinful heart does.

3. Jesus **accepted** the Father's plan. *"Yet not as I will, but as You will."* On His face, He surrendered, directing His will to obey in spite of agonizing feelings. He went to the cross for our sins, enduring shame and death because of the joy on the other side.[211] He obeyed His Father rather than His feelings. I'm so grateful He didn't follow His feelings!

When the Warning Light Goes Off

When you pull over and pop the hood, ask yourself what's the emotion? Why is the warning light flashing? Honestly admit how you feel. Look under your own hood first, before you look at someone else's engine or the bad circumstances: "*...**first** take the plank (or log) out of your own eye...*"[212] The plank is sin, twisted thinking, black dots, blindness from the old nature, bad habits, etc. You don't know how bad your reactions are until you spend a week with someone (like your mother-in-law) in a stressful situation (like a hospital), with everyone's emotions going full-tilt. Then God says, "Uh-huh, I've been seeing that in you a lot lately. Glad you noticed it too."

In grade 7, I lost a front tooth during a baseball game at recess, so I wore a plate with a fake tooth for years. When the plate was removed, I could hardly eat for the pain; food was SUPER hot or SUPER cold! Why? I had had a protective covering over the roof of my mouth but when it was gone, the skin was ultra-sensitive. Fortunately, it only took a week for it to toughen up after I got a permanent bridge. Friend, your heart may be super-sensitive too. When you remove the cover and stop hiding your emotions, your heart may feel tender and raw. But remember, it's only temporary.

Ask God to intervene. Ask Him to change the circumstance: heal the sickness, give you money or a job, save your parent, change your life, remove the thorn in your side, help you change your thinking, fix your spouse, end that destructive relationship… all fair prayers. God may answer "yes," or He may answer "no," but we can always ask.

Accept God's will. When you submit to His plan, you show His Lordship over your life: He's God and you're not. His plans are based on holiness, so they will always be right, always better than yours.[213] God will call you and challenge you. He wants you to be free and mature in your faith. Being a servant of God means doing the Word as soon as you learn it, relying on His power. Do you know the right thing, memorize it, even teach it, but opt out of doing it if your feelings disagree? How well would you tip a waiter

---

211 Hebrews 12:2
212 Matthew 7:5
213 Isaiah 55:8-9

who said, "I'll get your coffee when I feel like it"? I think the lag time between God's command and our obedience is Satan's slippery slope.

Don't Act Up, Don't Act Out, But Act!

The Bible doesn't say to ignore your emotions, nor does it say to live by them. Admit how you feel, then act differently than you feel. You might say *but I'll be a hypocrite if I feel one way and act another*. Have you ever gone to work and not felt like it? I sure have. Did you *feel like* getting up at 2 a.m. to feed your newborn? No? That's not hypocrisy, it's maturity—doing the right thing whether your feelings are calm or kicking up. It is incredibly freeing when you can admit your feelings, but are not chained to acting them out.[214] I'm guessing you have spent a lifetime acting differently than you feel. But can you be honest about those feelings first?

Changing Your Reactions

Do you know you can change what you *feel* by changing what you *think*? Here's how I learned that: the small town where I lived is the one place in Canada where the two east/west train tracks cross each other. So everywhere you drive, you go over train tracks. I crossed four sets of double tracks to get to church, so I often got there late (which I hate). One Sunday, a woman pulled me aside and said that the trains weren't going away, so I needed to think about them differently. Every time I was stopped by a train, I should see it as God asking to spend time with me. If I kept a Bible and some praise songs in the car, when I got stopped, I could read and sing to Him. I did that, and guess what happened? Often, I had such a sweet time with God, the car behind me honked when the train was gone. Waiting became filling, instead of frustrating. Changing how I thought about it, and bringing God into it, changed my reactions.

The great Apostle Paul wrote, *'...I have learned to be content whatever the circumstances. ... whether well fed or hungry, whether living in plenty or in want. I can do everything through Him who gives me strength.'* (Phil. 4:11-13) Paul learned how to be content, not because his circumstances were great (he was in prison). He was content with what he had at hand. He believed he was in God's will and trusted God to give him strength to thrive there.

Remember my angry reaction to the song *Baby, it's Cold Outside* at the ladies' lunch? I wanted to storm out of the room. I sat on my hands, refusing to clap for the singers. My anger had a lot to do with my distorted interpretation of the song (black/white,

---
214 Romans 6:11-14

meaning all bad or all good): *she is going to be raped; he's overpowering her*. God showed me my twisted thinking. I missed the teasing, tender romance. I missed the playfulness; the couple loved each other and wanted to be together. When I changed what I *thought* about the song, I changed how I *felt* about it.

Because you may not know how to recognize your feelings, let's start by looking at basic emotions using four simple words Melanie gave me: mad, sad, glad and afraid.

MAD

Anger is a big problem for most people, but especially those who have been abused. We often justify our anger: *You would be angry too if you had the life I had.* Even though I can give a reason for my anger, that doesn't excuse it. Anger affects your relationships with God and others, your children, your body and your health. Look at the kinds of anger on the Galatians 5:20 list, all driven by the old engine: *hatred, discord, jealousy, fits of rage, selfish ambition, dissention, factions and envy.* What anger tools do you use? Yelling, swearing, powering up, door slamming, pouting, punishing, sulking, or the silent treatment? (Paul Tripp calls that "bloodless murder.") All those are flesh; the old sinful heart acting out through your feelings.

Anger may cover feelings of fear, pride, helplessness, shame or rejection. *A fool gives full vent to his anger, but a wise man keeps himself under control.*[215] Friend, this doesn't mean hiding your anger or trying harder. It means kneeling before God, receiving the Spirit's self-control, and choosing to obey Him, not your feelings. If you are angry and pretend that you are not, watch out. Pretending is from the family of lies; it can be faking and deception. And it doesn't really work, because anger leaks out sideways; we lash out at slow people, scary situations or stupid things. We say we're not angry, but friends are flattened against the wall. Uh-oh, engine overheating.

Your Wants Cause Your Fights

What causes fights and quarrels among you? ... your desires that battle within you. You want something but don't get it. You kill and covet, but cannot have what you want, so you quarrel and fight. (James 4:1-2)

One of the biggest causes of anger is not getting what we want. Got conflict in your life? Someone isn't getting what they want. I have seen 2-year-olds have temper tantrums and 82-year-olds have 80-years-of-practice temper tantrums. People and situations

---
[215] Proverbs 29:11

don't make you angry; they reveal what's already there. What is inside of you squeezes out, like toothpaste out of a tube. I always say *it's not who you are when you get what you want; it's who you are when you don't get what you want.* Then you show your true self.

When you feel yourself *getting* angry, or recognize you are angry, it's time to pull over and talk to God. What's going on under the hood? What did you want but didn't get?

>   Acknowledgement or praise?
>   Attention or special treatment?
>   A change in someone's behavior?
>   To wake up feeling good?
>   Life to be fair?
>   The past to go away?
>   A safe environment?
>   To have some problem vanish?

What is the desire that has morphed into a demand? What do you think you deserve? What do you expect people to do for you or God to give you?

Spring Cleaning

When Jim and I moved to the U.S., most of the packing was easy. But the basement piles of throw-it-there-because-I-don't-know-what-to-do-with-it boxes slowed me down. Cleaning and sorting every spring would have been helpful, but 15 years of ignoring a mess and hoping it would vanish made it tough. Ephesians 4:26 says we shouldn't go to bed angry. In other words, don't wait for spring-cleaning; clean up your messes daily.

That verse is realistic when it says *(You will) be angry… just don't sin in anger.* I learned that annoyed, frustrated, stressed and impatient were all on the track to anger but I could de-rail the train. After saying hurtful, angry words and having to confess my sin to person after person, I started pulling over and popping the hood faster. I asked the Holy Spirit to "tap me on the shoulder" sooner every time. Keeping short accounts with Jim took practice. I worked to use calm words without tearing him down, screaming, slamming doors or throwing things. I stopped fighting about my wants. I didn't act out my anger. I forgave him before I talked to him. Today, I can say, "Jim, I am angry with you," with the same tone as, "How was your day?" I can say, "I am hurt" and not lash out. I can feel sad but not sulk or sit in self-pity, because I have submitted to God and drawn on His self-control. Anger doesn't run me any more.

Have a Plan

Six months after moving here, we went home to spend Christmas at my brother's house. He always got to me: he made me blow up, then baited me for hours. I knew he would say, "Women should be barefoot and pregnant" right away. But I was at a loss on how to handle this "game" in a godly way. I told myself *I'm not crazy, he does want to provoke me.... now I have to walk through thi*s. I planned godly responses when I was clear-headed and wrote them on a recipe card: *You are entitled to your opinion. I think one way; you think another. I don't agree, but I'm not going to fight about it.* I kept running to the bathroom to read the card I kept in my back pocket. Even when my emotions kicked in, I was able to stay calm. I stopped playing his game.

Event/Action -> Reaction -> Feeling

(You can insert a choice at any point along this chain of events)

Plan Ahead for an Action -> Different Action = Different Feeling

Or

Plan Ahead for a Feeling -> Action -> Feeling = Smaller or no reaction

Your plan can be "Put feelings aside in the Poofy file, to look at later." When you have to work or be there for your kids, it's not a good time to examine feelings that may come out boiling. Give yourself permission to put them aside until you can look under the hood. I often put off grieving until I can cry for a while without interruption. I have heard this practiced many ways: let yourself be sad for ten minutes, then move on. Journal to look at it later. Plan a time to talk it through with your accountability partner. I have said, "I'm not fit for human company right now," and sent myself to my room. These are ways of controlling your feelings instead of letting them control you.

Here's a warning from my 40 years of experience working with men accountants: When a woman says something, however right, smart and helpful it is, if she says it with the smallest bit of emotion, the men will write her off. Sadly, I see this happen when counseling marriages too. Instead of waiting for the men to accept your emotions, work on controlling your emotions and expressing thoughts in clear and logical ways.

So what about righteous anger? Yes, righteous anger exists (like Jesus cleansing the Temple, or M.A.D.D.). Righteous anger means being more upset over God's reputation being trashed or His plan being ignored than whether I am right. But I think about 98% of anger is sinful and self-focused, revolving around me: I didn't get what I want so I am angry, just like James 4 said. I haven't mastered righteous anger yet. For now, my goal is to repent of the selfish desires that cause me to get angry.

Verses about Anger:

Let everyone be quick to hear, slow to speak and slow to anger. For the anger of man does not accomplish the righteousness of God. (James 1:19-20)

Get rid of all anger, clamor, slander, rage, malice and bitterness. Put on compassion, tenderheartedness, forgiving others as God forgave you in Christ. (Ephesians 4:29-31)

SAD

The Bible says a lot about sadness, grief and depression. They can come from disappointed expectations, just like anger. Depression can be anger that's turned inward (beating yourself up—*what a loser, I'll never get this, I'm all wrong*, etc.). We can also be sad, downcast or depressed because of our own disobedience—fallout from sin, like David seducing Bathsheba or Peter betraying Jesus.[216] I visited my mom one day before going away for a badminton tournament. She was sick and I had been worried about her all week. As I said goodbye, the Holy Spirit quietly said, "Hug her and say 'I love you.'" Well, my family didn't do that. It would have felt too awkward, so I didn't. That was the last chance I ever had, because she died the next night. Disobedience brings sorrow; I still regret my unwillingness to obey.[217] When our feelings supersede His plan, we can end up sad and depressed. God can release you from grief over your sin when you face it: admit your sin, place it into God's hands and receive His generous and immediate forgiveness.

Sometimes sorrow comes to us because someone else wronged us. David wrote Psalm 42 when he was being hunted by an enemy. In verses 9-10, he poured out his sorrow:

"I say to God my Rock, "Why have you forgotten me? Why must I go about mourning, oppressed by the enemy? My bones suffer mortal agony as my foes taunt me, saying to me all day long, 'Where is your God?'"

David always admitted how he felt, but he didn't get stuck in the depression. He looked under the hood, realizing that his eyes were glued on everything other than God (v.11):

---
[216] Matthew 26:75
[217] This was a sin of *omission*- something I *didn't* do to obey.

"Why are you downcast, O my soul? Why so disturbed within me? My soul is downcast within me; therefore I will remember you. Put your hope in God, for I will yet praise him, my Savior and my God."

Bringing God into his story and placing his thoughts on the Lord brought him back to praising. He talked to his soul, calling out right actions. Psalm 13:5-6 says: *"But I trust in your unfailing love; my heart rejoices in your salvation. I will sing to the Lord, for He has been good to me."* Even in the midst of heartache there is always at least one godly action according to 1 Cor. 10:13, and there can still be joy and peace. Taking your thoughts captive, and directing them to God, brings you back to faith. Dr. Martin Lloyd Jones said, "Stop listening to yourself and start talking to yourself."[218]

Sad For a Lifetime

In contrast to David's many hopeful endings is the story of his daughter, Tamar, who was raped by her half-brother, Amnon. She left the room weeping and never got over her grief; she was desolate for the rest of her life.[219] People will sin against you, the world may crush you and Satan seeks to devour you, but don't let sorrow steal your life away. You cannot build your life in such a way that sorrow will never call. A wall can't be high enough or thick enough to keep pain away. You can grieve the rest of your life or leave sorrow behind by forgiving and walking into your new life.

My Feelings are Hurt

In 1 Corinthians 5, Paul rebukes the believers in Corinth for tolerating sexual sin in the church, demanding that they expel the immoral brother. In his follow-up letter, he commends them for facing the problem and offers a strange-sounding apology:

Even if I caused you sorrow by my letter I do not regret it... I did regret it–I see that my letter hurt[220] you, but only for a little while–yet now I am happy, not because you were made sorry, but because your sorrow led you to repentance. You became sorrowful as God intended. (2 Corinthians 7:8-9)

The Message version says, *"I'm not glad that you were upset, but that you were jarred into turning things around. You let the distress bring you to God, not drive you from him."* Feelings weren't the issue for Paul, sin was. Women say, "You hurt my feelings" as a way to opt out of obedience. Friend, your feelings will get hurt. Expect it; it's not always

---

218 <u>Cross-Centered Life</u>, by C.J. Mahaney, Multnomah Books, © 2002
219 2 Samuel 13:21
220 'Hurt' is not in the original Greek – the word is 'made you sorrowful,' or Strong's #3076- inner grief

a bad thing. Look under the hood to see why. We can be "sorrowful as God intended;" compare our actions to the truth even when it's tough, face and admit sin, run to get or grant forgiveness. Grief is valuable if it leads to repentance. If *your* sin is sparking inside, humble yourself and repent. If *they* are sinning, forgive, or maybe confront. Sorrow from guilt can be short-lived. That's good news! See that pain as a gift—a chance to empty the trash that's rotting in your heart.

Normal Sadness

There is a time to weep and a time to laugh, a time to mourn and ... to dance. (Eccl. 3:4)

Some people struggle with depression more than others, but some periods of sadness and depression are normal; after childbirth, too much activity, adrenaline rushes, sleepless nights, worry or indecision, bad reactions to medications, PMS, fasting and more. It can be good and productive, instead of an enemy to avoid. It can signal a time for change: time to gather information or listen to your instincts; time to go to a friend to confess a bad habit or a selfish practice; time to say no to someone or get help. You may need to slow down; stop pushing your body and build time into your schedule. Or you may simply be grieving a loss. Acknowledge your feelings, but don't let them paralyze you. You can still function sad or depressed. You don't have to love 2 a.m. feedings, but you can do them faithfully. You can go to work, love on your kids, make lunch, do laundry, help with homework, be kind to your husband, pay bills and pray daily even if you are sad. Do what you can do and be thankful for that.

Then, consider the effect medication has on your body. The book Will Medicine Stop the Pain? has pages of information about how anti-depressants and anti-anxiety drugs can affect our emotions—actually increasing or magnifying the feelings they were supposed to erase—and it offers biblical alternatives like changing your thinking.[221]

The positive side of sadness is compassion. It's a good sign when you can feel sad for other people, and share their grief without demanding attention for yourself. God loves our tenderheartedness and our tears are precious to Him. It's not a bad thing when you start crying at commercials and sweet stories ... it means you have a soft heart instead of a stony one.

Verses about Sadness and Grief:

Sorrow lasts for the night, but joy comes in the morning. (Ps. 30:5)

---

[221] Elyse Fitzpatrick and Laura Hendrickson, MD, Will Medicine Stop the Pain? Chicago, Moody Publishers, ©2006

Do not fear, for I am with you; Do not anxiously look about you, for I am your God. I will strengthen you, surely I will help you. Surely I will uphold you with My righteous right hand. (Isaiah 41:10)

When you pass through the waters, I will be with you; And through the rivers, they will not overflow you. When you walk through the fire, you will not be scorched, nor will the flame burn you. (Isaiah 43:2)

Comfort in Grief

Jesus came to earth partly to *comfort those who mourn; to give them a crown of beauty instead of ashes, the oil of gladness instead of mourning, and a garment of praise instead of...despair.*[222] In my grief, I screamed at the unfairness of life. I turned to alcohol for comfort—I wanted the escape, the excuse to act out and the soothing numbness (only it wasn't the oil of gladness). But it enslaved me: it controlled me and added problems. I had to give up comforting myself in self-destructive ways and find a way that honored God. We all want to have people know us and touch our pain. But to receive true comfort and help, you will have to let go of the ashes, the mourning and the despair.

When life starts spinning and my emotions start bubbling, this brings me back to faith: "God is on the throne, He loves me and He is in control (the opposite of my earthly father)." No matter how black or bleak the situation seems, this always calms and strengthens me. Comfort is an inside job; words you receive as being comforting instead of rejecting. Everyone's comfort is different. What thought comforts you in a trial?

> God has a plan. He isn't taken by surprise. (Jeremiah 29:11-13)
> This won't last forever. It will pass. God will bring me out of it. (1 Corinthians 10:13)
> I did the best I could. God will make it all work out for my good. (Romans 8:28)
> God covers my failure with His more abundant grace. (Romans 5:20)
> I was making progress, so Satan tried to slow me down. (Gal. 5:7-9)
> God is doing a new thing in me. (1 Cor. 5:17, Ezek. 11:19, Isa. 42:9)
> God is the God of second chances. I can do it differently (or better) next time.
> God is with me. (Isaiah 41:8-13)

It's easy to fall in despair when you're being corrected and trying to change. After the Christmas lunch (and two weeks of processing it), I felt pretty stupid about my angry reaction to *a song*. I had to focus on healing, otherwise I would have felt like giving up. I comforted myself by thinking about having one less hook in my soul. It also comforts me

---
222 Matthew 5:4, referring to a prophecy in Isaiah 61:1-3

when I think I responded better compared to the last time: if a month ago I wouldn't have said that, I feel like I'm making progress.

AFRAID

Maybe instead of being mad or sad, you are mostly afraid. Peter addressed this core struggle for women in 1 Peter 3:6: *"you are Sarah's daughters, if you do what is right and do not give way to fear."* What are we afraid of? I could give you a directory, but for me, it boils down to fear of people, fear of pain and fear of the unknown. People freaked me out; I had no tools for handling pain; I hated surprises and couldn't handle a day, much less face years in the future. When Robbie was young, we watched Sesame Street together: I always felt like the little spacemen, shaking in fear, wanting to get back in their ship where they felt safe. But when I'm inside my ship, all I can see is myself shaking. When I step outside, I can see others; they too are shaking in fear.

I feel like if I_____then_____will happen.
I feel like if I confront my boss, then he will be angry.
I'm afraid of_____if I_____.
I'm afraid of not being able to handle it if I get fired.

Fear does not come from God, according to 2 Timothy 1:7: *For God did not give us a spirit of fear (timidity), but of power, love, and a sound mind (self-discipline).* His power—the same dynamic power that resurrected Christ from the dead—lives in you. His perfect love flows out of you. The mind of Christ rests in you; orderly, sound and disciplined.[223] Fear should not master you because Christ in you has mastered fear.

Choose Either Fear or Love

So we know and rely on the love God has for us. God is love….There is no fear in love, but perfect love drives out fear, because fear has to do with punishment. The one who fears is not made perfect in love. (1 John 4:16-18)

If you are living in fear, you aren't living in love—they both can't occupy the same space in your heart. Focusing on fear fans the flames; God's perfect love kicks it out. If you are afraid, you have not let His love completely dwell in you. For example, I have had to face my fear of intimacy with Jim in many small steps. I robbed him of the joy of sex because of my fear: I wasn't loving him well by giving and sharing myself with him; I made him pay for someone else's sin. I have chosen to love more and fear less in this area and many others.

---

[223] I Corinthians 2:16

In Matthew 6:25a, worry (or anxiety) means you are seeking first something other than God: *Do not worry about your life. Seek first the kingdom of God, and all these things will be given to you as well... do not worry about tomorrow* (6:33-34a). Fear is the opposite of faith; a lack of faith lets fear grow. Are you trusting in your ability instead of His, trying to do what only God can do? Seek God's wisdom first, then tackle today's problems. An old saying goes: "When your knees knock, kneel on them."

Fear of the unknown kept the Israelites out of the Promised Land. After they scoped out the land, ten of the twelve spies reported, *"We can't attack those people; they are stronger than we are... we are like grasshoppers in their sight."*[224] God repeatedly called Joshua (their leader) on his fear: *"Have I not commanded you? Be strong and courageous. Do not be terrified. Do not be discouraged, for the Lord your God will be with you wherever you go."*[225] Forty years later, the Israelites came back to the same place to face the same choice. If fear keeps you from obeying God, He may let you wander in the desert, then someday He will bring you back to make the same decision. If He says 'go,' then go—afraid or not.

Paralyzing Fear

Satan doesn't care if you are stuck in the past (which you can't change) or the future (5 terrible scenarios which can't all happen), as long as you're not living for today. If I believe my good, wise and sovereign God will be with me tomorrow and every day, I don't have to fear the future. God promises to take me into the Land and fight for me. If I ran the world, there would be no giants, but giants don't worry God.

If you push through a fearful situation (like talking to someone who may get angry, or admitting a failure), old feelings and thoughts will usually come back. Plan to fight old feelings with new truths (a red rose moment). Maybe the reaction was right in the past, but not today. Admit the screaming or whining feelings, then do the right thing in spite of them. Your fearful reaction is not everyone else's problem, and it's probably not their fault that you're at a 10. Own it, then examine your feelings and choices separately.[226]

Verses About Fear

Even though I walk through the darkest valley, I will fear no evil, for You are with me; Your rod and Your staff, they comfort me. (Psalm 23:4)

---

224 Numbers 13:31
225 All of Joshua chapter 1, especially verse 9
226 Read the article *Personal Reflections*, Dr. David Powlison, <u>Journal of Biblical Counseling</u>, ©2005, Christian Counseling and Education Foundation

Search me, O God, and know my heart; try me and know my anxious thoughts; and see if there is any hurtful way in me; and lead me in the everlasting way. (Ps. 139:23-24)

Peace Beyond Understanding

Do not be anxious about anything, but in everything, by prayer and petition, with thanksgiving, present your requests to God. And the peace of God, which passes all understanding, will guard your hearts and your minds in Christ Jesus. (Phil. 4:6-7)

I learned about God's peace through a story something like this: A contest was held to depict God's peace. Artists sent paintings of prairie sunsets, quiet meadows, breathtaking sunsets and calm streams. The picture that won was unique. It showed a fierce storm with lightning and rain slashing down, battered tree branches bowed in the wind. On one branch, a mother bird with outspread wings covered her tiny chicks. God's peace is not life without storms; it is His presence, power, protection, and provision in the midst of the storm. Jesus said *'Peace I leave with you, my peace I give to you…not as the world. Do not be troubled and do not be afraid.'*[227] Peace comes when His wings cover us.[228]

Sometimes you just need to "do things afraid." Writing this book is a good example. I am fearful as I write: afraid I will hurt you, afraid I will apply Scripture wrongly, afraid you will think "this woman can't write a grocery list," yet I persist. Why? I believe that God has called me, so I write, in spite of my fears. I am overcoming them by doing what I'm called to do. Work on pushing through your fear. Often you will find that when you face the fear, the smoke vanishes, the fear shrinks and the truth of the situation shines. If you reject the voices, find the truth, and hold God's hand, you can conquer a lot. A pastor once told me, "You can either live your Christian life bored or scared"—sitting on the couch or pulled outside your comfort zone. Fear says, "Stay." Faith says, "Go because God is there." I can't stop doing the right thing because I might get hurt.

Abuse often brings terror, dreadful fear times ten. Not *I'm afraid of cutting myself,* but *someone has a knife in my face*. It paralyzes your body, silences your voice and overpowers your mind. God used Psalm 18 to deliver my heart from terror.[229] David wrote it after God delivered him from Saul who was intent on killing him.

Challenge your fears: I believe that when I_____, God will be there with me, giving me His unlimited power and_____, so I can_____.

---

227 John 14:27
228 King David said *Hide me in the shadow of your wings*. (Psalm 17:8)
229 See Appendix on Psalm 18.

So, like anger, is there righteous fear? Yes, righteous fear means reverence and awe and holy respect. Proverbs 31:30 says *a woman who fears the Lord is to be praised.* Revelation 14:7 reminds us to *fear God and give Him glory*. Fear of falling makes us walk carefully. Fear of death motivates us to go to the doctor or buckle up.

GLADNESS AND JOY

So far, we have dealt with three of the four basic emotions; mad, sad, and afraid. Now let's look at the basic **good** emotion; gladness (joy). This isn't happiness that comes from something outside our control: having a baby after years of barrenness,[230] or a prodigal son coming back.[231] I was happy when we adopted our son, when I passed my exams, and when I got a new car. Happiness isn't bad, it just isn't the best.

Joy isn't from joyful circumstances--when we are part of a loving family, esteemed by others, treated fairly, blessed, kept from trials. Joy is not an outside promise. It is an inside gift from the Holy Spirit that comes with the new heart. It's fruit that grows, and can't be manufactured.[232] Your circumstances may not be joyful but you can still experience inner joy. You don't have to work at having joy: because Christ is in you, joy is in you. Your job is to let what is inside you flow out. Do this by changing your thinking: like David, tell yourself about God's mercies. Be grateful for what you have, and what you have been spared. You can increase joy by practicing thankfulness. This isn't taking your most terrifying moment and calling it fun. It's being thankful that it's over, or that you weren't alone, or that God is proud of how hard you tried.

Psalm 16:4 says *the sorrows of those will increase who run after other gods,* but v. 11 says *You have made known to me the path of life: You will fill me with joy in Your presence.* Want sorrow? Chase after the world. Want joy? Chase after God.

When you start to feel good feelings, it is so foreign that they may get delayed. There can be so much junk inside, it takes time for the right emotions to struggle through and rise to surface. I was in a prayer time once where the other two women were happy and bouncing at seeing God at work in my life. I didn't feel at all what they were feeling. I told them, "Wait for me! I think I will be excited, but I'm not there yet."

---

230 Leah in Genesis 30:13
231 Parable in Matthew 25:21
232 Galatians 5:22

BAD

I came up with a fifth emotion that Melanie didn't teach me: Bad. It's the flood of shame I talked about in Chapter 6, the feelings of *I am such a failure; if you really knew me, you would reject me; I'm filled with black slime; I am less than everyone else; I am beyond cure; I don't deserve to live; hide, hide, hide; I'll never be free; I'll never get it; I'm unworthy.*

Shame is not a small emotion; it goes deeper than sadness or depression. It is Satan's seed of despair in your fleshly nature. It is the root of much of our hiding, running, stagnating, frustration, self-condemnation, self-destruction and wall-building. If I have a small victory, shame says, *you should have learned that twenty years ago*. If you fail, shame gloats, *See? You're a failure*. Shame is a black hole that erases all your changes. No matter what you learn, shame wins. If you have one area of victory, shame screams that there are five more areas where you are doing wrong.

Shame is more than an emotion; it is a core value that infects the way I see myself. It's a feeling that's tied into my identity. It covers all of me with humiliation and condemnation. It hides under the surface until someone points out a sin, then it jumps out and punishes the other person in anger. It hides behind pride until someone exposes your weakness, then it turns on you and destroys your soul. It masks itself until you fail, then it screams at you for days or weeks without stopping.

Because shame lives in our flesh, Satan has plenty of ammunition to remind us of our failures. The flesh is never removed, it's just disconnected. So when we toggle back to the flesh with sinful choices (or when Satan lies to us and reminds us of our past), he lights a flash-fire of shame. We can't argue against it, but we can refuse to accept it. We can stand against shame and speak truth:

> God planted love, joy and peace in my soul.
> In Christ I am a new creation. The old (me) is gone. (2 Corinthians 5:17)
> There is no shame in my new spirit.
> Instead of shame I (have) received a double portion of everlasting joy (Isa. 61:7)
> Everyone who trusts in Him will never be put to shame. (Romans 10:11, quoting Isa. 28:16)

'I will repay you for the years the locusts have eaten....the Lord your God, who has worked wonders for you says... never again will my people be shamed.' (Joel 2:25-27)

Reject Shame

How could God declare that we would be without shame? Because Christ lives in us and He has defeated shame on the cross. Hebrews 12:2 says *Christ scorned shame*, refused to accept it. He heard Satan trying to pour shame on Him, but He refused to live under the condemnation. On the way to the cross, He knew He was right in the middle of the Father's will. He knew it was His purpose, to obtain peace with God for all of us. There was no shame in that.

Friend, you are not bad, you are a new creation. You are perfect because God declares you are perfect. (Hebrews 10:14) You are perfect, and you are also being made holy. *Be confident of this, that He who began a good work in you will carry it on to completion until the day of Christ Jesus.* (Phil 1:6)

Those who look to Him are radiant; their faces are never covered with shame. (Psalm 34:5)

The Spin

I can't leave this chapter without helping you understand spin-masters; people who work your emotions. Perhaps you want to address a friend's anger. You examine yourself, pray hard about having a conversation with them, and plan out your words. But as soon as you speak, you find yourself on the defensive. This is a bully spin-master, who attacks and blames. A bully's plan is to make you pay so much that you aren't willing to correct them again. They say things like:

"I am not deceived, *you* are deceived!"
"*You* are the cruelest person I know."
"*You* rip me open with your words."
"*You* are probably thinking____(or wanting____), so I can't have this discussion."
"You are wrong to feel that way. You're too sensitive."

Charming spin-masters would take the opposite approach, praising or flattering you while spinning a net around you. They play on your tender emotions until you feel guilty for even considering negative thoughts about them.

"You are so kind, so smart, so fun to be with, so godly…."
"I love you so much..."
"I know you are probably right and I am wrong."
"How do you know all those Scriptures? I can't even memorize one…"

Charmers draw you in and then painfully push you out. I often feel like charmers "slap your face" emotionally. The third kind, a manipulative spinner, avoids the problem by pushing you away, distracting and talking in bunny trails:

> "I have never been so hurt by anyone in my entire life."
> "It's such a bad time to talk about this."
> "I forgot to ask how was your date (class, project, headache…) the other night?"
> "You used the word 'frustrated;' what do you mean by that?"
> "You're just upset because of your mom."
> "Why are you so afraid?"

Spin-masters use your emotions against you. They want your emotions to kick in so they can blind you and control you. They twist your words, spin meanings, toss in emotionally-charged words, question your motives, tell you what you're thinking, and leave you feeling confused, crushed, or crazy. They play on your fears to keep you from speaking truth. They pile on shame to define you. Once your emotions are stirred up, they deny, retaliate, ignore, or pretend all is well. Spinners trust their feelings and ignore yours. They always point the finger of blame back at you (blame is a way of avoiding responsibility). Talks will end with nothing discussed, nothing resolved, and nothing changed. They may want to stir you up and push you toward someone (to fight their battles or take the fall or protect themselves). Then they can say (to a pastor or a boss), "See what I'm dealing with? See how bad she is?" You go in circles facing your own junk, but can't get to the real issues. *Rather than dealing with actual problems, you end up dealing with emotional responses; yours and theirs.* In fact, your problem is worse than before, because now you're a target for their wrath, rejection, slander or charm.

They often speak out of both sides of their mouth. He might say, "I don't want you to shop at _____ anymore." Later, he will say, "Sure you can shop there." You are in a lose/lose situation. If you shop there, he can say, "I told you not to," and if you don't, he can say, "I said you could." By saying both things, they control you no matter what you do. And another warning: some spinners can switch from bully to victim to charmer in the blink of an eye. The pros can be all three at once.[233]

1) They are never wrong, are un-teachable, or always have an excuse.[234]
2) They are experts about your problems, but blind to their own.
3) They are unreasonable, or live in a made-up world in their head.

---
[233] One person said of a spinner, "They hold the Olympic record for the fastest 180° turn in any direction."
[234] The Bible calls them "fools." Read through Proverbs, marking every mention of *fool* or *foolish*.

4) They don't want to solve problems, look at themselves, or work things out.
5) They want to get your eyes off them, stir up your emotions and leave you whirling.

So how do you deal with a spin-master? There is no formula. Recognize when they are holding you captive with emotions; theirs or yours. Spinners can be your authority, your peer, your spouse or your child, employees, employers, teachers or pastors. You can work with one, love one, or share a pillow with one.[235] If you are a people-pleaser or deal with the fear of man, beware. Spinners will trap you. You will be susceptible to charmers, and because you were abused, you have a greater chance of being married to or divorced from one. You must be grounded in Christ so you don't get tossed into the minefield of their emotions. Detaching from their emotional whirlwind is critical and may keep you from being destroyed. (Like Satan, who spins, baiting you and stirring up emotions by rehashing your past sins, shaming and accusing.)

- Recognize the people you don't want to talk to because it's not worth it.
- Realize they are probably not going away—marriage, family members, job.
- Redefine the relationship—it's about pleasing God first, not them.
- Resist their tactics and ask God how, when or if you should talk to them.[236]
- Refuse to get involved in the same old conversation.
- Respond don't react—go in wearing your spiritual armor, knowing they will attack, play victim, charm, or play off your emotions. Make a plan before your emotions kick in. Work your plan (note card or planned phrases). Revise as necessary.
- Release yourself from their opinion and power over you.
- Refuse to let them define you. Everything they say is probably true—it's just about them,[237] not about you.
- Root yourself in how God sees you.
- Rejoice that God doesn't bully you.[238]
- Re-evaluate their words later (are they speaking out of both sides of their mouth?) Write down what they say to help you stay on track, to see the tactics and to confirm that you're not crazy.
- Repent if you are guilty of being a spin-master.

---

235 Fool-Proofing Your Life by Jan Silvious is life-changing. Waterbrook Press Multnomah, Colorado Springs, CO, © 1998
236 Proverbs 26:4-5; Proverbs 9:7-10
237 Luke 6:43-45, revealing their heart.
238 A great prayer is "Thank you Lord that you don't see me this way. Thank you that you are kind and loving and merciful, and when I mess up, you lovingly discipline me but never tear me to shreds. Thank you that you don't avoid me. Thank you that you see my sin but never treat me as my sin deserves."

Living From 4-to-7

Mostly, I am not an emotional woman anymore. I don't have real high highs or low lows (10's or 1's), and live most days between 4 and 7. I know how to bring down the screaming highs, and how to stop the downward slide of desperate lows. As I walk in forgiveness of sins and live in the truth, problems have less power and I have deep, sweet joy in my soul. *He who goes out weeping, carrying seed to sow, will return with songs of joy, carrying sheaves with Him.* (Psalm 126:6) That was me: I planted good seed even when I was crying and now I carry more fruit than I ever dreamed. *The Lord has done great things for us, and we are filled with joy.* (Psalm 126:3)

Now, I can identify most of my feelings, and there are many more than five. I feel excitement, longing, satisfaction, relief, confidence, pleasure, joking, curiosity, contentment, passion, wonder…..

Bottom Lines:

1. Follow His heart? Yes. Follow your heart? No.
2. Emotions are the warning signal that something is happening in our souls.
3. Look under the hood. Identify and fix the problem.
4. Emotions can be on either list—flesh or spirit.
5. Acknowledge but don't act out.

Discussion Questions:

1. Which one of the five emotions do you live in most often? How does it show up and when?

2. What reaction did you have this week that was negative, surprising or out-of-control and strong? Is this a familiar reaction? What is the first time you remember feeling this way?

3. What do you want that you are not getting? What do you expect other people to do for you?

4. What would keep you from acting differently than you feel?

To the Friend of the Traveler:

1. Do you see your friend living by her emotions or based on the Word of God? Listen and pray. Ask questions, give her your observations.

2. Be a true mirror: help her recognize how mad, sad, glad, afraid and bad show up. Encourage her faith and reason in daily situations. Find options on the good Galatians list; help her plan other ways of doing things.

3. Do not give into her requests or demands to worship her fear. Do not arrange your world for her world, so she will never be afraid or unsafe. Keep showing her how big God is, and how He can strengthen her.

4. Don't be surprised if she reaches a certain level of control or peace and wants to quit. Barb wanted to keep going until she reached a Level 10 Freedom, but that's rare. Your friend may get to one level better than she has been, and stop. Can you accept this and love her, even if you hoped for even greater functioning and freedom?

Worship Song: *Counting on God* by Phillips, Craig and Dean[239]

---

[239] By Desperation Band at New Life Church, © Integrity's Vertical Music, https://www.youtube.com/watch?v=E6C-J_gP1C4 Desperation Band at New Life Church © 2007

Chapter 8
Baggage Handling

Two weeks into the Bible study, new truths about marriage's roles and responsibilities crashed through my mind: a good marriage takes hard work from both people; God called me to love Jim with His love; a marriage license doesn't grant mind-reading powers. I reviewed my growing list of sins: hardness towards God; hatred towards my father; anger, resentment and unforgiveness towards men; cruel, cutting words in response to pain; drinking; controlling people; hiding, withdrawing.

My list made me mad. Since I was abused, I had a reason—and a right—to be angry. I mean *poor me*, look at the cards I had been dealt. If my dad had done it right, I wouldn't have been hurt. He broke my life, so he should fix it. But he was dead, and I was stuck with one tool: blame-shifting. I blamed everyone else; telling my story just rehearsed their faults. Self-pity slid into self-indulgence. I held a powerful "permission to behave badly" card.[240] Then God had spoken through Melanie's teaching. She said my sinful choices could change with sincere repentance. I couldn't change my past, but I could change myself. I told her, "I am really angry at you." I think she sighed as she asked why. "*Because you have taken away all my excuses*. I have no one else to blame now."

Heavy Bags

For a journey, you pack things in a suitcase; responsibility means carrying it. To ask "Who is responsible for this?" assigns credit or blame for an action: which one person will answer to God for this choice? Responsibility is one of the "Big 3" concepts in sexual abuse (along with Deception and Forgiveness). Most people wrestle with their responsibility, but abused women flat out resent it. I can almost write the script for my counselees: they take responsibility for things that aren't theirs, and abdicate responsibility for things that are. If you are unsure about what to work on next, look at your sense of responsibility. That brought me to a big "aha!" moment. I held the key to freedom the day I realized *I have seen the enemy and the enemy is me*. I had to change myself before my life could change.

The responsibility for an action is usually divided between me, God and/or others. I can <u>carry my own</u> suitcase, push it on someone else, take another person's bag, or try to lift

[240] See Appendix B.

God's case. Vine's Bible Dictionary calls it "the blood" or "blood-guiltiness," which means "the guilt and punishment for a violent act (is) on the perpetrator."[241] Galatians 6:1 calls it *carrying the burden*. We can help others carry their big loads, but in the end, we must each carry our own burden. (Gal. 6:5) All through the Bible, people struggled with responsibility—crediting themselves and blaming everyone else:

Eve blamed the serpent for her choice. (Gen. 3:13)
Adam stood silently beside Eve, ate the fruit, then blamed God and Eve for his choice. (Gen. 3:6,12)
Aaron blamed the fire for creating a golden calf and the people for wanting it. (Ex. 32:22-24)
Saul blamed the people when he disobeyed God and spared the enemy tribes. (1 Sam. 15:15)

It's All My Fault

I lived like a child slave, carrying everybody's bags. My parents said if I just obeyed quicker, spoke softer, sat stiller, or agreed faster, they would be happy. As usual, abuse twisted my sense of blame but wasn't the source. It mangled my sense of what I had to carry. Children are egocentric: they think they are the center of the world. A child thinks *something bad happened to me because I was bad; if they say I can fix this, I can; they gave me this job, so I have to do it.* It felt like my parents gave me "the keys to the kingdom:" I thought I had all the power to control the craziness. I tried and tried to turn the key, but it didn't matter how quick, soft, still or fast I acted; nothing changed.

As a child, I thought I couldn't fix our family because I failed. Now I know I failed because I believed a lie: I had no power over anything and no power to change anybody. God was not at the center of our home. People were unhappy because they turned away from God's ways and chose alcohol and abuse. *And*, it was not my responsibility to make anyone happy. Perhaps, like me, you thought you had the keys to the kingdom. Did you try and try to fix things? Did it seem to work sometimes? Did you give up because you couldn't make it stick? Did you blame yourself?

Deut. 24:16, Ezekiel 18: Each person's blood (responsibility) will be *on his own head*. He will be responsible for *his own sins*, not for his father's or anyone else's. This is two-sided: you do not bear the penalty for your parents' sins, but you can't blame your sins on your father or grandfather. Each person will be held accountable for his/her own actions.

God has given you the keys to a kingdom; *your* heart and *your* life. You are responsible for all your own actions and reactions but not the actions and reactions of others. This

---
241 Vine's Bible Dictionary, "blood," *dam*, #1818, p. 20, Thomas Nelson Publishers, © 1984, 1996, Nashville, TN

should be a relief. You are not responsible for your husband, your kids, your mother or mother-in-law, your friends, your boss, your sister, world peace, the national debt, wars or cancer. You only have to answer for your choices. Carry your own suitcase and choose to walk in ways that please God.

When you try to please man rather than God, you either give people too much power (idolize them) or take too much power on yourself (act like God). You choose to carry their baggage. Here are things we feel responsible for (and some truth about them):

> Keeping people happy—Each person holds their own key.
> Protecting others from pain—There is pain in the world.
> Failed relationships—It takes two people to make a relationship.
> Tragic accidents—God has numbered everyone's days.
> People treating you badly—People treat you how you let them.
> Perfection, never failing—We mature; perfection is only in heaven.
> Keeping peace—Some people don't want peace.

It's Not My Fault/It's All Your Fault

When I got married, my problems all became Jim's fault or God's fault (how convenient). When Jim hurt my feelings, it was my job to even the score: he hurt me, so I could retaliate. I never "started it," but once he crossed me, I brought revenge: I didn't holdback critical, cutting, spiteful sarcasm. But the Bible says that is God's job: *'Revenge is Mine.'* (Rom. 12) So I took on God's part and didn't live in His economy.

But when I had to control my anger, I thought it was God's job to change my feelings. I prayed pleading, begging, pouting demands and blamed Him for not "doing it" for me. It was a stand-off: I wanted to do God's part (get revenge), and I wanted Him to do my part (make me not angry). The problem was I didn't do *my job*. When you expect God to do your part, you may feel frustrated, hurt and disappointed. When you work hard but are trying to do God's part, it will invariably fail, so you feel mad or betrayed. God is a gentleman. He never forces us against our will and He always gives choices. But He can also be a brick wall; He allows the natural consequences for our choices to fall on us, and waits for us to do our part.

The marriage Bible study had showed me the log in my eye—my sinful thoughts, actions and attitudes. My choices led to my sin, which brought on my consequences. I couldn't blame Jim for them. Instead of being a fixer or a fighter, a puppet or a pacifier, God called me to change myself and gave me the tools to do it; admit my anger didn't make me right;[242] take my thoughts captive to obey Christ.[243] I hadn't done any of this: I had ignored my part.

Exodus 20:5-6: The sins of the father are visited on the 3rd and 4th generations of those who hate God. But God limits how long it lasts and provides a way of escape: love Him.

In the movie *The Last Sin Eater*,[244] a small village handled sins in an ancient way; they appointed an innocent man to "eat their sin" and carry it away. He was cloaked in shame and lived alone—no one could look on him, talk to him or speak his name. He was a tortured soul until the gospel message of forgiveness penetrated the villagers' hearts. Their way didn't work, partly because God wants us to carry our own burdens. But the good news of Exodus 20 said when I surrender my life to His direction, I change my life and my descendants' lives. I start a new cycle of love for thousands of generations.

How Does Responsibility Tie to Sin?

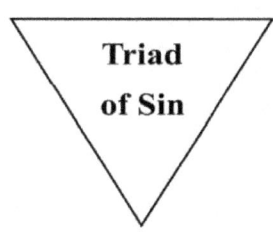

The first side of the Triad of Sin looked at the sin nature all people are born with (the flesh). God dealt with it in two ways: disconnected the old engine (made it powerless) and transplanted a new engine into your heart. This chapter examines the second side of the Triad: the sins and sinful choices we are responsible for, whether done on purpose or unknowingly. Taking responsibility for my actions means I "own" all my choices; what I do or don't do, and whether or not I keep God's commands. When you walk toward people, you have to learn how to handle sin—first yours, then other peoples.' You will sin against people and they will sin against you. Sinners sin, and they are very good at it. We shouldn't be surprised when people sin.

When our choices are sinful (break God's law, cross the line, fail to hit the standard of holiness, etc.), we will feel guilt. Guilt is a God-given sense of failure for doing bad or wrong things, or not doing a good thing.[245] When we choose to sin, we also owe a penalty. God provided a solution for this second side too: Jesus' death on the cross paid our debts. By paying the debt for our sinful choices, two-thirds of the Triad of Sin has been dealt with in Christ. Over half the work is done! Then He gives us tools to deal with our sinful choices and the power to change.

---

242 James 1:19-20
243 2 Corinthians 10:5
244 *Last Sin Eater*, book by Francine Rivers, Tyndale House Publishers, Inc. © 1998
245 Called Sins of Commission (bad things we do) and Sins of Omission (good things we don't do). We can also feel false guilt, where we didn't do anything wrong, but we have been trained to feel bad.

Instead of blaming God for how you were born (*I'm Italian, so I have a temper*) or how He made you *(I'm a choleric, so I want it my way)*, carry the suitcase of your own choices. Admit: *I got angry when he lied; I acted wrong, I repent; I took the selfish way out instead of the righteous one; I can act differently.*

It's Their Fault

The weight of responsibility is almost always divided, but abused women seldom get it right. Usually they take all the responsibility for the abuse. When I tell women that the abuser is all to blame, and his blame-shifting won't stand up before God, they look at me like I'm crazy. Abusers have the same Triad of Sin, the same sin nature. They struggle with sinful choices; to protect innocence or expose a child to pornography; to have sex with a partner or a vulnerable girl; to exercise self-control and crucify his fleshly desires or give in to them; to wait until marriage to explore sex; to take his thoughts captive—*no, it's wrong to want anyone who is not my wife*; or stay out of the neighbor's bedroom. His sinful, selfish choices devastated you. But the abuser will have to answer to God for that wickedness: his blood will be on his own head. You won't have to explain any of it. Can you drop their baggage yet?

Power and Control

Power and control are core issues in abuse. Rape is not about sex; it's about power. The abuser overpowered you. If you believe you caused the abuse to happen, "power" in abuse meant you could bring your abuser to orgasm. Or you made the abuser happy. Maybe you became promiscuous to hurt men by having power over them.

You may think the abuse happened because you were attractive, or too sexy or because you were in a vulnerable place (a bed or a bathtub) or you asked for it. If you can correct your "fault" (being sexy, attractive, vulnerable, asking) you can prevent abuse from happening again. You change your circumstances—become unattractive (gain fifty pounds) or never take a bath again—and take power for yourself. That's letting the giants keep you out of the land instead of fighting for it. Also, it doesn't take into account the wickedness of man (the abuser who chose to abuse).

No Power

On the other hand, if you were overpowered in the abuse (robbed of your choices), you may believe you were powerless to stop it or prevent it. You just took it; laid down and died, became a victim. *My body just reacted. There was no sense fighting.*

You changed so much until you didn't know who you were, what you liked, or what to think. You did nothing, or maybe waited for someone to rescue you or for God to change it.

Maybe you were powerless to stop it when you were young, but now you are not. Often, we need to save ourselves—speak, confront, challenge lies, expose sin, call the police, kick a defiant child out of the house. And, remember, you always have choices. You can choose your actions and reactions and get yourself out of sinful or scary situations. What situation easily intimidates you? What shuts you down? What talks you out of choosing? Where do you think *I can't do this*? When do you think *everybody else can do this better than I can*?

Is your helplessness an act? If you want something, do you move heaven and earth to get it? If you don't want to do it, heaven help those who pressure you? There is *a righteous way through every trial*—the way to avoid sinning and take a stand (1 Cor. 10:13). Sometimes it seems like a tiny sliver of light on the edge of the dark. Although it's hard to realize you can't control or change anyone else, it's freeing to realize you can look at yourself first. That's our part now. Here are some questions to ask yourself about the abuse:

> What was the first choice? Who made it?
> Who started it?
> Did I tell them to do that? Or did I say I asked for it?
> Whose actions led to these consequences?
> Was this an action or a reaction/response?
> Was my choice obedient or rebellious?
> When did I realize it was sin (or wrong)?
> Did this choice help me or hurt me? How?
> Did I have a righteous way out then?
> What is one righteous way through now?

Dealing With Consequences

The abuse wasn't your fault, but it knocked you off your original path and sent you on a different path. You can't change that event, but your life was changed. If you hadn't been molested, you might not have started drinking. If the rape hadn't happened, you might have kept yourself for your husband. You are not held responsible for their sin, but there may be consequences (for their choices and yours) that will affect you until you die. *Affect* is the key word; although they have *changed* your life, they should not *control* it.

Here are some consequences for being sexually abused (effects of someone else's sin):

    Loss of innocence, feeling guilty and marked
    Frigidity, unable to respond sexually in marriage
    Sexually transmitted diseases, chronic infections, physical damage to sexual organs
    Pregnancy, abortion, infertility, miscarriage
    Fear of things connected to the abuse—the dark, touch, nakedness, smells, sounds
    Isolation, broken relationships, fear of people, distrust of people's motives and authority
    The abuser was taken away through separation, divorce or jail time

You aren't responsible for the detour off the path, but you are called to make godly choices here, where you stand. You can find the righteous ways to endure the consequences, even if they don't change.[246] The Bible doesn't say that someone with an STD can't serve and please God with her life. Even though you didn't ask for that consequence, and don't deserve it (as payment for sin), it is a fact of your life. Rebellion or rage won't remove it any more than revenge or regret or running will. The only way out is through. Steady obedience to God's directions can diminish the effects. If you continue to do right even while enduring bad consequences, you will experience God's blessings.

It's the difference between a thermometer and a thermostat: a thermometer states the temperature, whether it is 75° or -30°. A thermostat reads the temperature, but it can also change it. You can change the situation by changing yourself. Life's situations may be out of your control, but you can always choose your own thoughts, words and actions. Your responses will show your level of maturity. Determine what your responsibilities are, then do them well.

What Are You Planting?

Do not be deceived: God cannot be mocked. A man reaps what he sows. The one who sows to please his sinful nature, from that nature will reap destruction; the one who sows to please the Spirit, from the Spirit will reap eternal life. Let us not become weary in doing good, for at the proper time we will reap a harvest if we do not give up. (Galatians 6:7-10)

You have hundreds of choices every day. You can choose your thoughts, words, actions, beliefs, attitudes, friends, food, sleep and laundry schedules. You can choose whether or not to answer the phone, and whether to talk or listen. You can choose what voices to listen to and how to show love to people around you. Every choice brings consequences.

---

246 1 Corinthians 10:13

When you choose your action, you choose your consequences.[247] Making a choice is like a farmer planting seeds (sowing). When the plants are fully grown, he cuts down the crop and gathers it in the storehouse (reaping). The crop you gather is your consequences (called the law of the harvest):

1. You will reap **what** you sow. If you judge without mercy, you will be judged without mercy. If you sow anger, you will reap anger. If you sow lies, you will be lied to. Also positively: if you sow patience, people will be patient with you. If you forgive, you will be forgiven.

2. You will reap **more** than you sow. If you sow a seed, you will reap a plant. If you sow ten angry words, you will reap 100. If you steal $5, you may have $500 stolen from you. Positively, if you are kind to one person, you may receive kindness from five.

3. You will reap **later** than you sow. There is a growing season. If you plant in spring, you will harvest in the fall. Because the harvest is delayed, some people think they can get away with sowing seeds of the flesh; others think they're not making any progress. But God will judge every action (your sins, and your abuser's sins). The good harvest is huge compared to the tiny seed.

This law comforted me when one of our son's friends stole $400 from us. We confronted the boy without results. We forgave him and warned our son. Because God is not mocked, I know he will face the harvest of his actions: others will steal from him, more than he stole. He is deceived; he thinks he got away with it, but I know he won't like the crop he pulls out of the ground someday.

If you don't like your crop, change what you're planting. If my dad planted barley in my soul and ten years later, I still grow barley, he is no longer responsible for my harvest and I can't keep blaming him. I can change my crop and plant wheat or sunflowers or strawberries. Here's a caution: it's not a formula to make someone change. I used to think that if I was kind to my son, he would be kind back to me. But sowing kindness into someone doesn't mean kindness will come back through them. God will bless you, but there are no guarantees about who He will use—total strangers, in-laws, radio programs.

What is God's Part?

Pastor Wayne Barber said, "Responsibility is our response to His ability." We can do our part through His ability; His divine nature, His engine, His magnet, His power source, His

---
[247] Concept from <u>Growing Kid's God's Way</u>, Gary and Anne Marie Ezzo, Growing Families International © 1998.

operating system. He began a good work in you and He will faithfully complete it.[248] He FOUGHT and won the battle for your spirit. As I list what God has done for you, slow down and ponder two questions: Do you believe this? Have you received it? Here is the acronym for God's responsibility:

Forgave
Overcame
Unique You
Grace
Holy Spirit
Truth

Forgave–God forgave **all** your sins. You are clean before the Lord, holy, righteous, shameless, blameless, unsoiled. Do you believe? Have you received?

Overcame–Christ won the battle on the cross, and overcame the enemy. He crushed sin's power over you. He was victorious so you are. Do you believe? Have you received?

Unique–You have a Unique identity. You are His child, born into the family of God, with a unique voice, special gifts and talents and a unique outlook. He has a custom-made plan and purpose for you. Do you believe? Have you received?

Grace–God gave you grace for salvation and for living. His divine power flows through you. He gives you the ability to say no to sin and yes to godliness. He treats you kindly and helps with consequences of bad choices. Do you believe? Have you received?

Holy Spirit–God gave you the indwelling Truth-Teacher, the Counselor and Comforter who points out sin and points the way back to God. Do you believe? Have you received?

Truth–God gave you the Bible. Eternal, perfect, flawless, unchangeable; the source of Truth that sets you free. Do you believe? Have you received?

What is Our Part? FIGHT From His Victory

Like the children of Israel marching into the Promised Land, we have to follow God's ways and His timing in order to claim our inheritance. Many Christians want the Promised Land but don't want to fight. Or they fight the wrong battles with old tactics.[249]

---
248 Philippians 1:6
249 Numbers 14

If we don't fight, we are in danger of becoming ineffective and unproductive.[250] There is no place for excuses: He has given us everything we need for life and godliness.[251] We follow, then we FIGHT to possess the land He has given us. Here is the acronym for our part:

Faith
Identity
Gratitude
Heart
Telling

Faith: Your job is to walk by faith, not by sight. Faith replaces frantic efforts to control. Trust God, His purposes and ways, His sovereignty, goodness and wisdom. There is only one God and you are not Him. Nothing happens to you that hasn't first passed through God's filter. Trust Him on things you can't control (the future, other people). He may be waiting for all the pieces to come together at the perfect time. God will use this for your good and His glory.

I learned to trust in baby steps. One year, I needed a winter coat but I was broke. So with childlike faith, I prayed for a new one. Ten days later, a rich friend gave me a beautiful coat she didn't need. I felt His love more, saw prayers answered and heard people's stories of faith, then my fear got smaller. It seemed a bigger risk not to trust Him. I often prayed, "Lord, I believe; help my unbelief." I have trusted God for my marriage, a baby and a new country, but I started with a coat.

Identity: You are responsible to live your new identity. Formerly a child of wrath, now a child of God. How has Kate Middleton learned to be royalty? She had lessons, she observed the royals, grew in her husband's love and lived in her identity. You are a saint, an ambassador, beloved Bride, adopted into His family, joint heir with Christ. Look for God's purpose, participate in it. I first served in puppet ministry so I could hide. Then I wrote some scripts, now I'm writing this book. I've grown into my new identity. I don't want to be a healed caterpillar, but a transformed butterfly. I won't let Satan keep me on the ground. I'm learning to relate as a new person, free from my awful past.

Gratitude: It's your responsibility to be grateful. Pray with thanksgiving in and for and through every situation. Be content in all circumstances. Weep with joy over forgiveness. See opportunities God has put in front of you and walk into them. Journal "5 or 10 things I

---
250 2 Peter 1:8
251 2 Peter 1:3

am grateful for today." *Thank you God for eyes to read, I can pray and listen, I have a job, clean water, the Bible so I can learn, God's perfect justice and mercy, a good future waiting in Heaven.* Any mother of a teenager wishes they were grateful for their allowance or food or clothes. Be thankful for unexpected blessings. What you can have is greater than what you lost. Practice laughing.

Heart: Recognize the battle within. Starve your old heart and feed the new one. Repent of actions on the first Galatians list that stop the flow of God's power. He won't make you walk in the Spirit, only you can let the new heart drive: follow righteous desires, thoughts, and actions. Love unlovable people. Be God "with skin on" to hurting people. Die to yourself, confess your sins, sacrifice your idols, submit to God, do things His way. Love your spouse. Forgive now. Don't gossip.

Telling: Share the treasure you found, what God has done for you. God doesn't send postcards; He asks you to be His ambassador to the world. Speak His words of hope, healing and truth. Disciple someone. Tell one person how you overcame abuse; tell another about the joy of forgiveness. Tell your Bible study group how you are growing. Teach the law of the harvest to someone in a trial. Share Romans 5 with a sufferer.

Carrying Your Responsibility

You have to decide where to apply Faith, Identity, Gratitude, Heart and Telling to your daily responsibilities. You plan how to spend your money, your time and your energy, comparing your actions to this list of priorities (in order of importance):

1. **Your relationship with God.** Our primary purpose is to have vibrant, ongoing fellowship with the Creator. (Gen. 3:8) Glorify God and praise Him. (Is. 43:7, Rev. 4:11) Fall in love with Love. If you know Him, you will love Him. If you love Him, you will obey. If you obey, you will know Him more, a sweet upward spiral.
2. **Be a godly Person.** Be conformed into the image of Christ. (Romans 8:28-9) Bear much fruit. (John 15:16) Obey His commands. Die to self. (Luke 9:23-4)
3. **Be a godly Partner.** The husband—a loving leader; the wife—a submissive, Spirit-led helper. (Ephesians 5) Be faithful to your spouse, forsake all others. Forgive. Serve each other.
4. **Be a godly Parent.** Teach and train, model, be patient and reasonable. (Eph. 6:4)
5. **Be a godly Employee.** Honest, dependable, hard-working, creative, an ambassador for Christ, representing Him at work.
6. **Be a godly Parishioner.** Be a vital part of the church, serve in ministry. (Eph. 4:16) For example, God says to love your neighbor as yourself. There are hundreds of ways

you could obey; bake her a pie, watch her kids while she has an afternoon away, cook dinner for her, house watch, take her to church, give her a ride to the mall, help her paint, shop for her, etc. Or pray for her, speak wholesome words, forgive her…

Loving God When I Fail

What happens when I try to do this but I have an epic failure? On the last night of His life, Jesus was betrayed by two of His disciples. Both Judas and Peter betrayed His love, His trust and friendship. Both turned their backs on Him: Judas betrayed Him and turned Him over to the authorities; Peter swore three times he didn't know Him. Both men's choices brought guilt and condemnation; both despaired; both wept. So why did one become the rock on which the church was built and the other committed suicide? Because one repented unto life, the other despaired unto death. One ran *to* Jesus, the other ran *away*. I think Judas thought, "You should have claimed Your kingdom. It's Your fault for stalling." He did things his way, not God's.

We do our duties the best we can, but even when we fail or sin, we still have choices. When I don't do well, God doesn't condemn me: He says *it's okay you didn't do that well*, then offers His grace (power and help to do what I should), mercy (lessens the consequences for what I do wrong), and compassion (*I know it's hard, I still love you*) to help us carry our burdens.

> Why did you choose that action? What was your goal/motive? Did you accomplish it?
> What did you fail to do; obey God or make someone happy?
> Was it a sin or a disappointment? Unreasonable expectation? Lack of knowledge?
> What does the Bible say about it? Which side of Galatians 5:19-22 did this action show?
> Does this please God? How do I know? What would Jesus do?
> How would this help me to do the Word? What should my attitude be?
> Do I need to do anything first? (confess my sin, forgive, be kind, get more information)
> What do I need to do to restore this relationship?
> Am I waiting for them to do right first? Why am I putting off making a decision?

Carrying Your Stuff in Marriage

Responsibility in marriage plays out in many complicated ways. When I change courses—carry my own duties, admit my deception, don't blame my spouse or take on anyone else's roles—it affects both of us. In marriage the husband often blames the wife for the marriage problems. Yet God tells men that they are the head, the CEO, of the marriage union. God holds the men accountable for the state of marriage. Your husband may blame you (like Adam) yet God does not buy into it (Adam was still cursed).

I am called to be a helper to my husband but ultimately it is my husband who stands before God to answer for his actions as servant-leader. I will stand before God and answer only for my role as a wife, mother, friend, daughter, sister. Although I am one-flesh with my husband, I am still held accountable for my own actions.

What is my responsibility within the marriage? Obey God. Grow in love with God and my husband. Submit to the Holy Spirit, let fruit grow. I may not be able to change Jim, but I can change myself. I can't expect Jim to meet all my needs (the Bible says God does that, not my husband). It's my duty to push through my fears and share my thoughts and feelings with him (because he can't read my mind). I can't demand it or force his actions. I give him a chance to respond because he loves me. But if he doesn't meet my needs, I run to God to receive from Him. And keep talking to Jim.

I can speak truth in love to him when he is deceived and encourage him when he is fearful. In Acts 5, Sapphira agreed with her husband to withhold money from their offering and lie to the church elders. I have heard it taught that she should have been exonerated because of her submission. But the Scripture proves otherwise: God held her accountable for her choices. She agreed to sin and it cost her life. Wives can't always just submit to their husbands; they have to pray about their own choices before God. Are their opinions or words more important to you than God's?

Not Sins

In our closest relationship (marriage or close friendship), there are many opportunities for disagreement, conflict, judging each other's actions and words. God uses these people as "iron sharpening iron." (Prov. 27:17) Remember, that there will be many things you don't like that are differences in personality (optimist vs. pessimist), training (neat freaks or messies), experiences (love to travel, hate to travel), and style (afraid of conflict vs. used to conflict) that are not sinful. Different doesn't mean sinful or bad, it's just different. Just because you don't like something about your husband doesn't make him sinful (or make you sinful). Accept your differences and try to come to win-win solutions about things (like how neat to keep the house). Take turns submitting to each other in love. (Eph.5:21) Talk until you can come to a compromise or a win/win solution.

I Can Do it Better

Control freaks try to control people's opinions and actions, thoughts and feelings, perceptions, and even God's hand. *If everyone did it my way, no one would get hurt.* They are constantly watching for the next person, problem or challenge that may get out from under their thumb. They control with manipulation (whining, sickness, helplessness, withdrawing) or intimidation (*you're a loser, I'm right*) even reaching into the future to control what comes to them. Isaiah 41:21-24 talks about the sinfulness of people who think they can predict the future based on events in the past. Ignoring today's speed bumps while looking far down the road is sin—it violates Matt. 6:33. It doesn't put God's power into the equation. No matter how hard you try, you can't make someone do it your way. You can change yourself and pray, but does that seem ineffective compared to your anger and manipulation?

Do you think if you don't do a job, it won't get done (because no one else will do it, or do it as well)? You can be a super-mom, super-wife, super-worker, super-Christian—you get your "strokes" from doing so much/so well, jealously guarding these jobs; burning out for God, working at a pace that guarantees breakdowns. Often your husband, friends, church, and your kids have figured this out and will work you to the point of exhaustion. Or you may be the martyr, working hard and complaining all the way. Do you feel like you "have to"? Does a perfectly clean house protect you from abuse? Does this **relate to** the abuser's idea of "your performance will bring my approval"? This may be wires- jammed-in-a-jar thinking.

> If I don't control my life, I will be abused again.
> If I am submissive, some bad man will take advantage of me again.
> God has let me down, so now I'm on my own (lie from the enemy).
> People will admire me if my house is perfect.
> I'll never trust anyone again.

I can stop being the kingpin and become the servant of the King. One woman said it well: "I am in charge of making the peanut butter and jelly sandwiches and God is in charge of the universe."[252] I want to do only what God calls me to do. I am not the Savior; I can only point you to the Savior.

Carrying Your Kids' Backpacks

I once cried to a pastor, "I had my childhood stolen from me." His gentle answer was, "Yes, but you can give your son a great childhood." I'm responsible to be a good mom, teaching my son the Bible and training him to do right. I am responsible *to* him before God (for my actions) but not *for* him (his actions). (It's easier to pick up socks than to train kids, but kids need to pick up their own socks). I hope he will carry his own stuff, and not be caught in the Blame Game. But he has a sin nature that has nothing to do with **how I**

---

[252] Blue Like Jazz, Donald Miller, Thomas Nelson Publishers, © 2003

parented him. Let's say he decides to speed. I taught him good driving habits, so it's not my fault if he chooses to push pedal to the metal. He bears full responsibility for a speeding ticket. Even if he says it's my fault, I am not responsible for his life (like his decision to walk away (at least at this time) from God).[253] (Now replace "speeding" with taking drugs, lying, stealing, being disrespectful or not doing homework.) If your kids don't learn from instruction, they will experience consequences.

Rescuing

Will you fight for others but run away from your problems? Being a rescuer can be a wrong use of control and a powerful distraction from dealing with your issues. You didn't have the power to stop your abuse, but now: *I'm the boss, I'm in control and by God, no one will get hurt on my watch.* One mom said it was like being a super hero:"As soon as I heard that cry for help, instantly— ZZZZIIIPPPP—out flashed my cape! SuperMe to the rescue!" It was *See the pain! Go fix it!* But she hadn't asked God if she was the one who was supposed to help, if He had other plans for this trial, if she should just watch and pray, or what her kids needed to learn. So she kept getting disciplined (receiving someone else's consequences) for getting in God's way. Always painful.

Here's one scenario: Your son's car is broken and your husband keeps promising to fix it "this weekend," but hasn't. So you are the one without a car. If you let the consequences for procrastinating fall on his head, suggest that the next time Junior's car breaks down, you will be happy to drive Hubby to work but you need your car. Could he ride to work with the guys? Could Son take Dad to work, then pick up the car parts?

Bag Snatching

It's not always good to rescue people. For example, if you clean Johnny's room because he won't do it, rather than training him to keep his room clean (by expecting clean rooms and addressing messy rooms), you have taken over his job. What has Johnny learned? Perhaps, *if I wait long enough, someone else will do my work.* In fact, you are paying his consequences for his sin. He failed to clean his room but rather than having to stay home one night and clean it (be held responsible for his lack of action), you let him off the hook. It is loving (sometimes it's tough love) to let the consequences fall on the guilty person's head. Consequences can be God's hand drawing a sinner back to Himself.

---

[253] Every year, he gets a little better. We have had good talks, and he has admitted he was rebellious.

Practice godly responses to problems so you don't automatically pick up someone's bag:

> "Hmm, that's interesting. Why do you say that?"
> "I've never thought of it that way. Could you explain some more?"
> "That's a new thought for me. I'll have to think about that for a while."
> "I see it differently, but I don't want to argue about it."
> "Can I get back to you later?"
> "Thank you for telling me, even though I'm sure it was hard to do."

I constantly fight with myself to let people carry their own bags. When you are used to carrying every bag, it seems unfair that your kids should suffer. Or you think they don't have any tools for handling hurt, because you didn't (or still don't). You think you are responsible for protecting your family (and it's loving). We have a duty to keep our children safe from physical harm, and we shouldn't expose them to abuse. But the reality is we live in a world under the power of an evil being—a sin-filled world ruled by sinful folks. Give your kids opportunities to face their own choices and consequences. Teach them to be thermostats. Let them make small, then bigger bad choices and fail while they have back-up (you); re-evaluate, get input, pray, then change.

Stepping Out

Often the Bible says if we do something right then God will do something in response. I once told Melanie I could never honor my parents: they didn't deserve it. She asked me to read Ephesians 6:2-3: *Honor your father and mother–which is the first commandment with a promise; that it may go well with you and you may enjoy long life on the earth*. Then she said, "Funny, my Bible doesn't say anything about 'if they deserve it.'" Whoa, that was a low blow: I couldn't re-write the Bible. If I honored my parents, *then* my life would be long and good. In the Bible, God gives choices, most of the information you need to make the choice, and warns of the consequences. He says, "if you do this, this will happen... if you don't do this, this will happen." If... then...

> **If** *the priests carrying the ark step into the water, (then) I will part it for you.* (Joshua 3:13)
> *If you believe in Me, (then) I will grant you eternal life.* (John 3:15, 1 John 3:11-13)

Sometimes your prayers aren't answered because God is waiting for you to do something. Maybe God has physical healing planned for you, but you have to walk a mile every day. Maybe He gave you the ability to earn money by making cards or tacos, greeting people or answering phones. Maybe you need to train your kids before you have peace. Maybe you must give love first before you will be loved in return.

Mix-up in Baggage Claim

Author Carissa Phelps, sold as a prostitute at age twelve, said one in seven American children will run away from home, and within forty-eighty hours, one in three will be asked to "take care" of someone in exchange for food, money, clothes, shelter and sexual favors.[254] This is twisted responsibility.

More confusion about responsibility comes in the areas of guilt and shame. Often we feel shame for someone else's actions more than for our own sin. Cris calls this an "over-active guilt gland." You may be ashamed of a part of your body, or your personality—whatever you think caused the abuse. I bathed in shame for things I wasn't responsible for: I was used sexually; I couldn't make my dad love me; I couldn't give Jim a child. You may feel guilty for keeping the secret or for letting it happen. It always stuns me when a woman, torn and broken by someone else's sin, feels shame in saying she was raped. Rape is shameful, but the shame is all on the rapist.

Pain Connected to Pleasure

When a teenager is molested, there may be physical pleasure. She accepts the pain of the abuse (guilt, shame, secrecy, self-loathing, regret) because she likes the pleasure, so she feels like she seduced him. Then she is "hooked;" she believes it was all her fault: she started it or caused it. The abuser gladly lets her take the blame and may say: "You know you wanted it," or "I would have stopped after the first time, but you kept after me." The longer it goes on, the more blame she accepts; the more pleasure she feels, the more responsible she feels. The proportion of guilt for the first time: she was 100% innocent and he was 100% guilty. But after that, the weight shifted. The division of guilt may be 70/30 or 60/40. They both sin in their choices. She seduced him but he fell willingly.

Carrying Contraband

Threats and physical violence also magnify the confusion about responsibility. It drives the lie in deeper that "it's all my fault." The abuser said, "If you didn't make me so angry,I wouldn't have to hurt you" or "you will do it or you will pay." My dad said if I told, my mother would die, so keeping her alive became my job. My silence could keep her alive,

---

254 Carissa Phelps, <u>Runaway Girl</u>, The Penguin Group, New York, © 2012, p. 288-9.

so I stayed silent with a vengeance. It was my responsibility to please my abuser, and not expose him. That was a crushing load for an 8-year-old.

Are you still carrying out the abuser's words, keeping his threats alive with self-punishment? You believe that your sin deserves to be punished, so you act as judge and jury. If you punish yourself, you can make it up to God for "being bad," or if you beat yourself up first, you think the punishment from God or people will be less? You may withdraw from fellowship; impose strict fasting on yourself; deny yourself a pleasure; take away a privilege; mentally berate yourself. Remember Romans 12:20 says only God has the right to punish sin? You are taking God's place.

Pack and Carry the Right Things

I travel a lot, and packing is always a challenge. When I realize I have packed just the right things—not forgotten something or packed unneeded things—I enjoy the trip much more. It's a lighter load just carrying my own duties. I hope you get there too!

Bottom Lines:

1. I have a part and God has one; I do my part and I trust God to do His.
2. I am responsible for all my thoughts, actions, words, attitudes and beliefs.
3. I cannot abdicate my responsibility.
4. There are no excuses for ungodly behavior (sin).
5. If I don't like my crop, I need to change what I am planting.

Discussion Questions:

1. How did the abuse knock you off the original path, and what path did you land on? What were you like before the abuse? How did it change you?

2. What luggage have you been carrying that doesn't belong to you? What responsibilities have you been dodging?

3. Who or what have you been blaming for your life?

4. What choices did you make after the abuse that have affected your life?

5. What are some different ways you could respond to a situation? What would your best friend/ pastor's wife/ Christian sister/ mentor do?

To the Friend of the Traveler:

1. Help her sort out where responsibility falls. Return to it often, any time you are stumped. Don't let her take the blame for stuff that isn't hers. Does she feel responsible for the future, her family's happiness, being perfect? This isn't just an abused woman's problem, it's a woman problem: share where your struggles lie. Remind her about God's grace. Praise little steps of obedience, encourage another step.

2. Most people hate and fear change. "I like the way I am and I don't want to give that up." *Better the devil you know than the devil you don't.* Allow her a lot of time to make adjustments. It takes time for her mind to have different connections, different memories, different thoughts. Remind her about the good crop that's coming.

3. Plan out ways to get out of other people's jobs/duties that she has taken on. Write out on cards the conversation she needs to have with husband, mother-in-law, friends, etc.

4. Is there anything she did during the abuse that makes her feel guilty or ashamed? Help her to see what was her responsibility, and what was the abuser's choice.

Worship Song- *Overcomer* by Mandisa[255]

---

[255] Mandisa, Sparrow Records, © 2013, https://www.youtube.com/watch?v=b8VoUYtx0kw

Chapter 9
Your Permanent Traveling Companion

After living in the States eight years, I had a crushing disappointment. Jim and I tried to adopt three at-risk children: we did all the paperwork and interviews and passed all the classes. After praying over pictures of the kids, we went for our final interview. Because of a situation that happened five years earlier, the process was stopped dead. We were judged unfit to adopt because a former friend had escalated a small thing when we were baby-sitting her daughter, ultimately involving the police. Nothing could be done, period. So I lay on the couch crying my heart out. I wailed to God about how unfair it was, how wrong and hurtful she had been. I ached for the children I would never get to hold. The more I thought about it, the harder I cried.

Hours later, my cat jumped up on my chest. I opened my swollen eyes and saw her butt in my face, tail straight in the air. *Well, that is a fine thing to be looking at.* Then I heard God's quiet voice say *Well, that is what you are looking at.* I was stunned, but God was right: I was focusing on the negative, licking my wounds. Slowly, I grabbed my thoughts and changed directions. I reminded myself that although my friend had betrayed me, God never would. He cared for me and only had my best interests in mind. Although my friend had lied, He never would: He always spoke truth, never exaggerated or twisted words. I praised God for His sweet love, and for always having my back. I turned away from disappointment and worked on trust. I said how great it was to "know that I know that I know" He was rock-solid and trustworthy. When I put my mind on Jesus and looked full in His wonderful face, I was able to get up and go on living.[256]

A New Thought

I was stunned when my first counselor taught me I could change my thoughts. Weren't my thoughts just my thoughts? Before I understood how my thoughts controlled me (and how to control them), life was just hard. With no tools and no hope, I didn't want to get up in the morning; I had no energy to fight my thoughts all day. But my changes didn't just happen because of determination; they happened because I applied biblical principles— scriptures like Romans 12:2: *Do not conform any longer to the pattern of this world, but be transformed by the renewing of your mind.*

---

256 Weeks later, I found peace when I realized that if God wanted us to have those children, nothing could have prevented us from adopting them. I didn't like the manner that "no" came, but I knew it was His no.

I have practiced changing my thoughts ever since the Barb revolution (chapter 2), when I learned to reevaluate all my thoughts based on the Word of God. Everything I believed, experienced and based my life on was molded by God's truths. The Greek word for *be transformed*[257] is a command—something you keep on doing and doing. You actively, continually obey, constantly changing your thinking. You keep on being transformed by choosing different thoughts. And—of course—it's a battle, one that is fought in your mind. Beth Moore calls it wall-papering your mind with God's thoughts. "Think new thoughts about the old things."[258] Are you ready to be transformed and revolutionized? Stop listening to the old tapes, the old voices, the old lies. Stop the toxic self-talk. Don't allow yourself to think old ways. Keep your mind occupied with telling yourself the truth about God, the truth about you, and how those truths impact your life. Rather than being spun by the ever-changing theories of the world,[259] let the eternal Word of God change you.

Listening in on David's Thoughts

King David—the man after God's heart—wrestled with his thoughts. He was not passive; he cried out raw to the Lord, pouring out words of despair, grief and confusion. He didn't run from pain or hide it or ignore it, but he quickly called out the two key words in our new vocabulary: But God. All through the book of Psalms, we can listen in on how he changed his thoughts:[260]

Psalm 13
How long, O Lord? Will you forget me forever? How long will You hide Your face from me? How long must I wrestle with my thoughts and every day have sorrow in my heart? How long will my enemy triumph over me? Look on me and answer, O Lord my God. Give light to my eyes, or I will sleep in death; my enemy will say, "I have overcome him," and my foes will rejoice when I fall. (v.1-4)
But *I trust in your unfailing love; my heart rejoices in your salvation. (v. 5)*
I will sing to the Lord, for He has been good to me. (v. 6)

Psalm 69
I am worn out calling for help; my throat is parched. My eyes fail, looking for my God. Scorn has broken my heart and left me helpless; I looked for sympathy, but there was none; for comforters, but I found none. (v. 3, 20)

---

257 The Greek tense is present (constant), imperative (a command), active (you have the power).
258 Beth Moore, Breaking Free, Lifeway Christian Resources; Workbook edition © 1999
259 The main issue in sexual abuse used to be multiple personality disorder and repressed memories. For a time, it was re-parenting your inner child. Later, it was diagnosed adrenal fatigue syndrome, recently PTSD. The world's problem and solutions keep changing. But they don't work because they don't embrace the One who came to heal and set us free.
260 Psalm 3, Psalm 10, Psalm13, Psalm 22, Psalm 37, Psalm 42 to name a few.

***But** I pray to You, O Lord, in the time of Your favor; in Your great love, O God, answer me with Your sure salvation. (v. 13)*
I will praise God's name in song and glorify Him with thanksgiving. (v. 30)

Psalm 116
The cords of death entangled me… I was overcome by trouble and sorrow. (v. 3)
***Then** I called on the name of the Lord; 'O Lord, save me!' (v. 4)*

He refocused—took his eyes off the problem, the pain and the enemies—and he reminded himself of more powerful truths; God's faithful presence and promises. Then he switched gears, moving from flesh to spirit, from torment to trust, from groaning to praising. He praised God for His goodness and help in the trial.

King David did what Dr. Martin Lloyd Jones wrote, "We need to stop listening to ourselves and start talking to ourselves. Tell yourself what is not coming into your mind naturally." Preach the good news of the gospel to yourself every morning in the shower or at breakfast:[261]

God, You renewed my life even when I was dead in my trespasses and sins. Jesus took on all my sins and paid my debt on the cross. He took all of God's wrath for them, so I am not under wrath today. You gave me new life as a gift, one I don't have to earn. Thank You for revealing Yourself to me through the Bible, the written Word so I won't lose it. God, I am in awe of the extent of Your forgiving grace for my sinful deeds today.

Fighting to Think

… take captive every thought to make it obedient to Christ. (2 Cor. 10:5)

Have you ever meant to stop at the grocery store on the way home from work but found yourself parked in the driveway? Without "thinking," a habit took you home. The mind has thinking habits like auto-pilot that don't require us to be aware of what we are doing. "The longer we think along any given line, the stronger that thought pattern becomes,"[262] and the deeper it gets carved into our mind. Bad habits are the lazy way of driving through life. Taking every thought captive means first tuning in, like you tune in to a radio station. Listen to what you think, then compare it with the Bible: are your thoughts consistent with what God says? If not, change your thinking. Lasso unruly thoughts; drag

---
261 The Cross-Centered Life by C.J. Mahaney, Multnomah Books, © 2002
262 Changing Your Thought Patterns, George Sanchez, NavPress. This is true of any thoughts- it's why pornography is so gripping. [my comment]

them out of the old ruts and down a new path. Tell yourself what to think. Focus on grace, mercy, kindness and compassion. Start praising God instead of saying "poor me." When a memory hits, think, *Thank You God that time in my life is over, and Your mercies toward me are brand new today.* And—especially when I'm facing something hard or scary—I think *this is not the hardest thing I've ever done*. I already did the hardest thing, so everything else is easier than that.

Imagine at the end of a day, you walk into a room and find every thought you have had all day written out on a blackboard for everyone to read. God hears all your thoughts like this. I wonder if you will be shocked by what's there when you try to take your thoughts captive?

"Danger, Danger, Will Robinson!"[263]

Jesus said, "Why do you entertain evil thoughts in your heart?" (Matt 9:4)

Most battles are won or lost in the mind. When you are at war, you expect the enemy to attack your fortress and try to take control. To keep an enemy soldier out of your house (your mind), you have to set up strong defenses. Remember in Chapter 3 we said the mind is the watchman of the soul? "The flesh plies deceit to knock out the watchman."[264] When you set a guard over your mind, not just any thought can enter the fortress of the soul. You have the mind of Christ, which is a sober, vigilant watchman,[265] calling out "Who goes there?" and identifying whether each thought is a friend or an enemy before allowing entrance. Instead of being captured by your thoughts, you take them captive. You direct which thoughts can stay and which must go.

Believe me, it's easier to keep the enemy out of your mind than to evict him once he has made it his home. This involves checking your input constantly; set up a guard against letting trash into your mind. Choose every moment of every day which thoughts to allow inside your head.

What do you feed your mind? What is your daily intake? How about your TV-watching? Do you learn about forgiveness and patience or selfishness and revenge? What do you think after seeing the nightly news, or scandalous, gossipy Internet clips? After reading a romance novel or watching a soap opera, which do you think about more: contentment or comparing your life with others? Do R-rated movies (or even PG ones) put lewd or violent thoughts into your mind? What *good* things do you learn from watching people fight? Does

---

[263] The robot's famous warning from the 60's TV show, *Lost in Space*.
[264] <u>The Enemy Within</u>, Kris Lundgaard, P & R Publication, Phillipsburg, NJ, © 1998, pp. 54-55
[265] 1 Peter 5:8

watching irresponsible sex start the cycle of temptation in your mind? The world tries to squeeze you into its mold (Rom. 12:1), by force-feeding you its thoughts.

Feeding or Starving Thoughts

I was once diagnosed with a systemic yeast infection and was put on what I call the "no-fun" diet. I couldn't have any yeast, sugar or vinegar. No yeast, in bread, my favorite food. No sugar–no carbs, cookies, chocolate or fruit. No vinegar, no ketchup, salad dressing, soy sauce or mayonnaise. I <u>could</u> eat sugar but it made the infection worse and kept me on the no-fun diet longer. So guess what I craved? Guess what I longed for?

Every time I put a slice of bread in my mouth, I was "aiding the enemy;" sugar fed my infection and prolonged the war. The infection had to be starved, like our flesh must die by withholding what it craves. Every time we give in to old thoughts, we nourish the flesh and make the battle worse. Thinking on the past keeps us weak and sick, and makes the battle drag on. Jesus said, *'If anyone would come after Me, he must deny himself, take up his cross daily and follow Me. For whoever wants to save his life will lose it, but whoever loses his life for Me will save it.'* (Luke 9:23-24) We will lose our life either way: by trying to fix the past or living for Him today. The way to abundant life is to deny yourself and say yes to Jesus: think the way He thinks.

Waging War Against Arguments

My thoughts are not your thoughts ... declares the Lord. (Isaiah 55:9)

Waging war means casting down (throwing out) arguments: we keep choosing to demolish them again and again. You, my friend, are a pro at arguments. You hear them in your mind; the "buts," and all the reasons why you think you can't change:

> *I have to be tough to keep from getting hurt.*
> *I will never be free—I am too damaged, too messed up.*
> *I am a victim forever. God helps others but not me.*
> *I can't deal with this. It's too hard, too unfair, too overwhelming.*
> *Someone else has to do it right first before I can do it right.*
> *If I deny my feelings, I will be a hypocrite.*
> *I am just bad, there's no hope for me.*

These are not God's thoughts; they are strongholds (strong lies). But our weapons have divine power that can demolish the Enemy's strongholds; divine power that can only be accessed by doing things God's way. What are the strongholds that hold you? What high walls are you are hiding behind? What lies do you believe that lash you to the pain?

Schemes of Satan – Red Button

Satan loves to keep us drowning in pain and grief. He plants a thought and we run with it. It is like we have a red button labeled "Pain and Weakness" that Satan hits. He targets us when we are down: he pushes the button as long as he gets a negative reaction. Renewing your mind means finding a new response to the old thoughts. When Satan pushes the red button, focus on God. *Draw near to Him so He will draw near to you.* Resist the devil by submitting to God and praising Him. (James 4:7) Pray for that person instead of worrying. In the adoption story, as soon as I saw I was thinking about the hurt again, I stopped the negative version and focused on how God loved me even in hard times. Guess how often the thoughts came when I stopped nursing the pain and started praising God? Satan doesn't want to trigger you to think about God; he only cares about triggering your old reactions. If you have a different/godly reaction, Satan will stop hitting the button.

You are responsible to direct your thoughts. Remember from Chapter 7, you can change how you *feel* by changing what you *think*? God doesn't want you to ignore your emotions or live by them. He calls you to a new standard: control your emotions by controlling your thoughts.

My Thoughts Make My Life

Our thoughts define who we are,[266] because they control what we do. What we believe in the heart affects and directs our actions. When we choose to sin, we welcome depraved thinking, and start a downward spiral. Romans 1 portrays bad people in a series of sinful thoughts, decisions and actions. They make choices, and God responds by giving them over to (or letting them be overcome by) natural consequences:

v. 20 For since the creation of the world God's invisible qualities—His eternal power and divine nature—have been clearly seen…from what has been made,
21 They knew God, but **neither glorified Him** as God **or gave thanks** to Him
22 Their **thinking became futile**, hearts were darkened. Claiming to be wise, they became fools
23 **They exchanged** the glory of God for images made like mortal man… and animals.
24 God **gave them over** in the sinful desires… to sexual impurity degrading their bodies.

---
[266] *As a man thinks within himself so he is.* Prov. 23:7

25 They **exchanged the truth** of God for a lie, worshiped and served created things rather than the Creator.

26 God **gave them over** to shameful lusts.

27 So they **exchanged** natural (sexual) relations for unnatural ones.

28 They did not think it worthwhile to retain the knowledge of God, so **He gave them over to a depraved mind**... to do what ought not to be done."

29 They have become filled with every kind of wickedness, evil, greed and depravity... envy, murder, strife, deceit and malice. They are gossips, **30** slanderers, God-haters, insolent, arrogant boastful; they **invent ways of doing evil**; they are disobedient to parents; senseless, faithless, heartless, ruthless.

32 Although they **know** God's righteous decree (those who do such things deserve death), they not only continue to do (them) but also approve of those who practice them.

God responded to their choices. First, He gave them over to sinful desires, then to shameful lusts and finally, to a depraved mind; they became vain in their imaginations, and their foolish hearts were darkened. They have minds—maybe brilliant minds according to the world's standards—but they don't work at all in the spiritual realm.

Living apart from God is devastating to the mind. Ephesians says Christians shouldn't live as the Gentiles do, *in the futility of their thinking.* One episode of *Say Yes to the Dress* showed this. The bride had tried on over 100 dresses, and brought her family in to help her decide, but ended up in a sobbing meltdown. She explained like this: "My OCD means I can't make up my mind. I'm so afraid of making a choice on impulse, but hating it later. I'm just waiting for my mind to tell me which one is the right dress." She was tormented by her thoughts. That is like the weak-willed woman from Chapter 4; she was a victim of her thoughts, believing she had no control over them. You can't always trust your thoughts, but you can always tell yourself what to think. You can control your thoughts.

Waging War Against the "Might-Be-Trues"

The enemy roams around seeking whom he may devour. He delights in filling their perceptions and senses with illusions that captivate them, paralyze them and destroy them. Avoid falling victim to these tactics by taking charge of EVERY thought that enters your mind. (1 Peter 5:8)

This is tricky—Satan at his best. An illusion is a pretension that sounds reasonable or right. It could be true, yet it is not; it's really twisted or fairy tale thinking. Here's an example: if I said I am a point guard for the Lakers, that is clearly not true. I am not a **professional** athlete and I am a woman in my 60's. However, if I said I am a professional quilter; that could be true. These partly-true ideas set themselves up against the knowledge of God. Our job is to demolish them all:

> *The world (my kids, husband, etc.) would be better off without me.*
> *My problem is low self-esteem.*
> *God's promises apply to everyone except me.*
> *God wants me to be happy, doesn't He?*
> *I just want to understand first.*
> *I want to wait until I'm stronger.*
> *She thinks _____ about me.*

When your thoughts are twisted, challenge them. Compare them to the Bible—what God says about you: you are His Beloved;[267] you will be complete in Him;[268] He has a plan and a purpose for you,[269] and so on.

Schemes of Satan – Anger at God

I have yet to meet a sexually abused woman who doesn't struggle with hostile, angry thoughts about God. *Why didn't God stop it? Did He not care? Does He care for others but not for me? Is He cruel? Is He punishing me? Is He powerless? Is He vengeful?*

So it's time to look at that core question through the lens of Scripture with adult eyes: Why did the abuse happen? It's time to pull that big question out of your Poofy file. If you believe it happened because of something you did, or said or deserved, then Satan has tricked you. Here are two powerful truths:

1. *The abuse happened because your abuser chose to sin.*
2. *You were vulnerable.*

Does God call sexual abuse sin? Yes. Does God hate sin? Yes. Does God always prevent sin? No. Why not? Friend, how you answer that question is critical to your growth. If you believe Satan's lies about God (He is cruel, angry, vengeful or weak, silent, uncaring), you will run away from God and stay angry for years. You can hate the sin, but not the sinner, and not God.

This challenges your core beliefs: is God sovereign or not? Faith is contrasted with sight;

---

[267] Deut. 33:12
[268] James 1:4
[269] Jeremiah 29:11

what you believe vs. what you see. Faith means hoping in what you don't see.[270] One way to express my faith is not letting my narrow vision of today eclipse God's vision of the future.

If I were God, there would be no suffering, no sin and no abuse. But our ways are not His ways.[271] God sees the big picture: He has a bigger plan and a bigger purpose in every trial. He is not afraid of sin or suffering. He doesn't remove pain from your past; He enters into it. God wasn't happy about the abuse, and He will judge the sin. You can fight God, cut off your source of help, run away and stoke your anger; or you can run to Him, let Him love you and help you. When you invite God in, He lives His story through your life. You may think that nothing good will ever come out of the abuse, but someday, it will be redeemed. You can't see it but it will happen.

> God will lift you out of the slimy pit and set your feet on solid ground. (Ps. 40:2)
> He will bind up the brokenhearted and set the captive free. (Isaiah 61:1)
> He will repay you for the years that the locusts have eaten. (Joel 2:25)
> He will give you rest, an easy yoke, and a light burden. (Matthew 11:28)
> He will provide a righteous way through every trial. (1 Corinthians 10:13)
> You will receive mercy and find grace to help in your time of need. (Hebrews 4:16)
> He is able to keep you from falling and present you blameless, with joy. (Jude v. 24)

I'm not happy that my abuse happened—neither is God—but God really has used it for my good and others' benefit; so I can counsel and minister to people, by reaching into their darkness and leading them out. I have a unique bridge to build relationships with hurting women.

Schemes of Satan – Traps

When I was the center of my universe—the King in the Kingdom of Me, the ruler of my life—I had a very small view of life. The world revolved around my thoughts, my hopes, my desires and dreams. Paul Tripp said, 'The whole world shrinks down to the size of my need.'[272] If your world is only as big as you, it is trivial indeed. How much time do you spend thinking about:

> Your thoughts vs. God's thoughts?
> Your betrayal vs. your blessings?
> Your health vs. someone else's disease?

---
[270] Hebrews 11:1
[271] Isaiah 55:8
[272] <u>Instruments in the Redeemer's Hand</u>, Paul David Tripp, P & R Publishing, Phillipsburg, NJ © 2002

Your diagnosis vs. God's promises for your future?
Your hair vs. your family's happiness?
Death/suicide/being out of the pain vs. new life?

To the same degree that you make your life about you, you will be unhappy with God, because it's not your party. The world mostly promotes the Kingdom of Self, not God's kingdom. But when you realize life is all about Him, you have greater peace and joy. When I bent my knee to God, declaring He was my Savior and my Lord, He became the King, the center of my world. When I decided to live for His glory instead of mine—when I declared to my soul that I must die so that He might live through me—everything changed for the good. Dying to self means letting go of rebellion and self-rule.

Fighting Back

The weapons we fight with are not the weapons of the world. On the contrary, they have divine power to demolish strongholds. (2 Cor. 10:4)

Once you realize you have bad thoughts, you have a choice: you can hold onto ungodly thoughts or change them. Colossians 3 says *set your mind on things above, where Christ is.* Thoughts that speed down the wrong track usually crash at the end. Ask the Holy Spirit to show you when your thoughts are speeding down the wrong line. He will. De-rail the train earlier every time, directing it down a different track. Plan a new route. Our thinking does not change overnight: renewing your mind is a journey. Choosing to capture your thoughts even once is a victory. If you build new thought patterns and habits, I promise, the bad thoughts will lessen. Over time, thinking biblically will be your new habit.

Spiritual Weapon – Self-Counseling

For every lie, argument and twisted thought, the Bible has a truth. Do you read His words often enough that they come to your mind in steady pulses? *Bring these all to mind.* (Deut. 30:1, ESV) Renewing your mind this way means recalling, reminding yourself, and retelling God's truths:

Remind yourself that you are redeemed, forgiven, chosen, empowered, loved, adopted.
   (Eph. 1)
Remember that you are a new creation, your old life is gone, the new one has come.
   (2 Cor. 5:17)
Recall His promises—He will never abandon you, never forsake you, never leave you.

Retell stories of how God has shown you love—the gift of a child, the love of a spouse, the faithfulness of a friend, a job provided, a beautiful sunset, a fun vacation, a joyous healing, answered prayer. Retell stories of God's good character.

Repeat the new thinking until it feels natural. (it can take six weeks of practice or more)

Spiritual Weapon – Reformat Your Thoughts

When we stop old thought patterns, we must replace them with new patterns. Ephesians 4:22-24 says to *put off old ways, and put on new ways*. Lasso your thoughts and place new thoughts in your mind. Imagine you leave a friend a voicemail telling her about the hard day you are having, but she doesn't call you back. As time marches on, what are your thoughts? What story do you tell yourself about her and the situation? This happened between Cris and me a few months after we met. Two days later when she finally called back, I was hurt, whiny and pouty. She addressed my ungodly thoughts: "The next time I don't call back, rather than having all those negative thoughts, *pray for me* because my day is probably out of control." (She was in her own crisis and didn't have a moment to call me back.) That thought has transformed my relationships ever since.

Paul says what I should have dwelt on in Philippians 4:8-9: *Finally, brothers, whatever is true, whatever is noble, whatever is right… pure…lovely…admirable…if anything is excellent or praiseworthy – think about such things*. My paraphrase: *Think before you think. And have innocent, kind, and positive thoughts until proven otherwise*. Here is how I could have applied this list when Cris didn't call me back on that hard day:

True—Do I know the truth? What is true? Am I trying to figure out why she did that without asking her? *I don't know, so until I ask her why, I am not going to go with my worst imaginations.*

Noble—Awe-inspiring and majestic? Am I thinking the highest about her? Do I assume her motives are honorable or evil? Or *she doesn't care…she hates me…she rejected me, she's tired of me.*

Right—Just? Have I given her justice or am I condemning her without the facts?

Pure—Holy and undefiled? Am I thinking what God would think about her? Have I defiled her by mentally dragging her reputation through the mud?

Lovely—Are my thoughts acceptable and friendly? Sweet and kind?

Admirable—Am I thinking well of my friend? Have I given her a good report? Have I extended her grace or judged her without mercy?

Excellent—Is it pleasing to God? Have I given my friend moral worth?

Praise-worthy—Is it commendable? Have I praised her mentally? Pulled her down or built her up? Would I want her to think the same things about me that I am thinking about her?

Spiritual Weapon – Praising

Just before the list of good thoughts to think, Paul gives other powerful ways to direct our thoughts:

Rejoice in the Lord always… again I say, Rejoice!....The Lord is near. Do not be anxious about anything, but in everything, by prayer and petition, with thanksgiving, present your requests to God. And the peace of God, which transcends all understanding, will guard your hearts and your minds in Christ Jesus. (Phil. 4:4-7)

Remember Paul's abuse, his trials and suffering?[273] Yet, he says *rejoice always*. Rejoice about the pain? No, rejoice that God is with you; you are not alone. He has not forgotten you or abandoned you. He lives in you, and He is for you. Thankfulness and prayer should be like breathing to a Christian; an ongoing, natural reflex. Don't worry about anything, but pray—start talking to God. Then you will receive God's promise: His peace will guard your heart and your mind. When you do it the flesh's way (worry, fret, rehash), you will have heartache and joylessness. When every trial becomes a chance to praise God, Satan will stop pushing on that big red button fast.

Spiritual Weapon – Choose Joy

> 'Even at the end of your rope, you still possess something very valuable: your attitude. You can choose your thoughts. You can default to pain, fear and anguish or you can proactively choose joy. You can focus on all that you do not have and all the stuff that's coming at you, or you can choose to rise above that and focus on what you do have—even if that is just the air that you breathe. Embrace it. Choose to think only about things that are lovely, true and pure.'[274]

I've practiced doing this for so long, my personality has changed for good: I used to be "the most bitter, angry woman," but now I am a grace-filled optimist. Now my thoughts sound like: *She's doing the best she can; I wonder what hurt her so much to make her so mad; Jim is just the way he is, and I accept him that way; I know we can work this out; It could have been worse.* My entire life has been transformed by renewing my mind.

---

273 In Romans, Corinthians, Philippians…
274 Mary Hunt's Everyday Cheapskate Newsletter, June 24, 2013

Counterattack – Using Your Sword

For years, I had asked God to change my life through His Word. But this went deeper when, early in counseling, Cris taught me to pray Scriptures. I learned to personalize a verse—put my name in place of "I," "you," "we," "he," "man" etc. These words had often comforted me but I did not know the power of praying them back to God. I prayed what I read, asking for abundant life (John 10:10); the same attitude as Christ (Phil. 2), or to be strong in the Lord (Eph. 6:10). Then I meditated on them all day or all week.

Barb has the mind of Christ. (1 Cor. 2:16)
Barb trusts the Lord with all her heart and leans not on her own understanding. In all her ways Barb acknowledges Him and He will make Barb's path straight. (Prov. 3:5-6)
When Barb gives heed to instruction, she prospers, and Barb is blessed when she trusts in the Lord. (Prov. 16:20)
Barb has chosen the way of truth; Barb has set her heart on Your laws. Barb holds fast to your statutes O Lord; do not let Barb be put to shame. (Ps. 119:30-31)
Barb turns her eyes away from worthless things; Barb renews her life according to your Word. (Ps. 119:37)
Barb was once an evildoer, but Barb was washed, Barb was sanctified, Barb was justified in the name of the Lord Jesus Christ and by the Spirit of her God. (1 Cor. 6:11)

Surprise Attack

Training and directing my thoughts is such a habit for me that the story I'm going to tell is a rare event. But I know it will help you. One day, I visited a friend's church to celebrate her fiancé's baptism. I had heard the preacher was a straight-shooter, and he was going to teach on Mark 5, which included the woman with the issue of blood, one of my all-time favorite Bible stories. I knew the worship would be awesome. I thought *this is going to be a great Sunday*. Then it happened: I got blindsided. I hit a time bomb in my soul, an emotional landmine.

The pastor shared how Jairus pleaded with Jesus to heal his twelve-year-old daughter, preaching persuasively about how a father should love his daughter. He spoke of his love for his own daughter, how precious she was to him, how he talked with her and held her and wanted to understand her. When he moved on to the desperate woman, he was describing me. He explained that her uncleanness meant she had been isolated for twelve years, but when she touched Jesus' hem, she did not make Him unclean; He made her clean instead. He said Jesus called her 'Daughter' because she did not have a father, a Jairus, to plead on her behalf. It was great stuff. Normally, it would have fed my soul.

But I didn't remember the last fifteen minutes of the sermon and I was startled when Jim got up at the end of the service.

We went to the celebration barbeque afterwards and I felt like I was drowning. We heard about their wedding plans and I felt panic. By 3:00 pm, I was crying but didn't know why. By 5, I had shut down. At 9, I carefully walked back through the day with Cris, trying to name the tidal wave of grief that had gripped me. Slowly, I fought my scattered thoughts and found a comment the pastor had tossed in. He said, "Some women have bad fathers or no fathers, and some fathers are so evil, they rob their daughters of their virginity by sexual abuse." That sentence was a fuse to a day-long battle with despair. The pastor's frankness knocked me off my feet and Satan's assault drowned me. I had never imagined I would hear my abuse exposed at church. I was stunned by the rawness of my emotions: a shock-wave coursed through my body that I didn't see coming.

Help! My Thoughts are Out of Control

Being blindsided is when the sun is shining, the sky is blue, the birds are singing, and BOOM— like a storm surge, a wave sweeps you out to sea. You can't find your footing or reach land. The world is dark and the only voice you hear is condemnation. *"My God, my God, why have you forsaken me? Why are you so far from saving me, so far from the words of my groaning? O my God, I cry out... but you do not answer; (I) am not silent."*[275] Here is a life rope for the time when this book or a person or life blindsides you:

1) **Cry and Cry Out**—*'Hear my cry, O God; listen to my prayer. From the ends of the earth I call to you... as my heart grows faint; lead me to the rock that is higher than I.*[276] Tears are the heart bleeding: it wouldn't bleed if it wasn't cut. *"I waited patiently for the Lord; He turned to me and heard my cry. He lifted me out of the slimy pit, out of the mud and mire; He set my feet on a rock and gave me a firm place to stand."*[277]

2) **Tell Yourself the Truth**—Not the truth you *feel* (*life is hopeless, I am hopeless, this journey is hopeless, all is lost*) but the truth that God says is true. Whether you are sad, hurt, confused or lost, be honest. What happened? When did you get blindsided? What was said? What scared you? What was hard to hear?

3) **Untangle the Knot**—How is the present tied to the past? What is the common word/fear/feeling/memory? What brought up old feelings? How did the present "rope in" the

---

[275] Psalm 22:1-2
[276] Psalm 61:1-2
[277] Psalm 40:1-2

past? What was the last thing you remember before the fog smothered you (whether 2 days or two weeks or a month earlier)? When do you remember feeling this way before now? When is the *first time* you remember feeling this way?

4) **Talk it Through**—Speak the fears/feelings/connections/thoughts; to your traveling companion or mentoring partner is best, but you can also voice memo yourself or journal them and read out loud. Listen to your words (thoughts). Then ask about each point, "Is this true now?" Say *I am not there anymore; my life is new and different today; I have tools, I can walk through this.* Say one part of what you are thinking out loud 20 times (it may sound pretty ridiculous by the end).

5) **Forgive and Release**—This "new" hurt reveals another sin to forgive. What new insight do you see? What truth has God revealed, to bring greater freedom? What specific hurt or sin do you need to rethink, let go, or give to God to deal with?

6) **Praise God**—Part of growing up (maturity) is learning to praise God even when life isn't going your way. It is easy to praise Him when the sun is shining and the grass is green; but you need to praise, even if it's a sacrifice. *Then will I ever sing praise to Your name and fulfill my vows day after day.*[278] Put on worship music—if you can't praise by yourself, let the music lead you. Praise God for more freedom from the past. Praise Him that He is the God of restoration.

When the World Tilts

You *will* be blindsided. You can't set up your life so it never happens. Oh, I know you have tried. I know you think if you could only steel yourself or protect yourself from the pain, you wouldn't have to feel it. But life doesn't work that way. Being blindsided is hard but staying there is harder. You won't always see the wave coming or know it has dragged you out to sea. But make a plan, a way back to land. Dog-ear this page.

One of the effects of trauma (sexual abuse; battlefield experience; witnessing domestic violence or a murder) is that the world becomes a scary place. We are forced to reconsider everything we have believed:

> Is the world really good?
> Is it a safe place, an okay place?
> What are people really like? What am I really like?
> There are good people and bad people in the world. How do I tell?

---

[278] Psalm 61:8

Is trauma normal, or is something else?
How do I handle my pain? How do I go on?
What am I responsible for? Who and what do I have to take care of?

You will have to answer each of these questions from God's perspective in order to live in freedom. Run to Jesus: *For You have been my refuge, a strong tower against the foe.*[279]

Being blindsided can feel like a time bomb (from Chapter 7). Be a detective with yourself, using the questions on page 55 or the lists on the previous three pages. *I can be okay even if the world isn't a safe place. I can choose and act and change. I can learn to deal with bad people and not lose myself. I can still honor God when...*

Memories

The shock wave of being blindsided comes to us in different ways. I had recurring nightmares for years that I was running to my mother for comfort, but when she turned around, she had changed into a vampire. I didn't know why. When I was in my 20's, the truth unrolled in my mind, like an old movie flickering on a screen: a memory of cuddling in bed with her when I was three. She put her hands on my head and pushed me down to kiss and touch her in ways that were confusing and frightening. The nightmares were my childish mind trying to figure out what happened.[280]

My worst abuse was revealed very differently. (**Warning:** this is graphic) In counseling with Cris, I had never even called my dad "bad," so when I called my babysitter's drunken husband "evil," her ears perked up. She pieced together a lot of quirks (I hated when Jim held my hips during sex; I have a morbid fear of blood), some "odd" comments ("sex means being absorbed into him"), some strongholds (I refused to speak to Jim during sex or about it) and more. When she asked what the connections were, I was swamped by a body memory (where I felt it again). When I was five, that man cut me and said, "Now you belong to me," and "You will never tell anyone." As horrific as this memory was, it was a small relief to know the truth. We walked through the blindsided questions. I slowly crawled out from under the weight of chains, and a mountain of quirks, rules, black dots and strongholds faded in a few days. Walking through the darkness and out the other side led me to greater freedom than I had ever experienced. And it only took me about two weeks to go through it, instead of twenty years.

---

279 Psalm 61:3
280 As I worked through this one-time event, I decided that she must have been zonked on pain pills.

Enemy Attack – Reliving the Past

Satan loves it when you think about the past, ponder it, review it and rehash it. He wants you to keep going back to the vomit until you understand it. But the past is dead: there is no hope and no life there, just pain and more pain. I call sexual abuse Satan's favorite tool; ten minutes of pain for a lifetime of agony. He wants you to believe this wave of pain is permanent—*you will never get better so just quit trying*. That's a lie: this is temporary. You have not gone backwards; you are moving forward.

After quoting Phil 3:13, author Ed Bulkley says,

> "I am not implying that memories must be repressed, but grace, forgiveness, and the power of God are sufficient to heal memories without deliberately ripping scars open. Often, returning to the past suffering, failure and pain can re-ignite the hatred and bitterness that God has already dealt with and can reopen the wounds that Christ has already healed."[281]

I always tell my counselees, "Examine, don't exhume. Don't go looking for memories. Pray that God will reveal what He wants you to know. And when He reveals something, walk through it, knowing He loves you and wants you to be free." You don't relive the past, re-write the past, regress to the past, or re-parent yourself. But you can re-evaluate the past and re-think it with new insight, in the light of new truths: *people are sinful; God is holy and good; I was hurt, but now I have a new life. God wants me to live in His Presence.* He wants us to have life abundantly; receive it and rejoice in it.

Bottom Lines:

1. Be transformed by renewing your mind—take every thought captive.
2. Stop listening to yourself and start talking to yourself.
3. Scripture is powerful. Pray it, personalize it, ponder it, memorize it.
4. Fight with spiritual weapons.

Discussion Questions:

1. Have you ever tuned into your thoughts? What do you hear daily? How do you explain that?

---

[281] <u>Why Christians Can't Trust Psychology</u>, Ed Bulkley, Harvest House Publishers, Eugene, OR © 1993, p. 156

2. What are your old thinking habits? Self-protection, suspicion, avoidance, hiding? Depression, holding grudges, bitterness, resentment, judging?

3. Use the Thinking Pattern with one situation in your life: Are your thoughts true, right, noble, good, noble, excellent, worthy of praise?

4. Make a card with the good news of the gospel found on page 157. Read those to yourself out loud every morning.

To the Friend of the Traveler:

1. Listen to your friend's words. Does she have scattered thoughts or a sound mind?

2. How does she see God in her story? Does she believe truth about God? Is God helpless to aid her? Is He more real in her story than when she first talked to you?

3. Ask her questions, give her your observations and be gentle but honest about what you think. Don't be surprised if she tells you what you have been thinking (even though she doesn't really know). She may think she knows what you think, or she may put her thoughts into your mind.

4. If she gets overwhelmed, talk her through it. Try to get to the truth. Don't react as she is talking, listen very carefully. Trust the Holy Spirit to reveal what He chooses, and trust Him to give you wisdom to help your friend.

5. This may be the week you will have an argument (or a heated discussion) about why the abuse happened. Listen to her words, mentally throw out words of despair, and try to discuss how the two truths (p. 162) apply to her situation. Don't take her anger or frustration personally. Forgive her quickly. Forgive the abuser. Remind her of God's love and care.

Worship Song: *Let the Words of My Mouth* by Fernando Ortega[282]

---

[282] https://www.youtube.com/watch?v=-TIgfoH_mzk from the album The Shadow of Your Wings

Chapter 10
Following the Map

As a young Christian, I put believers into two categories: GUBAs and RADs. GUBAs had Grown Up Born Again.[283] I made up the word RAD—one who was radically saved as a grown-up. GUBAs have Scripture in their DNA; they teach Sunday School and lead worship. But both GUBAs and RADs can both suffer from "Gubitis." The medical term "itis" means inflammation or swelling: "Gubitis" means a swelled head that causes a disconnect between your head and your hands. This condition develops when you know the Bible but don't practice it. Someone with Gubitis will say that gossip is a sin, and gossip in the next breath without realizing it. James 1:22 explains: *Do not merely listen to the Word. You must do what it says. Otherwise, you are only fooling yourself.* (NLT)

Here's how Gubitis works: A father told his teenage son "Clean up your room." He went in later to see if the boy had obeyed. He hadn't, but he told his father he was organizing a study group to determine what is "clean," what is the Greek word for clean, what is a "room," what does "your" mean, how often a room should be cleaned, can it be cleaned on Sunday and—with great joy—he announced that he could quote his father's words exactly: "Clean up your room."[284] That is Gubitis. The Father calls us to action, but it gets stuck in our heads. You may have Gubitis if you:

> Leave church saying, "That was a nice sermon."
> Listen to Christian radio for background noise.
> Do your Bible study homework but don't remember any of the points.
> Don't understand what "application" means.
> Listen to sermons to get arguments for someone else.
> Have no idea what "doing the Word" means.

Is there a cure for Gubitis? There are two: a greater love for the Father, and obedience.

Why Am I Here?

As the elect of God, holy and beloved, put on tender mercies, kindness, humility, meekness,

---
283 From an old book <u>Growing Up Born Again</u>, Patricia Klein, Fleming H Revell Co © 1987
284 Based on a story from Pastor Francis Chan

longsuffering, bearing with one another, and forgiving one another… Love… is the bond of perfection. (Col. 3:12-14)

You are chosen and loved, but why? What's your purpose for living? To be happy or have good relationships or an easy life? No, your reason for living is to glorify God and please Him, serving Him with every action. (Col. 1:10) Paul Tripp says, "We are not just God's spokespersons; we are his evidence."[285] We are His ambassadors, representing Him night and day. As the old saying goes, 'I would rather see a sermon than hear one.'[286] I tell people, "I can't hear what you are saying because your actions are shouting louder than your words."

Paul invited others to *Follow my example as I follow the example of Christ.* (1 Cor. 11:1) People should see you as Christ, with the qualities in Col. 3: kindness, humility, meekness, longsuffering, forgiveness and love. Life is not "I am empty, fill my cup Lord." Do you want to be filled? Break out the bottom of your glass and put your broken cup in the river of the Spirit, so He can flow through you. When you make life all about you—your wants or desires or feelings—people just see you, not Jesus.

But you weren't created to do good works as in the old engine with you driving. You were created to do good works in Christ Jesus; the new engine with Christ at the wheel. *"For I have come down from heaven not to do My will, but to do the will of Him who sent Me."*[287] If Jesus came to do His Father's will, and you are to be like Him, aren't you also here to do the will of Him who sent you?

Third Side of the Triangle: Sinful Responses

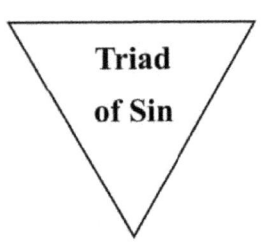

Many things can keep us from living in our purpose. Sexual abuse is a heinous sin where there is a sinner and one sinned against. But no sin is outside God's sphere of power. God isn't in heaven wringing His hands and pacing in worry because He doesn't know what to do. Maybe you were not abused, but you were divorced or betrayed, lied to, stolen from or cheated. All of us will be sinned against; some with big sins, some little. Your response to those sins will control your life.

The first side of the Triad of Sin dealt with your inborn sin nature that draws toward sin. The

---

285 Instrument in a Redeemers Hands workbook, Paul Tripp, P & R Publishing, Phillipsburg, NJ © 2002
286 Edgar A. Guest (1881-1959)
287 John 6:38

second side looked at your sins and sinful choices. This chapter will look at your reactions to sins; your sinful responses to being sinned against. Having dealt with two-thirds of your sin problems, God also helps you with this side. Jesus came to earth in human flesh that was pierced and punished because of those sins too. We bring God into our story, live in His hope as a new creation,[288] and access His power. Without God's intervention, sin only destroys. We can't change the past, but we do have tools and power and truth for a godly reaction to being sinned against.

It is not what happens to you but *how you respond to what happens to you* that dictates your future. You can respond in pain, in powerlessness or self-protection. You can respond in pride or punishment or by perishing. You can persecute others for what your abuser did to you…become a Pharisee…plague your life with heartache…pity yourself into paralysis…plot revenge…pitch a fit…pretend…plead with God to change things… please yourself and push God away…pollute your children with your bitterness or fear or anger…pressure your family into giving into your demands…preserve your hurt by nursing and rehearsing it. **Or…**

You can pursue Jesus, push past the pain and persevere. You can pray in faith. You can probe the depths of His love for you…proclaim your new identity…preach your Treasure and praise God for all He has done…practice forgiveness…plan new-heart words, thoughts, actions and attitudes…pull yourself out of the pit…prune off bitterness... peek into your future and the devil's punishment by reading Revelation…pray against spiritual attack…

When the flesh ruled us, we were dead in our sins and disobedience. (Eph. 2:1, NLT)
   You used to live in sin, and obey the devil. (Eph. 2:2)
     but now we are made alive with Christ. (Eph. 2:5)
       For we are God's workmanship, created in Christ Jesus to do good works. (Eph. 2:10)

Doing the Word

'Do not let this Book of the Law depart from your mouth; meditate on it day and night… be careful to do everything written in it. Then you will be prosperous and successful.' (Josh.1:8-9)

One way I sinned because of being sinned against was to live by rules. I changed by doing the opposite of what I wanted to do (180° rules): Be quiet when I felt like screaming. Stay when I wanted to run. Help others instead of taking from them. Instead of hurting

---
[288] 2 Corinthians 5:17

someone who hurt me, return good for evil.[289] But mostly, I did good things because my old ways didn't get me what I wanted. True Christianity is not about a changed life, but an exchanged life.[290] My heart was not transformed. I didn't love my enemy because of God's love flowing out. I did things out of duty.

I learned how to "do the Word" when Cris taught an in-depth discipleship program called Self-Confrontation,[291] based on James 1:22. Almost every word was based on a biblical principle. Her frequent words changed my life: "Open your Bible..." But Cris now admits she didn't know about God's love. She thought Christianity was performance; just do the right thing. But doing the Word isn't just keeping the commandments. It starts with the first commandment: *love God with all your heart, mind and soul.* (Deut. 30:6) *Then* you receive His love, grace, power and other gifts (Chapter 6). Then you do the Word.

Hear and Practice

'Everyone who hears these words of Mine and puts them into practice is like a wise man who built his house on the rock. The rain came down, the streams rose, and the winds blew...; yet it did not fall, because it had its foundation on the rock. But everyone who hears these words of Mine and does not put them into practice is like a foolish man who built his house on the sand. The rain came down, the streams rose, and the winds... beat against that house, and it fell with a great crash.'[292]

When storms came, my life "fell" in many ways. I had heard the words of Jesus, but I had still built my house on old thinking, a sandy foundation. Rules, walls, self-protection and anger didn't keep the rain, streams and wind out. If your life is crumbling, you need a new foundation. If you build your house on the rock—by hearing His words and doing them—*when* (not *if*) storms come, your life will stand. A house built on the rock may be battered and beaten by a storm, but it will not fall.

Hearing God's words and doing them means obeying His directions. George MacDonald (Scottish poet and preacher) said,

> "Men would understand; they do not care to obey. They try to understand where it is impossible (to) understand except by obeying. There is no salvation in correct opinions. A man's real belief is that by which he lives.

---

[289] Romans 12: 17-21
[290] Pastor Wayne Barber
[291] Now called Step-by-Step Discipleship, Biblical Counseling Foundation, Palm Desert, CA © 1998
[292] The Sermon on the Mount, Matthew 7:24-27

To do His work is to enter into a vital relationship with Jesus: to obey Him is the only way to be one with Him."[293]

Obeying means:

Doing God's way over my way—every day, every time, every situation.
Doing God's way in big things—going back to Jim or moving to another country.
Doing God's way in little things—controlling my temper, or praying instead of pouting.
Doing the right thing even if there's no immediate change in the situation.
Doing it God's way no matter what the other person does.
Doing right no matter what the circumstances (if you are attacked, misunderstood).
Obeying God no matter what you feel (tired, afraid, confused, annoyed).
Making a plan for practicing what the Bible says and working it daily. (book of 1 John)

I think that when you were saved, Satan lost the battle for your soul, so he tries to win the battle for your life. He can't keep you from eternal life with God but he can keep you from an effective life for God. Is he winning?

Release Sin, Rejoice in Christ

My response to being sinned against was to sin, from the minute it happened until today. I gripped past pain with all my strength, like hanging onto a cliff, convinced it was the only way to survive. Then Jesus climbed down the cliff on a rope and called out, "Let go, grab onto Me." But I was afraid. It felt safer to cling to the cliff than leap to Him. I wanted the Christ-life but I didn't want to let go of my pain. Since my goal was wrong, I was basically on my own. Only God can redeem broken lives, broken hopes, and broken dreams. He restores and renews and rebuilds. Compared to this, my goals of avoiding pain and being happy were way too small. *Count yourself dead to sin* (Rom. 6:11) means quit looking at the sin and the pain, and start looking at the Savior. Put *all* sin to death: the sins you have done, the sins you will do, and the sins done to you.

Overcoming Sin by Doing the Word

I've tried everything and nothing helps. I'm at the end of my rope. Is there no one who can do anything for me? (Romans 7, The Message)

Here's an example of a sinful response to being sinned against. Let's say, as part of my abuse, I was introduced to pornography. Now, the more I watch, the more I want. The more

---
[293] <u>Knowing the Heart of God</u>, © 1990 Bethany House Publishers, Minneapolis, MN, p. 11

I give in to it, the more degrading things I watch. That is all from the flesh. Then the Holy Spirit convicts me. I want to watch, yet I want to obey. I try to stop, so I pull the computer out of my house. That is a good step, but it won't solve my heart issue. My desire is still for porn.

How do I really change and do the Word? I read that pornography was on the list of Galatians 5 as counterfeit love. So I look to Christ: His purity, His sincerity, His desire for me. I think about Him and draw near to Him until I fall in love with Him. I repent of my controlling attitude and lustful actions and submit to Him. I ask Him to cleanse me. Then what happens when I think about pornography? In the light of God's holiness, pornography fades. I see it for what it is; cheap, fake self-love and selfish pleasure. Pastor Wayne Barber said, "Repentance isn't me overcoming sin; repentance is Christ overcoming me." It's not just trying harder, it's submitting to Him more fully. *God, help me to love You more and love my flesh less.* As the poem says:

> Do this and live, the law commands,
> But gives me neither feet nor hands.
> A better word the gospel brings;
> *It bids me fly and gives me wings.*[294]

Oswald Chambers directs us to the core issue: "…A Christian is under grace. (He) has had the power of the evil nature broken… (so he does not need to obey it anymore) and has been given the divine nature, which gives him both the desire and the power to do God's will…One can not think oneself out of a spiritual muddle, one must obey oneself out."[295]

A New Road

But now…we have been released from the law to serve in the new way of the Spirit, and not in the old way of the written code. (Romans 7:6)

We don't just stop sinning because of willpower or decisions; we can because we have new divine power. The old way, the Law, did not work. Adam and Eve had one rule, but they couldn't do it. God gave us ten rules, and we can't do it. The problem is with us, not with the Law. The Law proves that we cannot do what it asks. But Jesus kept all the rules. After He fulfilled the Law's requirements, the perfect Christ laid down His life and paid the penalty of our sins. We can make the great exchange because He did it for us. Now we have only one Law: *'A new command I give you: Love one another.*

---
[294] <u>Word Studies in the Greek New Testament</u>, Volume 1 by Kenneth Wuest, page 113, comments on Romans 7:1.
[295] Oswald Chambers

As I have loved you, so you must love one another.' (John 13:34) So our new command, our new rule, is love. If we get love right, everything else flows from it.

Now that I understand grace and how Christ lives in me, I can be vulnerable. I don't have to pretend or cling to my past, because I know that I am loved beyond reason by my good Father. Because He loves me, I don't want to bring shame to His name. I embrace my purpose: honoring Him for my great life. Since I have all these blessings, I can act in a new way. It comforts me to think I wouldn't make the same bad decisions again today. I would get more help; I would find the righteous way through.

Paul Knew Abuse

The Apostle Paul described his sufferings throughout the New Testament.[296] He accepted tremendous suffering because he saw the higher purpose and his sufferings gave credibility to his message. He was willing to suffer to preach Christ.

When you know his story, his joyful words seem even more amazing. He had *five times... received forty lashes minus one. Three times beaten with rods, stoned, shipwrecked, spent a night and a day in the sea, constantly on the move, in danger from rivers, bandits, my own countrymen, Gentiles and false brothers; in danger in the city, in the country, at sea.*[297] But he didn't start the letter to the Ephesians by listing his hurts: "Hi, my name is Paul and I have been abused." No, Paul's words almost sing about who we are in Christ. He begins with praise. He doesn't focus on the hardships; his eyes are firmly focused on his sweet Lord and Savior. He lives in his true identity as a child of the King.

I don't see Paul saying about his life, "It's too hard." Paul only talks about his past to have an excuse to praise God. Then he offers to help pull us out of the pit of pain and show us how to walk in maturity; how to live a life worthy of the Lord.

Paul Prayed for Us

In Ephesians 3:16-21, Paul (*the servant of this gospel by the gift of God's grace—3:7*) wrote an incredible prayer, my favorite in Scripture. Paul outlines a new life, one that's lived out of the new heart of love:

You are rooted and established in love,

---
296 Ephesians 3:13
297 2 Corinthians 11:24-26

> So you will come to know the full dimensions of Christ's love.
> You will come to know the love that surpasses knowledge.
> Christ is able to do more than you ask or imagine, and He will strengthen you with power.
> God works in you, all for His power, His purpose, and His glory.

When you receive and believe His provision, (first referring to Ephesians 1), then you can "do the Word" out of His abundant love (verses from the last 3 chapters of Ephesians).

> God's grace and peace are yours (1:2), so you can speak the truth in love. (4:15)
> God has blessed us with every spiritual blessing (1:3), so you can be humble and patient. (4:2)
> Because you are holy and blameless in His sight (1:4), you can get rid of anger, fighting. (4:31)
> You were adopted as His son in love (1:5), so you can bear with others in love. (3:2)
> You freely received His glorious grace (1:6), so you can show grace to your spouse. (5:33)
> We have redemption and the forgiveness of sins (1:7), so we can give up sexual immorality. (5:3)
> It pleased Him to make known the mystery of His will (1:9), so we won't be foolish. (5:15-17)
> We are chosen, predestined according to His plan (1:11), so we can live as children of light. (5:8)
> When you believed, you were sealed with the Holy Spirit (1:13), so don't grieve Him. (4:30)

Maturity is The Goal

We have the Holy Spirit to draw us to maturity. Then God gives us gifts to help others mature too. Ephesians 4:11-13 describes the goal of the gifts: to prepare God's people for works of service, so that 1) the body of Christ may be built up 2) we all reach unity in the faith 3) we grow in knowledge of the Son of God and 4) we become mature, attaining to the whole measure of the fullness of Christ. God has work for you to do —Kingdom work—and He needs you to mature enough to do it. I don't see any justification for Christians staying in the pain. I don't see any caveat for those who are too hurt to move.

Maturity means to be filled with the fullness of Christ; so you won't be blown away by every wind of teaching and deceitful schemes of men; speaking the truth in love; being built up in love so that you can do your part of God's bigger plan of redemption. Satan wants to isolate you, cripple you, and paralyze you. The world's thinking tosses you back and forth: repressed memory syndrome, healing from damaged emotions, PTSD, adrenal fatigue. They sound reasonable and they do explain some of your symptoms. But they are fixing the old engine. They don't help you mature in Christ. Don't settle for healing. It isn't big enough. Healing is still about you. Maturity is about living for Him.

Drive to Maturity

What gets in the way of living for God? Often it's responding to someone's sin by demanding life our way. Control becomes an idol. An idol of the heart is anything that rules me other than God. My heart desires something more than God. We migrate away from worshipping God (and toward worshipping self). Paul Tripp gives an insightful description of what happens:

> 'The problem with desire is that…it very quickly morphs into demand. ("I must") Demand is the closing of my fists over a desire…I have left my proper position of submission to God. I have decided that I must have what I have set my heart on and nothing can stand in the way. I am no longer comforted by God's desire for me; I am threatened by it, because God's will potentially stands in the way of my demand. I can no longer conceive a good life (moment, day, week, situation, location, relationship) without this thing. The morphing of my desires changes my relationships….Now I enter the room loaded with a silent demand: You must help me get what I want. If you are an obstacle, I will immediately be angry and impatient with you.'[298]

Demands interfere with serving, and keep the focus on ourselves. When God does not give us what we want, we stay angry at God. We want it never to have happened. But God says *I can redeem what has happened; I will give you a double portion; I can restore and rebuild; I can heal; I can show you the righteous way through the trial.*

The Casting Crowns song *Somewhere Caught in the Middle* says, "When will we trade our dreams for His?" After Cris' friend Gloria read When People are Big and God is Small,[299] she wrote in her journal: *How can I see Christ as so glorious that I forget about my perceived needs? What is my duty before the God who has loved me?*

Godly Response to Suffering

We also rejoice in our sufferings, because we know that suffering produces perseverance; perseverance, character, and character hope. And hope does not disappoint us, because God has poured out his love into our hearts by the Holy Spirit, who He has given us. (Romans 5:3-5)

When you are sinned against, there will be suffering. But have you responded sinfully

---

[298] Instruments in the Redeemer's Hands, Paul David Tripp P & R Publishing, Phillipsburg, NJ © 2002, page 86
[299] When People are Big and God is Small, Ed Welch, P & R Publishing, Phillipsburg, NJ, © 1997

to that suffering? That brings on more suffering. The godly response to suffering that replaces your old responses is rejoicing. You don't rejoice because you suffer, you rejoice because of what suffering will produce in you. If you respond to suffering in your new heart:

You will *persevere*: keep walking and doing the right thing; be knocked down but get back up.
    Doing that again and again builds *character* (faithfully do hard things with integrity).[300]
        Character produces *hope in Christ*, as you trust Him and His ways.
            As you hope in Christ, the Holy Spirit *pours* His love into your heart.

So if you respond to suffering in a godly way, you will become more loving. Some of the most loving people I know are Christians who have responded well to terrible trials. But if you respond in the flesh, the results are the opposite:

You become *paralyzed*, waiting for someone to change the circumstances.
    You respond out of *emotions*. You get angry, despairing, then act out how you feel.
        That leads to *hopelessness* when you see nothing is changing.
            That leads to bitterness, depression and hardness.

If you are bitter about your trial, you may have responded to it in a way that does not honor God. The most angry, bitter people I know have responded to trials in their flesh (that was me).

I changed my circumstances by moving to a different country, but that didn't stop my suffering, because of the anger and bitterness I held in my heart. Even if we can't end suffering, we can change our response in it. If we think differently about it, it can be used to develop strong character. I had to give up my ungodly response to pain and grow up. My new goal was God's: build spiritual muscles.

Practice, Practice, Speak

Solid food is for the mature, who by constant use have trained themselves to distinguish good and evil. (Hebrews 5:14)

As you practice doing the Word, your eyes will be open to see both good and sin: a brother who is in and out of jail, a tearful, manipulative mother, a weak but punishing father, a lazy co-worker, or a friend trapped in drugs or alcohol. Part of maturity may mean saying no to sin, not only yours but also other people's. In this chapter, we finally give you permission to go talk to someone who is sinning against you or someone else.

---

[300] The Greek word for character is *dokime* which means tested and found to be trustworthy.

If you're anything like me, confronting a sinning brother or sister is terrifying. How do you "do the Word" in these situations? Galatians 6:1 says to go gently. *Brothers, if someone is caught up in a sin, you who are spiritual should restore him gently. But watch yourself, or you also may be tempted.*

Some of you will resist the "go" part of this command. Others will resist the "gently" part. It does not say lie down and take it, or blow them up with God's righteousness. It says *be spiritual* (let the Holy Spirit control you, know right from wrong, etc.). It takes courage and humility to speak the truth in love into someone's life. You won't be good at this. You have years of hiding or exploding under your belt. But that was caterpillar living. Now you have been given wings and are learning to fly. God calls you to live a completely new life. Part of this new life includes having the courage to deal with bullies and manipulators and charmers in a godly way.

Evil Roadblocks

Romans 12:21 says *Do not be overcome by evil, but overcome evil with good.* Here's a scenario (imagine a mean ex-husband or a cruel boss or a sneaky friend): You're trying to work out something and they shoot you with a pop-gun. So you retaliate with a pop-gun. Then they bring out a cannon, so you fire a cannon back. Next, they drop an atomic bomb on your soul. About this time, the Holy Spirit speaks to you: *Beloved, you know this is wrong. You can't repay evil for evil.* You cannot "out-evil" an evil person and God won't let you. You are restrained: you must resist the vengeance game.

The only way Christians can overcome evil is with good. This doesn't mean you lie down and take it; it means you have the courage to say NO to sin. Jesus was gentle and kind with people who were hurt (woman at the well, little children, Peter and doubting Thomas) but He was bold and brutally honest with the Pharisees who were trying to kill Him and bring His followers back under the tyranny of the Law.[301] 1 Thessalonians 5:14 says *we urge you, brothers, warn those who are idle (unruly), encourage the timid, help the weak, be patient with everyone.* Society is so dark that if you're living for Jesus, you are so light. You stand out.

How will you live out your faith with people who don't get you? Knowing you are a loved child of the King, you may need to cut some people loose (the Pharisees, the old guard); let them stay in their sin or their performance, while you move onto what you know is godly truth, and live it.

---

301 Matthew 23

Put-offs and Put-ons (Biblical Change

You were taught, with regard to your former way of life, to put off your old self, which is being corrupted by its deceitful desires; to be made new in the attitude of your minds; and to put on the new self, created to be like God in true righteousness and holiness. (Ephesians 4:22-24)

In the counseling arena, this process is called *put-offs* and *put-ons*.

Step 1: *Put off your old self, which is being corrupted by its deceitful desires.*

Verse 22 warns us the old nature was corrupt before salvation and is still trying to corrupt us with its deceitful desires. "Put off" means to stop doing it, like peeling off old, ill-fitting, smelly clothes. It is a continual action–you put off sins at salvation, now do it, do it, and do it again.[302] You can't do in your own strength; you are enabled to because of Christ in you. Pastor Wayne says, "I can't, but He never said I could. He can, and always said He would." It's like a toddler who can't walk on his own, but with the father holding his hands, he can. But our Father is not on the outside, He is on the inside—holding our heart, directing us, enabling us, moving us to become more like Him.

White-Knuckle Christians

Have you ever tried changing your behavior without changing your heart? You want to be seen as kind so you do kind things, or pretend to be kind while you grit your teeth and grip the steering wheel to keep from sinning. God says to be kind because He is kind and Kindness lives in you. As you submit to God, His kindness will flow out of you. Some of us are really good at tying pretty Christmas ornaments on our lives. God wants fruit to flow out of us because we are rooted in His love. Pull your foot off the gas (stop feeding the flesh) so His patience can flow through you.

For instance, putting a guard over your mouth doesn't always mean stop talking; it means watching what goes out. It could also mean cleaning the trash out of your heart so it doesn't spill out of your mouth. Then maybe teach your kids about this principle. One mom told her kids, "I'm right in the middle of this just like you are. You struggle with this just like your mother."

Step 2: *Be made new in the attitude/ spirit of your minds.*

---

[302] Greek- Aorist imperative middle tense

That means change your thinking. Change your attitude to line up with what God says (again, keep doing it and doing it).[303] God will *enable* you to renew your mind but you have to read, memorize Scripture and change your thinking. You may need a new attitude because you are still living by your emotions. Living by your emotions stops your maturity in Christ. In fact, it's one of the main reasons you still have a broken spoon in your hand.

Step 3: *Put on the new self, created like God in true righteousness and holiness.*

Once you have removed the stinkin' thinking, then put on Christ, your new self. Start doing the right/godly action. The Greek tense is the same as the *put off*: you did it at salvation, now do it again and again. It is a command God enables you to do. Some common put-ons are:

    Meet other people's real needs
    Be patient with them
    Comfort others with the comfort you have received
    Speak kind, encouraging, graceful words
    Confront sin, say no to being involved
    Consider someone else as more important than yourself
    Being filled with the Holy Spirit instead of alcohol

When Is a Thief Not a Thief?

Ephesians 4 has several examples of put-offs/put-ons. Here's the example of stealing (vs. 28-29):

    He who has been stealing must steal no longer (put off)
    but must work, doing something useful with his own hands (put on)
    that he may have something to share with those in need (change in attitude)

So did you learn something from reading this? That's good, but don't just hear, let's *do the Word*. Based on that passage, ask yourself *am I stealing in any way?* Stealing supplies from work or stealing time to make personal phone calls? Stealing money from God, spending my 10% tithe instead of giving it to church? Stealing affection from your husband to give to someone else? Stealing God's glory and giving credit for your life to a person? Are you stealing attention in a group when someone else may need it more? You apply the Word that specifically.

---
303 The Greek tense is present infinitive middle.

Change Your Thoughts

This verse says *stop stealing*, so we know it's wrong. The main change in attitude is to see stealing as wrong instead of deserved: it violates the Ten Commandments and doesn't please or honor God. B*ecause it is wrong, I should never take part in it*. So the put-off is stealing.

The goal (the put-on) is work, but working isn't enough. And it is not enough to just stop stealing. A thief who is not stealing can just be a thief between jobs. Do an attitude check and look for desires that deceive you. Stop stealing and put on the righteous action: start working, so that you can share, give away money and help others. See yourself as part of the body of believers: money is a way to help people. Give generously, because God will generously take care of you. If you have been stealing in some way, what has your attitude been? *I deserve it* (the attention), *I can't afford it* (tithing), *I don't get paid enough, so I will do my thing* (make personal phone calls or take supplies), *I want an easy way to make money, or I can just take things I want.* How do I mentally defend my actions? If God asks me why I've done that, what would I answer?

Put-Ons for Stealing

The last step is to put on godly actions: how can you change your actions to line up with God's? Be filled with the Holy Spirit, led by the Spirit and live for Him. Then work— work with God's strength. Work hard and be ready to tell people why you work so hard (to honor God). Be faithful and dependable and trustworthy. If you have stolen anything, return it. Work knowing that you receive your paycheck from God, who sends it through your company. Work so you can return part of what God gives you by tithing. Work to share what you have with those who need it: food or gas money or lunches or the time to talk. Sharing is the opposite of stealing. Giving is the put-on for taking.

God wants you to line up with His Word in every area. His Word trumps your feelings, overpowers your excuses, and commands your obedience. God's Word is the final authority. But don't change your behavior without changing your heart. Live out of your new heart because you love Him and want to serve Him. Put-offs, changing your heart, and put-ons are how God changes you from the inside out.

Start With Yourself

One day I again complained to Melanie how someone I knew had failed to live right. I went on and on and she listened for a while, then said, "Barb, why don't you ask God to treat them as their sin deserves?" I was excited because she finally agreed with me. "Really?" Her answer was, "Sure, just start with yourself. Ask God to treat you as your sins deserve first, then pray the same for others." Ouch.

People who have been deceived by abuse are very sensitive when someone's words and actions don't line up. But here is maturity. Rather than getting angry, blowing them up, running away or whatever, *you* do the right thing. First get your life right with God, then once you have it right, you can start helping others. In other words, be responsible for your own actions; i.e., don't be guilty of the very thing that you are upset about with them.

Making it Permanent

God created us with habits. "Good habits and bad habits are…acquired by custom or a frequent repetition of the same act…."[304] To stop a bad habit, engage your will. Let's say you have a bad habit of yelling at your kids. First, pray. Ask the Holy Spirit to show you when you are yelling.[305] He will. When you realize you are yelling, you have a choice. You can keep yelling (sin) or choose to stop. If you stop yelling, you are doing the Word (repenting, putting off anger/ unwholesome words). (Eph. 4:29) Then ask for forgiveness. Then, ask the Holy Spirit to show you sooner the next time. Repeat this until you have stopped yelling. Warning! Satan the accuser will be close by, saying what a loser and a failure you are, what a bad Christian you are; you will never change. At those moments, you must say "Liar" and turn your eyes to Jesus. Tell God *Thank You for showing me my sin* and ask Him show me sooner next time. Rejoice that you chose to obey rather than despair that you did it again.

Speed Up, Slow Down

Be quick to listen, slow to speak and slow to become angry, for man's anger does not bring about the righteous life that God desires. (James 1:19-20)

Lead with your ears, follow up with your tongue, and let anger straggle along in the rear. God's righteousness doesn't grow from human anger. (James 1:19-20, The Message version)

When you talk with someone, do you "lead with your ears?" Here's a quick test: if you can't wait for them to finish talking to tell them what you think, you are not. If you lean in and lean back, waiting to tell your version, you may be doing your

---

304 Webster's 1828 Dictionary definition of habits, http://1828.mshaffer.com/
305 This works for any sin—lying, gossiping, slandering, quarreling, being unforgiving, etc.

will, instead of doing the Word. When you lead with your ears, there are moments of silence. There should be times when both are listening rather than both trying to talk. Listen to understand what they are saying; try to find clarification, understanding and common ground. Our discussions should be give-and-take instead of push-and-pull.

Here's the application: ask yourself *do I listen for a long time? Am I slow to speak? Where have I been angry?* Make a put-off, an attitude change and a put-on for each person or situation, then practice them as often as needed. Cling to God's love while doing this, and practice being like Jesus.

Love Your Enemy

When Jim and I met with Pastor and his wife to rebuild our marriage, he asked me, "Do you feel like Jim is your enemy?" I thought *Wow, he finally heard me. Yes, Jim is my enemy.* As I basked in his understanding, he asked me to open my Bible to Luke 6:27-28: *Love your enemies, do good to those who hate you, bless those who curse you, pray for those who mistreat you.* That meant meeting his real needs. I was stubbornly angry that God asked me to act in ways I didn't want to. I was okay loving people that I liked or loved naturally, but not when He called me to love people I didn't like. God does that, doesn't He?

Here's a way to do the Word here: put off hatred, cursing at them, returning evil for evil and retaliating. Put on doing good to them: meeting their needs, blessing them with your words and praying for them. Practice until it becomes second nature. You also may need to forgive, then go to them. Tell them they are sinning against God and you, and how you are going to change the relationship so you can obey God. Or, you may not trust them or have relationship with them, but still bless them with your words. Always pray for wisdom.

Am I loving my enemies, doing good to those who hate me, blessing those who curse me and praying for those who mistreat me? How does God see that person? Is there a way I can witness to them? Am I more concerned about their walk with God or how they hurt me?

When To Avoid Instead of Bless

Jan Silvous talks about three marks of a fool:[306]

1. Proverbs 12:15: *The way of fools seems right to them, but the wise listen to advice.* A foolish person thinks they are always right.
2. Proverbs 28:26: *Those who trust in themselves are fools, but those who walk in wisdom*

---
306 Fool-Proofing Your Life by Jan Silvious, Waterbrook Press, Colorado Springs, CO, © 1998

are kept safe. A foolish person only trusts himself (not God, not you, not anyone but only himself).
3. Proverbs 29:11: *Fools give full vent to their rage, but the wise bring calm in the end*. A foolish person controls you with anger.

When you are dealing with a foolish person, it is best to handle them with a "long-necked spoon."[307] Feed them but don't get too close. These people who only trust themselves and think they are always right will blow up when you don't think the same way they do. They are neither teachable nor willing to listen. We don't suggest that you write them off, but learn to speak the truth in love to them. Or your conversation may need to be limited to polite "Walmart cashier" conversation, "How are you, nice day outside..." You can't really have a relationship with a fool, you only have an arrangement, one based on their terms.

Anne Graham Lotz once asked her mom how to handle difficult people. She is reported to have said, "Ann, your heart is like your finger. On one side, it is so tender it can feel a hair, and the other side is so tough (due to the nail) it can handle a hammer hit." To some people you can show your tender side. Some you cannot. Your job is to learn who gets your tender heart and who needs that stronger side of your heart (because they swing hammers at you). Be careful with your heart around a fool.

Listen to Your Speech

Do not let any unwholesome talk come out of your mouth (put off), *but* (put on) *only what is helpful for building others up, according to their needs, that it may benefit those who listen* (attitude changes). (Eph. 4:29)

Have you given a piece of your mind, sworn, boasted, slandered, gossiped? Jesus' words were amazingly gracious (Luke 4:22) even though He was treated unfairly, accused falsely, and maligned. Sinful speech is part of gratifying the sinful nature (flesh) on the Galatians lists.[308]

Here are some other directions about our speech:

...the Lord's servant must not quarrel (put off); *instead, he must be kind to everyone, able to teach* (put ons), *not resentful, not quick to take offense* (put offs). (2 Timothy 2:24)

Love does not envy or boast, it is not proud, rude, self-seeking, easily angered; it keeps no record of wrongs (put offs). (1 Cor. 13:5)

---
307 Ibid.
308 Galatians 5, Romans 1 or 2 Timothy 3

If anyone considers himself religious and yet does not keep a tight rein on his tongue (put on), *he deceives himself and his religion is worthless.* (James 1:26)

Let the word of Christ dwell in you richly... teach and admonish one another with all wisdom.... (put-ons) (Colossians 3:16)

The Word should richly dwell in you, in every room and every closet of your heart. Here's how to do the Word with your speech:

>   Are your words wholesome, gracious, patient and kind?
>   Are they compassionate, gentle, sweet?
>   Do your words encourage people to love and good deeds?
>   Do they reflect worry (a lack of trust in God)?[309]
>   Are they jealous, boastful, resentful, angry or prideful?
>   How can your attitude display *the bond of the Spirit in humility, unity and peace?*[310]

What is your put-on instead of sinful words? Make a plan for one area or one person and practice until you don't have to think about it (it can be six weeks or more). That is new-heart living.

Since God does not just want behavior change, look at your heart as well. Luke 6:45 says o*ut of the overflow of your heart, your mouth speak*s. Examine your expectations and desires (Chapter 7). *Ask why was I angry, Lord? What did want that I did not get? What did I expect that didn't happen?*[311] What flows out of your mouth? Angry words reveal what you want. But you can't yell to have a good marriage. You can't accomplish God's goals man's way.

Put Me In, Coach

Because the abuse took place with my dad, an angry man in authority over me, I was hypersensitive to angry men in authority. As soon as I sensed anger, I reacted; either retreat and avoid or rise up to defend myself. This played out all over my life: I became a victim around an angry boss, I quit teams if the coach yelled, and I quit ministry if the pastor was a controller. So every time I began moving forward in my job, sports or ministry, guess what I bumped into? I was all right as long as I "sat on the bench," but the minute the coach sent me to carry the ball down the field, the Enemy sent an angry man who freaked me out. On the tackle, Satan always went for my banged-up

---

[309] Philippians 4:6- Worry is a sin
[310] Ephesians 4:2
[311] James 4:1-4

knee. Once hit, I would crawl back to the bench: out of the game, out of God's will, unusable and broken.

Satan will never stop going for my weak knee. So how can I play? I learned how to handle the hits in a righteous way, so I can stay in the game. I changed my responses to angry men and my thoughts about them. I became strong in God so I could persevere. If I didn't learn to take the hits, Satan won.

Victory in the Battle

After years of growing and shrinking, learning and forgetting, taking wrong turns and u-turns, I have learned how to respond to being sinned against in a way that glorifies God and sets me free. Doing the Word has matured me and changed my heart. Practicing put-offs and put-ons has brought me closer to looking like Jesus. I am not a prisoner; I am a loved daughter. I live in today, not clinging to the past. And I have joy.

Cris' favorite show was *The Biggest Loser*. Every week they showed people striving and struggling to overcome life-threatening obstacles. When you saw a contestant conquer something they said couldn't be done, it inspired you to say *Maybe I'm not done. Maybe I can get past this*. I hope my story inspires you.

Ephesians 5 Sums it Up

God doesn't just want changed behavior; He wants you to live out of His heart.

- *Be imitators of God*—As a child imitates his father, so we should imitate Christ.
- *As dearly loved children*—Living like a loved child of the King means letting the pain go. A loved child knows little fear of failure. They will try new things with confidence.
- *Live a life of love*— Receive His love, let it overflow to others. Walk every minute as if you are loved.
- *Christ loved us and gave himself up for us*—Christ loved by serving, teaching, praying, healing, forgiving.
- *As a fragrant offering and sacrifice to God*—What is your aroma?

Bottom Lines:

1. Love and obedience are the cures for Gubitis.
2. Put off sin/wrong, change your heart attitude, put on right actions.

3. Repentance isn't me overcoming sin, repentance is Christ overcoming me.
4. I can't, He never said I could; He can, and always said He would.

Discussion Questions:

1. Do you have symptoms of Gubitis? Is there something right you know to do, but don't do it? Why? Is there an area of your life where you are very obedient? Is there an area you need to work on?

2. Have you obeyed out of duty or love? Out of fear or respect? To avoid punishment or to please people? Is it surprising to find that God wants you to obey out of love? Do you know what this looks like?

3. Describe the concept of Put-offs and Put-ons from Ephesians 4. What does it mean to "change the attitude of your heart?" Name one example you will work on.

To the Friend of the Traveler:

1. Has God prompted your friend to **do** any of the verses in this chapter? Encourage her to obey, and come up with a plan if needed.

2. If she hasn't heard any specific verse, talk about an area she would like to change (Fear, anger, comfort, serving, praise, prayer, worship). Then use a Bible Concordance (Strong's or Young's) to find a verse about that area and help her plan to take baby steps daily.

3. As she practices doing the Word, help her watch for the joy and her growing sense of God's pleasure and journal about it.

4. Name an area where you too need to put off sin, change your attitude and put on righteous behavior. Let her pray for you in your obedience. Keep her posted about your progress.

Worship Song: *Speak O Lord* by Keith Getty and Stuart Townsend[312]

---

312 <u>Beautiful One CD</u>, Keith Getty & Stuart Townsend, Thankyou Music, © 2005, worshiptogether.com, www.kingsway.co.uk

Chapter 11
Destination: Forgiveness

Dear Friend, who has traveled so far. Your journey has rounded the final bend, heading toward your new home in the Land of Grace. Everything so far has carried you here. You stand before a wall and sweet freedom is on the other side. What is this wall? It is the wall of unforgiveness.

What do you hear when I say the word "forgiveness"? Do you hear "your hurt doesn't matter"? Do you hear "lie down and die"? Do you think I want you to be a doormat? Do you feel depression? Quick anger? "It's not fair"? Do you think if you forgive, the abuser got away with it? Do you feel more abuse coming? Will you listen as I explain what forgiveness means? Will you give me a chance to explain forgiveness from a biblical perspective? Let me show you the way through pain into Freedom. Beyond this high wall lies the Promised Land.

Fastened Tight to the Person Who Hurt You

To explain the concept of forgiveness to one of my classes, I took toy handcuffs, hooked two of the leaders together, and asked them to role-play. It was amazing. They pretended one had snubbed the other, who wouldn't forgive her friend. One wanted to get up and talk to the ladies but the other refused, so she had to sit down again. Tied together, they were stuck. They wouldn't cooperate with each other and were both unreasonable. Neither woman could function in the class until they both softened and worked it through.

Unforgiveness is like being handcuffed to someone who continues to sin; won't cooperate, won't be reasonable, and won't let you live. When we refuse to forgive, we are emotionally and spiritually chained to the person who hurt us. They go everywhere with us: we eat, sleep, talk, and walk with them. We take them into every relationship, every conversation and every situation. The only way to release yourself is to take the key—forgiveness—and undo the handcuffs. You alone can turn the key. No one else, not even God, can do it for you.

In ancient days, when a man was found guilty of murder, the dead person's body was strapped to the killer, so he carried the body everywhere. Eventually the decaying corpse rotted his body and he died. It was effective, deadly punishment. We are not murderers, but we can bear the offender's spirit on our backs for years. The person who hurt you had the power to hurt you once; sin caused pain that spread over your life. Unforgiveness keeps the hurt alive. Unforgiveness has been described as drinking a cup of poison and expecting the other person to die.[313] Bitterness (long-term unforgiveness over months or years) grows like soul cancer that eats you from the inside out. Is someone's sin rotting you?

Forgiveness: The Only Key

Forgiveness is the third of the Big 3 core issues in sexual abuse, along with Deception and Responsibility. It is the key to freedom from sin on both sides: forgiveness *from* God releases us from *our* sin. Forgiveness given *to* others releases us from *their* sin.

Jesus taught us to pray: *'If you forgive men when they sin against you, your heavenly Father will also forgive you. But if you do not forgive men their sins, your Father will not forgive your sins.'* Matthew Henry says,

> "This is not a plea for merit, but a plea of grace. Our duty is to forgive our debtors. We must forbear, forgive, and forget the affronts put upon us, and the wrongs done us; this is a moral qualification for pardon and peace; it encourages hope, that God will forgive us; it will be an evidence to us that He has forgiven us, having worked in us the condition of forgiveness."[314]

When Peter asked Jesus, "How often shall I forgive my brother?" Jesus answered, "seventy times seven," and told the Parable of the Unmerciful Servant. (Matt. 18:21-35) Here are the main points:

- A king wanted to settle accounts with his servants.
- One man owed him ten thousand talents (15-20 years of wages) but could not pay.
- The master ordered him to sell all that he had (incl. wife and children) to pay the debt.
- The servant fell on his knees and begged, "Be patient and I will pay back everything."
- The master took pity on him, canceled the debt and let him go.
- That servant found a fellow servant who owed him 100 denarii (2 months of wages).
- He grabbed and choked him, demanding payment. His fellow servant fell to his knees and begged him with the same words, "Be patient with me, and I will pay you everything."
- He refused, and had the man thrown into prison until he could pay the debt.

---
313 Original author unknown, quoted by Corrie Ten Boom, The Hiding Place, Chosen Books, © 1971
314 Matthew Henry Commentary

- Other servants saw this; they were greatly distressed and told their master what happened.
- The master called the first servant in. "You wicked servant, I canceled all that debt. Shouldn't you have had mercy on your fellow servant just as I had on you?"
- In anger the master turned him over to jailers (tormenters (NASB)) until he paid back all.

Lesson 1: You are the man who owes the debt you cannot pay

God doesn't compare your sin to your abuser's sin: He compares your sin to His holiness. Compared to the King's purity and righteousness, we desperately need His mercy and grace. Do you understand God's gift of mercy to you? Has the abuse blinded your eyes so you only see your abuser's sin and not your own? *If you claim to be without sin, you deceive yourself and the truth is not in you.* (1 John 1:8) Can you see the depth of your own sin?

Lesson 2: God took pity on you and canceled your debt

God forgave your sins because of His mercy, not because of your works. We all stand as beggars at the foot of the cross, desperate for God's forgiveness when we deserve punishment. Christ paid our debt on the cross[315] as a free gift.[316] When we fell to our knees pleading for mercy and forgiveness of sins, our debt was cancelled, paid in full. Receiving His forgiveness releases *us* from *our* sin.

Lesson 3: The King expects you to be merciful to others just like He is merciful to you

God calls you wicked when you won't forgive a fellow servant who asks for mercy. (Wicked here means evil in a moral sense, malicious). His logic: I cancelled your debt so I expect you to cancel others' debts. I gave you mercy, now you give mercy. People *will* sin against you. If you forgive them as Christ has forgiven you, you will walk in freedom. Forgiveness given *to* others *releases* us from *their* sin.

Lesson 4: If you don't forgive, you will be treated as unforgiven

The Master forgave the debt but the servant didn't receive it. When the servant refused to extend mercy to others, he revealed that he had rejected the gift. If you cannot extend mercy, you have not received it. *Extending* forgiveness is the proof—the fruit—that you have *received* forgiveness. Does this mean you can lose your salvation if you don't forgive? No, it means you didn't receive your salvation in the first place. You can't lose what you

---
315 1 Peter 3:18
316 Ephesians 2:8-9

don't have. How you forgive reflects what you have received. How you treat others shows how you think God treats you. Unforgiveness says at its core, "I don't trust God to be just." As the servant's unforgiveness shocked the watching slaves, your unforgiveness affect others. Don't you think it distresses those who hear you call yourself "Christian" when you are bitter, walled, self-protective, self-focused and unkind?

Lesson 5: If you don't forgive, you will be tormented

"This is how my heavenly Father will treat you unless you forgive your brother from your heart."

In the end, the King was able to turn the servant over to the jailers. He could because the transaction was incomplete and the debt was still in His hand. If you don't forgive, you will end up imprisoning yourself. You will build fantastic walls plastered with hatred. You will put heavy yokes on people, ruining relationships by expecting them to be perfect. You will become hard and bitter, and walk in torment and grief. And you will open a door for Satan to harass you.

What is Biblical Forgiveness?

Webster's Dictionary says forgiveness is "the act of forgiving; the pardon of an offender, by which he is considered and treated as not guilty. The forgiveness of enemies is a Christian duty." What are you thinking, Mr. Webster? How can I pardon the offender and treat him as not guilty? Christian duty? "I must??" Let's look at the ABCs (and D) of forgiveness.

Forgiveness is an Act of Sacrifice

Christ was sacrificed to take away the sins of many people... (Hebr. 9:28)
...without the shedding of blood there is no forgiveness. (Hebr. 9:22)

Imagine I am horsing around in your house and break a lamp. You say, "You broke my lamp, you owe me $200." I shake my head. "Too bad, I am not going to pay it." "But you broke my lamp, you owe me," you insist. I refuse. "It was your fault for letting me play around." You write an IOU for $200 and hand it to me. I tear it up. "Not paying," I yell. "But you owe me!" you scream back. "I don't care, forget it!" I shout as I slam the door. You carefully tape together the torn IOU. You know I owe you because I broke your lamp. You carry the IOU in your pocket, burning inside because I am so wrong. Every time you look at it, the offense grows. You show people the IOU, telling them how I won't pay. The IOU consumes you.

Then imagine Jesus walks in your house. You tell Him all about the broken lamp; show Him the damage and the taped-together IOU. He smiles slightly and says, "I'll pay for that, just give me the IOU." He opens His wallet and gives you the $200. What do you do? If you are like most people, you don't want the money from Jesus. You don't really want a new lamp; you only want me to pay for it. It's not about the debt anymore; it is about making *me* paying the debt.

When someone sins against you, there is a cost, a price tag or a debt. You know the cost of being sinned against: for some, like me, the cost forever altered your life. When there is a sin you need to forgive, you must be willing to admit the pain and absorb the cost. You may need to sacrifice the expectation of ever being repaid by the person who cost you. If you don't do this—accept the cost, then release it to God—you will carry it for life. Your hurts can then become your identity, your reason to live.

Our forgiveness was very costly—it cost Jesus His life to obtain it. He was our sacrificial lamb (John 1:29): He shed His blood for our sin. Hebrews 9:22 does not say "*without that bad person* shedding blood, there will be no forgiveness for sin." Jesus did it for all people, all sin.

Forgiveness is a Bridge Back to Relationship

Your iniquities have separated you from your God; your sins have hidden His face from you, so that He will not hear. (Isaiah 59:2)

Albuquerque's new Big I (where two freeways intersect) was completed after 25 years of discussion and three years of preparatory roadwork. The actual building seemed almost magical: the fly-over grew one section at a time, suspended in mid-air. Just when it looked like the soaring road would fall, the builder would add a tall support pillar of concrete and steel, anchored in bedrock. The long off-ramp was built quickly but was unfinished for almost a year. 2,000 feet of fly-over was useless because a one-foot gap kept it from connecting to the ground ramp.

Sin separates. Our sin separates us from God and from people. Christ is the bridge between God and man. God wants to have relationship with us so He built the bridge of forgiveness on the bedrock of Jesus' sacrifice. Starting from His side, the bridge soars over the gap—except for the last twelve inches. That is my work. My reconciliation with God hinges on whether I admit my sins and accept God's way back. I admit I cannot build a bridge He would find acceptable. When I confess my sins, I complete *His bridge*. I close the gap (make relationship possible).

Forgiveness does not say, "It doesn't matter." It does matter. Sin always matters to God. It matters so much that He sent His sinless Son to pay the penalty.

...forgiving each other, just as in Christ God forgave you. (Ephesians 4:32)

You forgive others just as God has forgiven you. If you act like Christ, you build the long bridge toward the person who has sinned against you. You forgive them, release the debt to God (because Christ died to forgive them too) and *offer a way back* to relationship. The goal of forgiveness is reconciliation (the relationship fully restored), but that can't happen unless both parties do it right; humbly face their sin: one repents, one forgives and both walk back toward unity and love. But if the relationship isn't restored to godliness, at least you will be free from the stench of the dead body.

If you are unwilling to forgive freely or "need time" to forgive, or wait to forgive, or forgive but stand back from people, what do you model? The world sees that God does not forgive freely, He needs time to forgive, He waits to forgive, or He forgives but He stands back. Is that "Christ in you" or the old man in the flesh? If you received grace from God but you don't extend it to others, you either chose to put your feelings ahead of your Lord, you didn't receive the gift, or you chose to live for yourself rather than the Savior. You toggled back to the flesh: "I'll handle it."

God has appointed believers to carry the message of reconciliation.[317] Choosing to forgive is a mark of a good ambassador. We are His agents of peace; He assigned us to bring friendship where there is strife. I believe when we accept Christ's terms of engagement—when we surrender to Him, fall on our face and ask for mercy when we deserve damnation, when we receive His free gift of grace—only then can we leave the old life and enter the Land of Grace. Then we invite others.

Forgiveness is a Command

Be kind and compassionate to one another, forgiving each other, just as in Christ, God forgave you. (Eph. 4:32)

And when you stand praying, if you hold anything against anyone, forgive him, so your Father in heaven may forgive you your sins. (Mark 11:25)

I didn't know it at the time, but when Melanie said I could get anger out of my heart by

317 2 Corinthians 5:19

forgiving, she was quoting Ephesians 4. The commands are: *get rid of all bitterness, rage, anger, brawling, slander...Then be kind and compassionate...forgive...as He forgave us.* The Greek word is *charizomai* – the root word *charis* means grace: we forgive to be gracious, to treat kindly, and to give as a willing gift.[318] God gave graciously to you, so you graciously give to others.

We will be sinned against. The world says when we are sinned against, we should get even, or destroy relationships or build walls and set boundaries. But God gave us one way to get through sin: forgiveness. It is all we have and all we need. First deal with it vertically, taking it to God and receiving His forgiveness. Then you can forgive the offense horizontally (a sinning brother or unbeliever).[319] To get rid of the anger and clean out your heart, don't let anger fester and bitterness ripen; obey the command to forgive. My anger was justified and legitimate, but *staying in it was my choice*. On my knees in Melanie's living room, I poured out all my venom, poison, anger and malice. I didn't have to face my heartache alone: I took it all to Christ and left it at the cross. He took it from me. Two hours later, I rose up a different woman.

If for no other reason, we forgive because we are commanded to. Forgiveness is an act of your will. *You make the choice, God makes the change*. If you refuse to obey God, you have chosen to sin and how are you different from your abuser? You want your way over God's way, which is exactly what they did. We forgive in spite of the feelings, wrestling rebellious flesh to the ground.

Forgiveness is a Duty

*"If your brother sins, rebuke him, and if he repents, forgive him. If he sins against you seven times in a day, and seven times comes back to you and says, "I repent" forgive him." The apostles said, "Increase our faith!" He replied, "Suppose one of you has a servant plowing or looking after sheep. Would he say to the servant when he comes in from the field, "Come along now and sit down to eat?" Would he not say, "Prepare my supper, get yourself ready and wait on me while I eat and drink; after that you may eat and drink?" Would he thank the servant because he did what he was told to do? So you, when you have done everything you were told to do, should say, 'We are unworthy servants; **we have only done our duty**.'"* (Luke 17:3b-10)

Do you think forgiveness is impossible? You are not alone. The disciples understood the call Jesus was making and asked for more faith to do it. You can't, but Christ in you can.

---

318 <u>Strong's Concordance</u> Thomas Nelson, © 1999, #5483, *grace*
319 Tim Lane, president of CCEF at CLARUS Conference, Desert Springs Church, Albuquerque, 2013.

Forgiveness begins as a duty. Your flesh does not want to forgive but you do what you are supposed to do. You drag your will to obey the Lord; *I don't want to but I must.* The servant didn't serve his own food, he served the Master's food. His **duty** is to serve. Obedience means "Yes, Lord" no matter the feelings, reasons, excuses, logic, or the actions of others. Your flesh is talking to you right now, saying *it's too hard or it's not fair or I don't want to or I don't feel like it.* You look like this: ☹

When you understand more, forgiveness can change to a debt payment. God forgave you so you can forgive the other person (like the story in Matthew 18). You look like this: 😐 It is a fair exchange: my big debt has been paid, so I will pay your little debt.

When you become a believer, God makes a huge deposit in your spiritual bank account. When someone sins against you, you go to the bank and withdraw what you need to cover the debt. If the abuser hurt you $2,000,000 worth of pain, then go withdraw it from your account. *When sin abounds, grace abounds much more.* (Romans 5:20) There will always be more money in your account than sin that needs to be paid. God will never leave you short! He has it covered.

Forgiveness at its best is a delight. We love God so much, we desire to be His ambassadors, representing Him in every arena of our life. It is our privilege: I *get* to forgive; I *get* to surprise them with the gift of grace, the gift of mercy, the gift of forgiveness. You look like ☺:

Restoring Relationships

If your brother sins against you, go to him and show him his fault. If he listens to you, you will have won your brother over. (Matthew 18:15)

Do you go just to point out his fault? No, it's to win your brother over. Th*e reason to go is reconciliation.* In order to restore a relationship, have open hearts and walk in fellowship, there needs to be repentance (*your brother listens*); an acknowledgement that he has sinned but now desires to change his behavior. If he doesn't repent, you are to get others involved (first a witness of the process, later the elders and the church) and keep trying. If he still refuses after a long period of time, you are to treat him as an unbeliever (witness to him, ask if he's repented, pray for him—Matt. 7:16-17). The intimacy of spiritual brotherhood is severed and the relationship is changed and guarded.[320]

Forgiveness is half of a very important spiritual equation:

---
[320] Treat the people like a grocery store clerk-pleasant, kind, small talk, not heart talk. Or speak the gospel message.

Forgiveness + repentance = reconciliation

Reconciliation can't take place if there is only forgiveness. It takes both sides doing their part to restore a relationship. The person who sinned must repent, the person sinned against must forgive. We have talked about your half (forgiving). The sinner (or abuser) has a part to play as well. In most abuse, the abuser never asks for forgiveness, so the relationship is never restored. If the abuser never repents, or has died, the relationship cannot be restored. But this principle is not just for abusers; it works for all relationships.

If there is no repentance, guard your heart.[321] If there is repentance, open your heart wide.[322] If they ask your forgiveness but you know they are totally unrepentant, or are trying to manipulate you, or it's a pattern with no change behind it, you can grant forgiveness, but have no relationship with them.

A "New" Relationship

Will the relationship be restored back to what it was? No, if you work from forgiveness through to reconciliation, it can be better than it was before. When you are in a relationship long enough to go through the honeymoon stage (or "dating behavior"), there will be some hurt, betrayal, harsh words, hard judgments or disappointment. You cannot be close to someone without getting hurt. At some point, the flesh (either theirs or yours) will rule and the relationship will be broken; the reality of sin will stain the relationship. *It is not a question of if; it is a reality of when.*

What happens next will dictate the future. If you follow God's principles and quickly, humbly go to your brother and he repents, the relationship will be restored—you will have won your brother over. As restoration takes place, the relationship is stronger where it has been welded back together. *The relationship is not based on good behavior but on godly behavior.* When you understand that each of you has a pull towards sin (fleshly desires) but sin can be overcome with good and erased with forgiveness, you can have great relationships. Forgiveness and repentance rebuild the relationship based on reality of the sinful nature rather than on the pretense that we are nice people. Even godly people sin.[323]

If you only have a relationship with someone *until they sin against you*, your heart will be broken often and your relationships will be short-lived. You won't reflect God's patience (long-suffering), or merciful, generous, grace-filled forgiveness and you will be brittle or

---

321 Proverbs 4:23
322 2 Corinthians 6:13
323 1 John 1:8

hard. My marriage is stronger today because we have walked through the restoration process so often. We know that either one of us can give into our flesh. We also know there is nothing we can't resolve. There are no hidden skeletons in the closet and no unrealistic expectations. There is comfort in knowing we can solve our problems in a way that glorifies God.

Ongoing Unforgiveness

Ephesians 4:26 warns us to not let the sun go down on our anger, *lest we give Satan a foothold.* So how many nights has the sun gone down on your anger? (Or how many years?) No wonder we struggle to forgive; we haven't given Satan a one-night foothold, we have given him night after night of footholds. A foothold is like giving Satan a place. Imagine giving Satan a chair at the family dinner table for days or weeks. Or worse, letting him sleep inbetween you and your husband. Forgiveness is *the* weapon of spiritual warfare.

Imagine you are a house. Everyday living produces trash. At first the trash goes into the trashcan, then it overflows, so you have to find other places to put it—in the basement or the garage. Sometimes you create trash; sometimes people knock on your door and hand you trash; other times it's like a drive-by, where people throw it through your front window. Like it or not, you have trash. When you don't remove the trash, the house begins to stink. The stench comes through the floorboards so you decorate your house, add air-freshener, and buy flowers to cover it. Eventually, you need to get to the root of the problem: you have old trash in your house. The solution? Get the trash *out*. Jesus is the trash man: He will take it away forever. For some of you, that may mean a major spring-cleaning (like I did for two hours). Then, when you have done major cleaning, take the trash out daily to keep your house clean.

One summer, I neglected weeding my small rose garden. In Canada, with lots of rain, weeds grow like crazy. I quickly plucked out the little ones, then I noticed one weed that stood over three feet high. I pulled it. Nothing. I planted my feet, grabbed it low at the bottom with both hands, bent my knees and gave it all I had. Nothing. I lost that battle, so I got a shovel and tried digging the roots out. I loosened the soil around the thick roots, then grabbed it again and heaved. Nothing moved. I got an axe and cut the roots off the best I could. I finally had victory.

Parking Lot Forgiveness

See the spiritual application of that weed? How easy it is to pull out little weeds, but what work it is to pull out the "tree" that has grown for months. *Don't let the sun go down on your anger*, deal with it quickly. *The longer it grows, the deeper it goes.* Say there is a man at work who drives me crazy. Unreasonable, self-focused, blind, vindictive, arrogant and mean, he gives me lots of chances to practice forgiveness. If I don't forgive as God commands, I sin and grieve the Holy Spirit. I am not willing to give away my peace and joy because of him. *He is SO not worth ruining my relationship with God.* I purpose at the end of every workday, before I start the car, to forgive him. As I leave the parking lot, I leave it all with Jesus: I don't take it home to poison my evenings or my family. Is there someone you need to forgive at the end of each day? Flesh will not forgive, but in our Spirit we can. Forgive quickly and often. Forgiveness is like breathing; it should be natural and automatic.

Forgiveness Brings Release

When Jim and I moved back in together, we learned to forgive on a daily basis and keep short accounts. One Sunday, we hit a red light heading to church. When it turned green, Jim didn't go. We sat through the green light, then the red light again. I gripped my seat, trying not to say anything unkind or critical. When Jim realized we had been there for some time, he asked if he sat through the green light. I quietly said yes. Then he said, "And I suppose you're thinking, 'it's not going to get any greener'" (what I usually said). I blew up—how dare he put me down when I was trying so hard to be kind? He didn't give me credit for keeping my mouth shut. He parked the car, and said, "You were right. Would you forgive me?" I couldn't even speak. "Go," I choked. I watched him walk into the church, a free man, forgiven and clean, while I struggled to find a godly attitude. We laugh about it now, but it shows that even when you want to do it right, it's sometimes hard.

God Will Repay

My accounting partner and I had two bills we couldn't collect; a music store and a carpet store. Rather than wait for payment, my partner got a piano and I got new carpet. I quit work when my son came along, so several months passed. When I finally got to the store, I found out my former partner had taken my carpet. I called but he refused to reimburse me. I went to Melanie with the IOU clenched in my hand. She said to forgive the debt. "No, you don't understand," I said, "This is legitimate. He owes me." She assured me she understood and challenged me to forgive him.

I pondered it. Clearly he was not going to pay me back, so I could carry this IOU for years. I decided *Why not give it to Jesus*? What have I got to lose? I dragged my will to the altar of sacrifice and put my IOU there. It wasn't easy, but I obeyed; I gave it to Jesus and walked away. Over the months, I struggled to take my thoughts captive but as I refused to think about the IOU, the anger subsided. I mostly forgot about it.

A few months later, a man called me with an odd question. I had counseled his two daughters, who had been sweetly reconciled. He was so happy that he prayed for two weeks about how to bless me. God gave him one word: "Does the word "carpet" mean anything to you?" I just cried. He gratefully did my whole living room and up the stairs, giving me far more than what I had lost. I was glad I had obeyed God. Do you have torn, taped-up IOUs in your heart's pocket? Put them on the altar as a sacrifice to God, trusting that He is a just accountant. He keeps the books.

Debt Collector

Imagine this meeting: Jesus stands between you and the abuser, with you on the right, he is on the left. He tells your abuser to repent but he chooses not to. Then Jesus turns to you and tells you to forgive. When you forgive, you hand the sin debt over to Jesus the mediator and debt collector, completing your side of the transaction. He receives the debt and repays you for it. He heals your heart and restores the years the locusts have eaten. You are free to live. Jesus then turns to the abuser with your sin debt in His hand. The Holy Spirit convicts the abuser of the sin that he has done to you. Yet he still refuses to repent.

If the abuser will not repent for Jesus, do you really think he will repent for you? Get on with your life; forgive and leave the sin debt with Jesus. Take him off your hook and put him on Jesus' hook. God is far more effective in convicting of sin then you will ever be. In fact, conviction of sin is not your part of the equation; it is God's part. Your part is to forgive.

Front Door Forgiveness

Warning: **This is a graphic story** that illustrates a conflict Christians have. Imagine you are living in the country. It is late one evening; your husband is out of town, your baby boy is tucked in bed and you are watching TV alone. Suddenly, there is a loud knock at the door. You open it carefully, and see a man who is clearly distraught. He says he had a fight with his wife earlier so he went for a drive to cool down. As he drove, he spotted your car in the lane, which was the same as his wife's. In a blind rage, he jumped out and slashed your tires. He is at the door asking for forgiveness. He knows he was wrong and hands you cash to pay to have your tires repaired. You take a deep breath, trying to take in the emotional story. You take the money to fix your car and tell him you forgive him. He leaves.

You are still shaking as you head upstairs to bed. You turn into your son's room to check on him before you go to bed. When you see him, you realize that the man has not only slashed your car tires but also has slashed your baby's wrists. You are frantic as you realize you don't have a way to get him to the hospital.

I know this is a horrible story. But it sets up a big question: does the forgiveness you extended *at the front door cover the discovery upstairs*? I believe not. As you begin to forgive sexual abuse (or divorce or betrayal) you will find yourself looking again and again at some issues. You may have forgiven one sin, but find another, much more serious one, popping up that needs to be forgiven separately. Don't believe the enemy's lie that you never forgave in the first place.

Where Do I Collect?

Imagine I lose control of my car and hit your car, causing extensive damage. You are hurt, angry and upset. We exchange information and take our claims to my insurance company. I pay the deductible and the insurance company pays the rest—a considerable amount. If you call me and say I owe you more, I would say, "Go discuss it with my insurance company–they will handle it." No matter how often you brought it up, or demand that I pay you, my answer would be the same: go to the insurance company. That is why I have insurance, to cover what I can't afford in case of an accident.

Forgiveness is similar. God knows we will have accidents; we will sin against others (sometimes accidentally, sometimes on purpose). When we do, we have to pay our deductible: repent of our sin, ask God to forgive us, ask the person to forgive us, take responsibility for our actions, and repay any reasonable and obvious debt (which can be very costly). However, once we have "paid" our deductible, we are released from the obligation. If they demand more payment, we are under no obligation to pay. They must go to God (our insurance company) to get their car fixed. There are things only God can do: restore their life, make heart changes. There are things you cannot do for the person you sinned against; change their attitude, turn the key to their happiness. But you can buy them a new lamp (replace what you damaged).

Sometimes spouses refuse to let go of their IOU. They hold it over their spouse's head for years demanding full payment again and again. Thank God I do not have to pay the full price of my sin, the full debt. Thank God He paid for sin on my behalf. That is grace.

Four Promises of Granting Forgiveness

Forgiveness is a promise not to tell. Don't continue to talk about it, to others or the sinner. If you say you have forgiven, but you still talk to others about your suffering, you have not biblically forgiven. Your words say you have forgiven but your actions give a lie. When the prodigal returned home, the father did not tell others all that the boy had done (unlike the elder brother who relayed his sins in great detail); he simply said, "*He was lost and is found.*"[324]

Forgiveness is a promise not to yell. Don't scream at the person who hurt you. If it lays dormant until a fight erupts, and pops up full-strength, you have not biblically forgiven. Forgiveness is a promise to leave it buried permanently, not save it until you need it. Pastor Skip Heitzig says we often bury the hatchet, but leave the handle above ground. *As far as the east is from the west, so far has God removed your sins from you.*[325]

Forgiveness is a promise not to dwell. Don't nurse it and rehearse in your mind. Don't play it over and over again. God chooses not to remember our sins. (Jer. 31:34) You choose not to remember theirs as well. Take your thoughts captive. If you replay it in your mind over and over, that is not biblical forgiveness.

Forgiveness is a promise not to quell.* Don't kill the relationship or hide behind walls. *If the other person has repented and you have forgiven, then you can rebuild the relationship back to honesty, openness and love.* 2 Cor. 2:7-8 says to *forgive and comfort* the (repentant) *sinner,* (reaffirm their love for him) *so he will not be overwhelmed by excessive sorrow.* Then, a warning in verse 10: *(Forgive) in order that Satan might not outwit you.* If you are unwilling to bring down the wall, you have not biblically forgiven and you are a tool in Satan's hand. (So, why the * after quell? Because, remember, forgiveness is only half of the solution.)

Bargain-Basement Forgiveness: Worldly Sorrow

People tend to say "I'm sorry" without looking at the full extent of what has happened: "I SAID I was SORRY." But godly sorrow and worldly sorrow are very different. *Worldly sorrow wants to sweep it under the rug* instead of hearing an account of the sin done. "I said I was sorry, that should be enough." *Worldly sorrow has a "but"* or implication hiding in its message. "It's your fault I sinned." "If you wouldn't have done this, I wouldn't have done that." *There is no ownership of the sin*, just a marginal agreement that "maybe I did something wrong." They may be sorry they got caught. *Worldly sorrow gets angry at the idea that it takes time to rebuild trust* and demands intimacy immediately. One husband yelled, "God forgave me immediately but you don't," calling his wife sinful. If we pay the cost (the

---

[324] Luke 15:24
[325] Psalm 103:12

sacrifice), we demand the person understand and appreciate it. We want their kindness and respect, and demand they never hurt us again. It's a Christian version of manipulation. Finally *worldly sorrow doesn't want to deal with consequences.* They want it to go away quickly.

Godly sorrow owns their sin and calls it sin. Sinners want to play "forgiveness volleyball." In volleyball, you never "catch" or "hold" the ball. You deflect it with your arms. In basketball, you catch the ball, hold it, bounce it, then pass it. In order for true forgiveness to take place, there is a moment when the sin is "owned." You grab the truth: You sinned or were sinned against. You don't ignore it, deflect it, or pass it over. This might sound like, *"Please forgive me for my words of gossip. I know I tore you down and damaged your reputation. I realize it caused you a lot of pain."*

Godly sorrow does not finger-point. In Psalm 51, David did not blame his wife for not meeting his needs or Uriah for having a bathtub on his roof without a fence. He did not blame God for making Bathsheba so beautiful. He did not say he was only being a man enjoying the beauty of a woman. He understood it was his sin. *"For I know my transgressions and my sin is always before me* (v. 3)." *"I know it was my choice to scream at you. I realize that showed anger in my heart."*

Godly sorrow accepts responsibility for sin. There are consequences for sin. When David and Bathsheba's baby died, David did not rage at God. He accepted the loss, stopped praying, got up and comforted his wife.[326] In Psalm 51, David was concerned about his relationship with the Lord: *Do not cast me from your presence or take your Holy Spirit from me.* (v. 13) He knew his sin (adultery) had marred the relationship and he asked for grace.[327] The person you sinned against often controls the consequences. *"I understand that even though I have stopped the affair, you will want to check my texts and emails. I realize that it will take time for you to believe my words. I know your family hates me and I will try my best to love them with God's love."*

Fourth, *godly sorrow recognizes that it takes time to rebuild the relationship.* The Bible says we should look for the *fruit* of repentance[328] and deeds of repentance.[329] With broken marriages or sinning boyfriends, many women see blossoms on the tree but don't wait for the fruit. Fruit takes time to grow. While God is omniscient and knows immediately if the sinner is repentant, we don't, so we must wait for the fruit.[330] *"I understand it will take time to trust me again since I have lied to you so often."*

---
326 2 Samuel 12:18-24
327 2 Samuel 12:22
328 Matthew 3:8
329 Acts 26:20
330 Matthew 7:20

Details of Asking for Forgiveness

So what does a conversation sound like where you ask for forgiveness? Here are some steps:
- Set aside a time when you can be alone, without distractions with time to talk it through.
- When you meet, ask the person to tell you how you hurt them.
- Listen—don't defend your actions or sidestep or blame her (write them down if needed).
- If s/he gets quiet, say you are listening and ask if there is more.
- Ask them specifically to forgive you for each offense you committed. "I know I hurt you and disappointed you by my actions. I know I sinned against you and God and I want to change so I never do it again. *Please forgive me*."
- Add more sins if they are brought up. Own your sins, don't explain.
- Rather than demanding their trust immediately, accept that as your consequence.
- Tell your plan to not sin against them again. Include put-offs, put-ons and attitude changes.
- Maybe ask for another meeting in a week or a month to get input on how you are doing.

If both parties are willing to keep talking and you are faithful to change, you have a chance to grow and rebuild the friendship based on godly behavior. You develop a track record of working things out rather than ignoring them. You don't stop at pseudo-forgiveness.[331]

"What Are You Talking About?"

Jesus said, "Father, forgive them, for they do not know what they are doing." (Luke 23:34)

There is a third category of people who need forgiveness: those who don't know they have sinned. These people aren't from the 2 Timothy 3 list; unrepentant, lovers of themselves, proud, abusive, ungrateful, unholy, without love, slanderous, brutal… (guard your heart). Nor are they like the repentant prodigal ("I have sinned against heaven and against you")[332] that you open your heart to. These people are unaware that they have sinned at all. They believe their actions, words, attitudes and emotions are justified. They are children in the spiritual sense; they lack the maturity (or self-discipline) to see their sin. We handle them like Jesus did on the cross: *"Forgive them, for they do not know what they are doing."* He not only took them off His hook, but He prayed for God the Father to take them off His hook too.

---

[331] A loud explanation of "why I sinned against you *because you had sinned against me first*."
[332] Luke 15:21

This is the ultimate forgiveness, the highest goal. We forgive, taking them off our hook and putting them on God's hook. We give the IOU to Jesus and trust God to deal with their sin. We desire to see them receive mercy from God even though they don't understand their need to repent. Then, by the power of the Holy Spirit flowing through us, we ask God to not treat them as their sins deserve. We forgive and intercede; we seek God's mercy for them.

Forgiveness = Love

In Luke 7, Jesus tells a story to Simon, a Pharisee who had invited Him to dinner. To Simon's disgust, a sinful (sexually immoral) woman came and knelt at Jesus' feet weeping, wet His feet with her tears, wiped them with her hair, kissed them and poured perfume on them. So Jesus told a story about two men who owed debts to a money-lender, one a huge sum, another a small sum. The moneylender forgave both debts. Jesus asked Simon who would love the moneylender more, and he correctly replied, "The one who had the bigger debt cancelled." Jesus challenged Simon's attitude and ended the discourse with these words, "*Therefore, I tell you, her many sins have been forgiven–for she loved much. But he who has been forgiven little* (you, Simon) *loves little.*" (v. 47)

Without Christ's forgiveness, we are damned. With it, we receive priceless forgiveness, and are enabled to forgive those who sin against us. The more we have been forgiven, the more we will love. Perhaps we don't love others because we don't see our need for forgiveness. To the extent we understand how much God has forgiven us, to the extent we see our sin nature correctly, to the extent we admit our sin—to that extent we will love God.

I am convinced that forgiveness is the greatest proof of our Christianity. If we are forgiven by grace—a free gift, not earned—and received that gift, then we can share what we have. Having received forgiveness, we agree with God that forgiveness is no longer based on justice, or rights, or deserving, but on mercy. We are a new creation with a new economy.

Blameless

What a gift the Savior has given us. Once sin-stained, now white as snow. Once shameful and guilty, we are now blameless and righteous. Once lost, now found. Once hopeless, now with hope eternal. Once condemned, now accepted. Yes, the joy of the gospel belongs to us.

Proclaim these declarations out loud every day:

I AM A FORGIVING PERSON (or I want to be a forgiving person).
I can forgive, knowing God will judge.
I will forgive and trust God to repay them according to their deeds.
I will forgive because I have been forgiven so much.
I will forgive and not walk under sin's shadow anymore.
I will forgive and bury that dead body.

Take the sharp pointy end of the cross, and drive it like a stake in the memory of the abuse. Christ died to forgive that sin too, even if the abuser is not aware of His sacrifice. That sin was covered at the cross. Who are you to keep it alive? It is their responsibility to accept (or reject) His death in their place, as what they deserve for that sin. Leave it right here… Don't carry it forward after you turn the page to the next chapter.

Bottom Lines:

1. Forgiveness is an Act of sacrifice, a Bridge to relationship, a Command and a Duty.
2. Don't tell, yell, dwell or quell.
3. If you don't forgive, you imprison yourself.
4. If you can't forgive, have you been forgiven?

Discussion Questions:

1. Have you experienced this kind of forgiveness? Did it restore the relationship?

2. Are you a "debt, duty or delight" forgiver? What hinders you?

3. Right now, do you need to forgive someone who knows their sin, ignores their sin or is unaware of their sin?

4. Have you received God's forgiveness for your sins? Have you extended it to others?

5. First thing when you wake up, ask yourself, "Is there anyone I need to forgive or ask forgiveness of? Is there anything on my conscience? Is there any way I am not at peace with God or man?" (from a Joyce Meyer teaching)

To the Friend of Traveler:

1. Forgiveness is something you cannot do for your friend. You can encourage them, remind them, teach them, but forgiveness is an individual choice.

2. Forgiveness is primarily a transaction before God. You forgive, give it to God and He takes it. Always talk about forgiveness with God's presence in mind.

3. You will need to forgive the abuser too—as her story unfolds, you will hear horrifying details, things that make you weep for her pain. Don't carry them with you… forgive as soon as you possibly can. At least forgive immediately, then if you need to forgive more deeply you can do that after she leaves.

4. It's not unusual if the two of you will have some unforgiveness between you; some hurtful comment, some miscommunication, some selfish or unloving action. Go through the steps carefully and try to carry out some of the trash together.

Worship Song *Forgiveness* by Matthew West[333]

---

[333] From album Into the Light, © 2012 Sparrow Records Songs of Southside Independent Music Publishing, Songs for Delaney, External Combustion Music

Chapter 12
Mountain Passes

"Would you come to the church and meet with a gal who's going through the 12-Step program?" my pastor asked. "She needs someone to listen to her Step 5."[334] I didn't know the 12 Steps in AA, but I wanted to help. But as she listed her wrongs, I called the whole thing to a stop. Since she was a Christian, there was little sense in listing the sins if she didn't ask God to forgive them as she went. Why talk about them without bringing them to Jesus? So she started again, and after each item, she humbly asked God to forgive her. She left the meeting released and revived. Later, I found out we had jumped ahead to Step 7.[335] Christians don't just list sins; we can receive forgiveness right away (without waiting for the right Steps). So in this chapter, as we look at the mess either we made or others made, let's not just name it; let's call it trash and get it out of the house.

Your Old Journey

You were "bumped off" the original course onto the path of pain because a person (i.e., your abuser) chose to disobey God and turn to abuse. You were forced to live a new reality and make impossible choices. At the time of the abuse, you had no tools, no truth, and no power to get off the path. No one brought you to Jesus. You didn't hear truth about the abuse. You held onto wrong thoughts and beliefs. You didn't know what to do or how to fix it.

Then you stayed there because you made some bad choices. You lied, pretended, ran away from people, ran to drugs, or ran to immorality. You became angry or sullen or frightened or mean; you lost your way by letting people control you, or you pushed ahead by controlling them. You decided God couldn't be trusted or man couldn't be trusted—only you could be trusted. Friend, in these ways and many others, you responded to being sinned against by sinning. Most people I meet do not have the tools to respond to being sinned against without sinning. People who are sinned against usually will sin back. The popular saying goes, "Hurt people hurt people."

Your New Journey

<u>With the Word</u> of God teaching and the Holy Spirit helping, you can step into the Promised

---

334 Admit to God, to ourselves, and to another human being the exact nature of our wrongs.
335 Humbly ask God to remove our shortcomings.

Land, leave the path of pain and live in Freedom. You can shred lies and boldly face some tough facts, knowing that God will enable you to walk through it in a righteous way.[336] Forgiveness releases us both from sins that were done to us and from our own sinful choices. Forgiveness brings freedom; it frees us from past pain and sets us back on the right path, free to make new, good choices.

We have broken the process of forgiveness down into two different actions. You need to choose your own way through:

Part 1 – Ask forgiveness for my sinful choices
Part 2 – Look at the pool of pain and then forgive the sins done to you

Paths Around the Mountain

There are two paths through forgiveness in this chapter; you will choose one. Both will look at your sins and sins done to you. Both will lead you through forgiveness. Both will take you to Jesus. Both will end at the foot of the cross. Both will get you to greater freedom.

Path to the Right

You can follow the path to the Right if you want to follow the **biblical order**: first confess *the sins you did* in response to being sinned against (remove the log from your own eye, Matt. 7:1-5). This path first addresses your need to be forgiven for your sinful thoughts, words, attitudes and actions. Then in the second step, you will look at the abuse: name the sins, hurts, feelings and outcomes, then forgive it (give it to Jesus to deal with). I believe to the same extent you receive forgiveness from the Father for your sinful choices, you will extend forgiveness to others.

The Right path means receive forgiveness for your own sins then examine the abuse, then forgive the abuse. If you choose this path, you will do Part 1 (p. 216) then Part 2 (p. 222).

Path to the Left

The path to the Left is for those who want to deal with the abuse in **chronological** order: first deal with the abuse, then your sinful responses to it. You are ready to pour it out and do serious spring-cleaning. You don't want to hold trash in your house one more minute. Once you have named all that was done to you—looked at the abuse through adult eyes and a heart filled with Christ—you will take it to Jesus, forgive it specifically and let it go. Then you will circle back and look at your own sinful responses to being sinned against.

---
336 1 Corinthians 10:13

The Left path means examine the abuse, forgive it, then receive forgiveness for your sinful responses. If you choose this path, you will do Part 2 (p. 222) then Part 1 (p. 216).

Path in the Middle

The Middle path is for those who are stuck. For whatever reason (fear, anger, resentment, etc.) you are unwilling to look at the sin done to you, and you don't want to look at your sinful responses to those sins. So rather than staying stuck, we want you to pray. Pray for courage and power. Then once you have prayed through your section, you can circle back and go down either path.

Taking the Middle path means asking for God's help to go down either the Left or the Right path. If you are here, read the following prayers, then with God's help, you may be able to get onto a path around the mountain.

Help, I'm Stuck and I Can't Move

Oh friend, I know forgiveness is hard. You look around and wonder how others can forgive. You aren't ready yet. You are still stuck. So friend, let's help you walk closer to freedom now.

1) Do you still believe old thoughts about the abuse? Thoughts like: *it's not fair because he hasn't repented. I want him to pay for his part. I hate him. I don't want to let it go. He hasn't changed. He is still hurting me. It's too hard.* Pray for your thoughts to line up with God's: *Lord, thank You for giving me the mind of Christ. Please renew my mind from the inside as I take control of it with new habits. Give me the courage to believe what Your Word says. The Bible says again and again You are just.*[337] *Forgive me for thinking You are not just. You ARE. The Bible says that vengeance is Yours.*[338] *Forgive me for trying to avenge what happened to me. I trust that You will avenge me and repay me for the years the locusts destroyed.*[339] *Forgive me for getting in the way of Your wrath. The Bible says I can do all things when You strengthen me.*[340] *Forgive me for not running to the throne of Grace to receive mercy and grace when I need them. Lord, help me think about forgiveness differently. Forgive me for the wrong ways I have thought about forgiveness.*

2) Are you still running old tapes about God? *God doesn't care for me. God didn't protect me.* Pray: *Lord, open my eyes to see You right here with me. The Bible says You care for*

---
337 Deut. 32:4, 2 Chr. 12:6, Jer. 22:15, 2 Thess. 1:6, Rev 15:3
338 Isaiah 34:8, Rom 12:19
339 Joel 2:25
340 Philippians 4:13

me.[341] *Forgive me for telling myself that You don't. Forgive me for thinking that You have to act in a certain way to prove You care for me. Lord, forgive me for trying to put You into a box. All through the Bible, it says You will protect me.*[342] *Forgive me for believing my walls or my toughness will protect me. The Bible says You will keep me safe.*[343] *Forgive me Lord for believing that safety means no pain. Forgive me for wanting safety more than holiness. Forgive me for fighting Your process for growth when it includes suffering and trials. Forgive me for thinking my way is the right way and Your way is wrong. I believe You have kept my soul and that's why I'm alive today. Please hold me, Lord. Give me bigger faith to forgive.*

3) Are you walking in condemnation? *I am such a loser, such a mess. I can't do anything right.* You need to pray like this: *Lord, forgive me for believing that You reject me. Your Word says that there is NO condemnation for those who are in Christ Jesus.*[344] *Lord, I want to accept Your approval. Forgive me for being a tool in Satan's hand as I have beat myself up. Forgive me for calling You a liar, because I have condemned myself when You love me. Forgive me for devaluing myself, when You valued me so much that You died for me, bought me with Your precious blood. Forgive me for thinking I have to fix myself before I am any good. Your Word says no one is good.*[345] *Your Word says that You died for me while I was still a sinner.*[346] *Forgive me for believing I can earn Your love or deserve Your love. I open my hands to receive it as a free gracious gift.*[347] *I believe You are working in my heart. Increase my faith, Father.*

4) Do you let emotions run your life? Are you waiting to forgive because you don't feel like doing it? *Lord I am too hurt to forgive. It's too hard to forgive.*

You need to pray: *Lord, give me the courage to do my part and faith to believe what Your Word says. In the Garden, You did not let your emotions rule Your actions; You obeyed. How grateful I am, Jesus, that You did not walk away from the cross because it was hard. Give me the courage to deny myself, take up my cross and follow You.*[348] *I want to be Your follower. Forgive me for saying "No" to my Lord. I want to say "Yes." I know if God is not Lord of all of me, He is not Lord at all. So forgive me Lord, for being the center of my universe. Forgive me for letting my emotions, my desires or my thinking be my god. I know You oppose the proud. I want Your grace, Lord, the grace You give to the humble. Lord,*

---
341 1 Peter 5:7
342 Ps 32:7, Ps 41:2
343 Ps 16:1, Ps 18:2
344 Romans 8:1
345 Romans 3:12
346 Romans 5:8
347 Ephesians 2:8
348 Luke 9:23

forgive me for not submitting to you, as I choose, right now as an act of my will, to submit to you.[349] *The Bible says when I sin, your grace is greater.*[350] *Lord, restore to me the joy of Your salvation and grant me a willing spirit to sustain me.*[351] *Yes, Lord, yes, I will choose to forgive.*

5) Do you still believe your shame-based identity? You think *Shame is who I really am. God can't overcome my shame. It's too big, too real, too overpowering.*

Pray against the lies of the flesh: *Lord, forgive me for not receiving your gift of adoption. Forgive me for believing I am "less than." Forgive me for believing the lies of Satan that I am a shameful person. Lord, I know You have given me a new identity. I know that I am a new creation. Help me to receive this new identity and live in the wonder of it. Help me to remember I belong to You. Help me to keep growing. Help me not become ineffective and unproductive because I have forgotten what You have done for me. Open my eyes Lord that I may see Your truth. Tear down my walls so I can believe truth and be set free.*

Friend, staying in the pain, stuck on the dark side of the spiral, will rob you of your life. Our prayer is that you are now ready to move forward. Remember, the biblical order is do Part1 then Part 2, while the chronological order is to do Part 2 then Part 1.

Part 1- Asking Forgiveness for My Sinful Choices

One day, I told Melanie that I seemed to be getting worse not better; I was more sinful instead of less. She smiled and said when a person walks toward a streetlight, the closer they get to the light, the dirtier they seem. In the darkness, they couldn't see the stains and filth, but the more the light shines, the more dirt it shows.

In this part, you will "do the Word" in the biblical order. First confess sinful ways you have responded to the abuse. Sit with your loving Father and take the log out of your eye by taking responsibility for your sins. This is a big spring-cleaning moment of 10/20/30/40 years of sinful responses. I am so proud of you for having the courage to step out in obedience. Some of you are dragging your will here, doing your duty as Christ said. Others of you are so sick of your life, you are obeying out of desperation. Some may be here because of the Debt moment: Jesus will forgive my sins so I can forgive others. Yet here you are, ready to walk in the light. What is the process? I have listed sins from Chapters 1-10 of the book, including wrong thoughts, bad words and sinful actions. You can write on a piece of

---

349 James 4:6-7
350 Romans 5:20
351 Psalm 51:12

paper or in your journal, or you can tell Jesus what you have done: acknowledge the sin, tell Him your feelings, then ask Him to forgive you. If you don't know whether something is a sin, it's better to confess it and let God remove it. Don't let fear of that slow you down. I know some of you struggle with how unfair this all is. I know this is hard, but Freedom is waiting for you. Engage your will. Submit to God. Do things His way.

Here's an example: *I believed the lie that God didn't care about me* (from Chapter 3): *Lord, please forgive me for believing the lie that You don't care for me. I know now it is untrue. You shed Your blood for me because You care for me. You stepped in and took my punishment on the cross because You care for me. Forgive me Lord for not seeing Your care for me and for disobeying You by not bringing my cares to You. Thank You for Your sweet forgiveness, Lord, I receive it fully.*

You can confess each sin separately or each section/chapter as a whole. The first few chapters may be tough slugging as they are more detailed. The last few will be easier, because many of them are repeats from earlier chapters. You may choose to do it alone with God or bring your friend with you. You can get on your knees or walk and talk. There is no right way, except to bring it all to the cross. Remember, you are confessing sinful ways you have responded to being sinned against.

Lord thank You that You are here with me. Be gentle but be firm. Open my ears to hear the Holy Spirit's voice and my eyes to see the areas that hold me. Show me the lies I have believed, the actions I have done that don't glorify God, and the ways I have tried to deal with the abuse in my own strength and by my own way. Forgive me, Lord.

Chapter 1 – Sins from a Sinful Life

- I kept secrets, hiding sin, pretending everything was okay. I didn't tell or expose sin.
- I believed the voices in my head that taunted me: *You're weak, you're not normal.*
- I poured condemnation on myself: *I don't have a right to exist, you're a failure. Give up.*
- I made inner vows: *never be stupid and vulnerable again, never be a sexual being, never be used again, never trust people. I will get approval by my performance. I must be perfect.*
- I believed the lie that my Heavenly Father was like my earthly father (or my abuser).
- I tried ungodly ways to run away from the pain: ignoring, pretending, numbing, drinking, hiding, dumping, sidestepping around it. (Did you cut, masturbate, have an affair or an abortion, become homosexual, gain weight, to self-protect, become anorexic or bulimic or a perfectionist?)
- I believed lies about myself. *My love is poison. I'll never be free, I am beyond help*

I'll never be a real woman. If only I could keep him from being angry, he wouldn't hurt me. If only I had been born a boy, this would never have happened. If only I could keep my legs together, he wouldn't force himself on me. It's all my fault. (Did you reject yourself and others?)

- I had suicidal thoughts and believed it was the only way to end the pain. I attempted suicide.
- I joined my abuser's team by hurting people.
- I rejected the way God made me (a woman) and dressed and acted like a man.

Chapter 2 – Sinful Responses to Correction

- I was a closed circuit, unwilling to receive input from anyone.
- I believed I didn't have to trust anyone. I treated everyone, including God, as untrustworthy.
- I trusted only my thoughts, feelings, opinions, ideas and plans.
- I received correction as condemnation and beat myself (or others) up for failures made.
- I doubted God's love because He did not follow my formula for life:
    God's Love + Protection = Nothing Bad Happening to me
- I wanted man's approval more than I wanted God's approval.
- I hurt people who tried to correct me. I punished people if they hurt me.

Chapter 3 – Sins Based on Lies I Believed and Acted on

- I ran from God rather than to Him.
- I looked at God with a jaundiced eye. *God doesn't keep His promises.*
- I refused to receive God's good gifts. *You haven't earned it.*
- I trusted my feelings rather than obeying God. *It's too scary, you don't have to obey.*
- I questioned whether the Bible was relevant to my abuse. *It's not for today.*
- I followed my desires. *You deserve it.*
- I excused myself from following God's commands. *It's too hard.*
- I rewrote history according to my perspective. *God is never there for you.*
- I refused the gift of love from others. *They don't really mean it. They wish you would go away. They only tolerate you because they have to.*
- I believed lies rather than truth:
    My abuser loved me; he just didn't know how to show it.
    My abuser was drunk and didn't know what he was doing.
- I was too afraid to look at the pain.
    I could never survive. If I start crying I will never stop.
- I listened to Satan's voice.

> *This will comfort me* (going away, cutting, drinking, sex, etc.)
> *I'm bad, black inside, slimy, a bad seed, damaged goods. I'm only good for being used.*
> *I have no voice. No one loves me.*

- I believed lies about God, that He didn't care about what happened.
   > *If He loved me He would have stopped the abuse.*
- I justified my sin *(I yelled because I was hurt)*; minimized it *(I only yelled once)*; and blame-shifted *(you yelled first)*.

Chapter 4 – Sins from Not Exercising My Will

- I did not take control of my own life and was controlled by other people.
   > *I allowed bad men into my life; I didn't avoid them, confront them, or reject their control; I didn't stand up for God's ways; I rejected responsibility for my life and my choices; I looked to others for rescue or waited for people to change first.*
- I was weighed down by sins and moved by sinful desires (my own and other people's):
   > *I complained and wallowed in bitterness or self-pity; I blamed circumstances for my problems; I tried to fix my life by following fantasies or desires; I didn't repent and receive God's forgiveness; I believed shame was permanent; I drank (or drugged) to escape; I lied to cover up; I forgot the call to love and serve others.*
- I did not see the truth:
   About myself, God, the other person, the domination of sin, what needed to change
   About biblical commands to avoid bad company and walk in the light
   About my changed identity as a believer in Christ
   About my purpose and uniqueness
- I lost control because I gave control to an evil person:
   I stayed trapped by keeping my will disengaged; I wore a victim badge, forgetting the victory Christ offers; I was adrift and lost.
- I did not draw on God's enabling power, to respond to being sinned against in a Biblical way. I did not stand firm and speak like Abigail.[352] I did not run like Joseph.[353] I did not fight like David.[354] I did not put the past behind me and look ahead at what God had planned for me[355] or walk forward as Paul did.
- I let fear of man ensnare me. (Proverbs 29:25)
- I chose to be paralyzed rather than to act in God's power
- I chose to reject God's authority and rebel against Him rather than submit to Him

---
[352] 1 Samuel 25
[353] Genesis 39
[354] 1 Samuel 17
[355] Philippians 3:13-14

- I chose to worship a person, my feelings, or my fantasies rather than God
- I chose to plan revenge or hold onto a grievance rather than forgive
- I chose to give into temptation rather than deny it
- I chose to tear people down in anger rather than love them
- I chose to draw back in fear rather than walk forward in faith

Chapter 5 – Sins of My Sinful Flesh

- I chose again and again to act in the flesh rather than in the Spirit. I was on the wrong list in Galatians.
- The Old Man – the acts of the sinful nature: (5:19-20)
  Sexual immorality, impurity and debauchery; idolatry and witchcraft; hatred, discord, jealousy, fits of rage, selfish ambition, dissentions, factions, and envy; drunkenness, orgies, and the like.
  Rather than The New Man – the fruit of the Spirit: (Galatians 5:22-23) *Love, joy, peace, patience, kindness, goodness, faithfulness, gentleness, and self-control.*
- I have been unloving, discontented and greedy, depressed, impatient, selfish, unkind, hateful, demanding, bad, impure, disloyal, unfaithful, unreliable, unavailable, harsh, cruel, mean, rage-filled, out of control, impulsive, fantasizing, self-justified, self-focused, self-destructive, self-pleasuring, self-condemning.
- I have been involved in witchcraft, drugs, or idol worship of people and things.
- I have lived in fear of man, pleasing people more than God.
- I have been a gossip, a slanderer, envious.
- I have loved fighting, taking sides and forcing people to choose.
- I have been sexually immoral, and have had sex without the covenant of marriage.
- I have been prideful about my sins.

Chapter 6 – Sins from a Sinfully Closed Heart

- I refused to believe and receive the new life and other gifts God has given me: Eternal Life, Relief and Rest, Antidote for Fear, Peace, Adoption, a Generous Inheritance, Comfort, Wisdom, Mercy and Grace, Choices, Maturity, Holiness, Freedom, Healing, etc.
- I have demanded more and more from God while rejecting what He has already given.
- I have blamed Him for not providing for me, while worshipping my idol (safety, understanding, etc.).
- I believed lies about God's forgiveness—*I owe the wages of sin; I deserve condemnation; I have to do penance; I have to be serious about my sin; I can't run*

to the throne of grace and find mercy; I am under the law not grace; I am dead in my transgressions, not alive in Christ.
- I let my identity be shame-based. I forgot who I was in Christ. I believed Satan's lies about me. I did not scorn the shame. I let my flesh define who I am.

Chapter 7 – Sinful Responses to Emotions

- I ignored my emotions (masking tape): I put on a mask—pretended, hid, lied, had a double life.
- I let my emotions destroy (the hammer): I ignored my emotions and the problems they caused. I ignored what I did to people. I refused to agree with friends when they confronted me. I blamed people and situations for my emotions. I ignored my God-given emotions.
- I worshiped my emotions (an idol): I was paralyzed, or let my emotions rule my life. I became fear-driven and depressed, or I yelled, screamed and took revenge. I have not done what was right in spite of my emotions.
- I justified my emotional reactions. My emotions were always right and defendable.
- I believed and lived by my emotions rather than on the Word of God.
- I didn't listen to the Holy Spirit when He spoke to me about sinful emotions (anger, fear, worry, pride, lust, etc.)

Chapter 8 – Sinful Responses to Responsibility

- I sinned by taking responsibility for things that were others people's responsibility.
  The abuse was my fault. I shouldn't have_____(gone in the room, etc.).
- I took responsibility for things that are God's.
- I abdicated responsibility for things I needed to do to obey God.
- I sinfully tried to make people happy. I manipulated or controlled people.
- I was fearful or a peacemaker who didn't expose sin.
- I made other people feel responsible for my stuff. I liked/hated their attention.
- I blamed other people for my sins.
- I played God in people's lives.
  I was protecting my sister/mother.

Chapter 9 – Sinful Responses to My Thoughts

- I sinned by not taking my thoughts captive to the obedience of Christ. I let my mind float. I did not stop the toxic self-talk.
- I played bad old tape reruns in my mind, listened to many voices.

- I did not think on true, pure, lovely, good, excellent, praiseworthy things
- I did not guard my mind, or watch the things I let into my mind. I took in bad, harmful, wicked or sinful input.

Chapter 10 – Sinful Responses to Being Sinned Against

- I responded in pain, powerlessness, self-protection, pride, punishment, perishing, persecuting others for what my abuser did to me, becoming a Pharisee, plaguing my life with heartache, pitying myself into paralysis, plotting revenge, pitching a fit, pretending, pleading with God to rewrite history, pleasing myself and pushing God away, polluting my children with my bitterness or fear or anger, pressuring my family into giving into my demands, preserving my hurt by nursing and rehearsing it.
- I sinned by not doing the Word—I knew it but didn't practice it. I have acted as if I was powerless when I didn't want to obey. I have rejected Your directions and done my own thing. I have quoted verses but not applied them. Like a Pharisee, I have held others to a standard of godliness that I didn't keep.
- I sinfully returned evil for evil; given a piece of my mind, retaliated, undermined, threw someone under the bus, ruined their reputation, slandered, gossiped, boasted, didn't help them.
- I didn't obey God's commands to love my enemy or speak wholesome words.
- I sinned in the following ways that were not on the pages…

Good job Friend! 1 John 1:9 says, "If we confess our sins, He is faithful and just and will forgive us our sins and purify us from all unrighteousness." Right now, you stand squeaky clean at the cross. You have been forgiven for every sin you confessed, and every act of unrighteousness that went along with it. You have been washed and cleansed and are holier now than you were an hour ago. You look purer, too. Rejoice! Receive!

Part 2- Looking at the Pool of Pain and Forgiving

Oh, the agony of the abuse. The depths of the pain are unfathomable to someone who has not walked this path. Yet now is the time to pull the trash out of the basement and look at what happened, in truth and with adult eyes. Jesus is with you, waiting to carry the trash away. We want you to keep giving it to Him, don't stop or make a bed in the messy pile. Just name the sins that were done to you, then hand them over.

Show me the truth about the abuse. I want this out of my life Lord. I believe in 30 minutes or an hour, I can get this poison out of my soul and be washed and clean. I know it is not my shame, not my fault, not my sin. Please Lord, let me look honestly at what happened to me; don't let me minimize, ignore, or defend. Let me see it through Your eyes of truth.

Show me as much as You want me to know today. Thank You God that I am not alone and we will walk into this pain together. Carry me through to the other side of this shadow of death. Let me not stay in the pain one second longer than You want me to, but don't let me run away from it either. Give me courage. I know Jesus that You understand the agony of facing pain. You wrestled with God about pain in the Garden. Yet You walked toward pain of crucifixion because it would buy our freedom and release us from the sins done to us. Thank You for everything, Lord.

Write out about **one incident of** abuse. Be specific but go through it quickly. What happened? How old were you? Do you remember any details of the room/car/field/barn/office/backyard/alley/bed/basement? Smells, pictures, noises, colors? When you think of that place, what do you feel?

Was there more than **one time** with this person, or more than one instance of abuse? Go through one event/person. Were you overpowered? Were you tricked by someone you trusted? What were you promised? Did you get it? What were you told you would lose? Did that fear/threat control you?

Look at the **words**: Did he[356] flatter you or praise you? Did he say filthy things or make you say things you knew were wrong? Were there weapons or force involved? Did he threaten you? Did he tell you it was your fault? Did he tell you you failed or pleased him? Did he talk about your body in shameful or degrading or humiliating ways? Is there a word or phrase you hate?

Look at the **actions**: Did he give you a gift? Did you participate because there was no escape? Did he touch you, penetrate you, perform oral or anal sex? Did it move from looking to touching to fondling to full-on sex? Did he tie you down, hold you down, drug you, take pictures or make a movie? Did he give you to someone else?

What did you **do**? Did you scream, cry, yell, lie there quietly, cooperate, fight, say anything, say "stop"? Did you "go away" or shut down? If it was ongoing, how did your reaction change? Did you make it happen or initiate? How did you comfort yourself afterwards?

What did you **feel** like? Confused, terrified, mad? Little and lost? Like you were going to die? Hateful, powerful, powerless? Trapped? Exposed, ashamed, humiliated, violated, betrayed? Guilty? Shamed? Used, rejected? Did you feel some pleasure? What was your strongest emotion?

---
356 I use "he" but it could be "she" or "they"

Did you lie or pretend to cover up the abuse? Did you tell anyone? How did they respond? Did they blame you, not believe you, call you a liar, ignore you, overreact and frighten you, let it go on, get help, confront the abuser? Were there people who could have helped but didn't? Why couldn't you tell your parents or their friends or a teacher or a minister or a coach? Did you do to someone younger what was done to you?

Were you told this is a game? Were you told this would be fun? Were you told this is what grown-ups do and you wanted to be grown-up? Did he tell you why he did it? *You asked for it when you had that drink/ the way you dressed/ you kissed me. Your mommy said I could. You wanted to. You have to because I am your dad/pastor/coach/teacher. Everybody does it. You said yes so you can't change your mind.*

Why do **you** think it happened? *Brown eyed men are evil, I wore too low a top, I was in the wrong place, I disobeyed my parents, I deserved it, I should never have gone upstairs/ downstairs/ into the bedroom/ in the car.*

Here are some effects of someone else's sin (**consequences** for being sexually abused). Did any of these things happen to you? Forgive these effects that you didn't ask for.

- Loss of innocence, feeling guilty, marked, different
- Frigidity, unable to respond sexually in marriage
- Promiscuity, dangerous or unsafe sexual partners, inability to say no, used to being used.
- Sexually transmitted diseases, chronic infections, physical damage to sexual organs
- Pregnancy, abortion, infertility, miscarriage
- Fear of things connected to the abuse–the dark, touch, nakedness, smells, sounds
- Isolation, broken relationships, fear of people, distrust of people's motives
- Defiance of authority figures (teachers, coaches, pastors) or rules and laws.
- The abuser was taken away through separation, divorce or jail time.

Friend, keep writing or keep talking. Go through the list again quickly if you think you missed something. Don't deflect it: you are getting ready to give it all away. Don't miss this chance to put it all on the table. Are you done? I am sure you are exhausted. Yet we must finish. Like the woman in the opening story, let's not bring up the mess without taking it to the cross and giving it away.

Handing Over the Trash

Having looked at the pool of pain, let's follow God's command to forgive. My friend, here is the final step to freedom. It's time to bury that dead body. It's time to give Jesus the worn

IOU. It's time to take it to the Supreme Court—the True Judge who is Just. It's time to be set free from the torment.

Go through the list of what you wrote or said about the abuse and release every detail, the whole thing, to God by forgiving specifically. You may want to physically hand it to God. Here is my example of forgiving the neighbor boys who held me down:

(I prayed) *Lord, I forgive the neighbor boys for holding me down and touching me. I felt overpowered because there were two of them. I felt tricked because we were playing and they turned on me. I felt ashamed as they looked at my naked body. I felt cold and frightened. It made me mad. I didn't know whom to trust anymore. I felt like an object and not a person. I felt different after they touched me. I remember the smell of the cut grass. The flowers were blooming around my head and I was angry that I was dying when they were blooming. I remember hanging my teddy bear after it was over. I was angry that I had been so naive. I was angry that I was so vulnerable and they wouldn't listen to me when I said stop. I felt like there was no safe place anymore. Beds weren't safe but now backyards weren't safe anymore either. I felt that all men were evil. I felt betrayed. I felt like it would not have happened if I had been a boy. I was angry at You, God, for making me a girl.*

I give you this whole horrible event Lord. I give You my pain, my tears, my anger, the abuse, the boys, the fear, the betrayal, the lies. I forgive them for robbing me of the joy of playing. I forgive them for making me feel like nobody. I forgive them for making me feel I had to protect myself from all boys because even friends who were boys were unsafe. I forgive them for stealing my safe place, for throwing darkness over the whole world. Lord I release it all into Your hand. Thank You for paying for their sin on the cross so I may walk in freedom and in truth; that I may be holy and blameless in Your sight; that I may not be forever marked by what man did to me but can live my life as You made me to be. Thank You Lord, that Your light overpowers darkness. I give You this dark place in my soul and receive Your loving light into my life. I receive Your love, Your joy, and Your peace. Thank you for making me a girl Lord, I receive this as a gift. Help me to see every day how You will work through me for my good, to glorify You and to help other people.

Do you see how specific I am? Give it all, give it all to Jesus. **Pray and go through your list**. Forgive each detail—every word, action, thought, feeling and response—and hand it to God. Then leave it all at the foot of the cross. Pray as you begin this process:

My Good Shepherd, please walk through this with me. Be gentle but be firm. Give me the courage to face the pain honestly. Don't let me rewrite history, or hold anything back.

I want to give it all to You. I want to open my hand to release it to You and receive with that open hand all the healing You have for me. I know it is an event (what I am doing today) and a process (more things will come to mind that I must forgive). But I stand today, ready to give it all to You.

Thank you, Jesus, that you paid for it all. I forgive the ways someone else's sin has affected me. I ask Your forgiveness for my sinful responses. Thank You that You came to bind the broken-hearted and set the captives free. Change my heart, oh God.

Well done! Do you feel like a train wreck? We call it "being run over by a Mack truck." You have done hard, spiritual work today. Take time to rest. Take a bath or a walk or a drive. Spend some time with Jesus. If you feel joy, then run with joy. If you feel sadness, then rest. If you feel free, then dance. You have done your part and God is doing His.

Finally, Freedom

We all stand together at the foot of the cross. You have been forgiven, and you forgave. You have pulled out weeds (were some of them trees?). You have cleaned out the basement and handed the trash to the Trash Man. Now, you no longer have the smell of smoke (abuse); you have the sweet aroma of Christ. Now you are clean—washed in the blood of Christ. You are a radiant Bride.

Mark this date in your journal, when you did a major work of forgiveness. Satan will try to tell you it was not effective, but I assure you (and God promises) that it was powerful spring-cleaning! Rest dear ones, rest in the bosom of your Lord. Then rise up to continue fighting for your freedom.

To the Friend of the Traveler:

1. Forgiveness is not something you can do for your friend. You can encourage or pray or remind them, but until they are ready, they won't do it. It doesn't help them to nag, badger, force or guilt them. Just be patient and pray, and don't rescue them from the negative consequences they will experience for being unforgiving. Be ready to walk with them when they are finally ready.

2. Even if they could only forgive one step or one part, it's still progress. Yes, they need to do more, but can you rejoice with them about what they did?

3. Remind them forgiveness doesn't make it okay, and doesn't mean they have to have

a relationship with an abuser. It means they don't carry the dead body with them anymore.

4. Has this chapter brought up anything in your life that is stinking up your basement? Do you need to go through the process about a divorce, or a wayward child, an accident or an unfair termination? Go through and forgive, and share that good news with your friend. All Christians need to forgive and receive forgiveness on a daily basis, not just abused people. Thankfully, God's mercy and grace are new for us every morning!

Worship Song: *In Christ Alone* by Travis Cottrell[357]

---

[357] Travis Cottrell, Jesus Saves Live, © 2010, Word Records www.youtube.com/watch?v=-RecJ79t4Oo (with lyrics) or www.youtube.com/watch?v=YhIatwjAxXo

Chapter 13
Intimacy—Drawing Close

Dear friend, how are you? Recovered from the "Mack truck" last week? I know last week was bitter/sweet: bitter from looking at the pain and sweet because you handed it to God. I wish I could say forgiveness was all behind you, but you should be prepared to revisit Chapter 12 again and again for different offenses (from the abuse and life). I think God in His mercy only gives us little bits at a time to forgive. I don't think we could handle all the effects of abuse if they were revealed at once. So as God reveals, we must forgive. Remember, forgiveness is both an event and a process.

The last turn in the road takes us through Sexual Intimacy before we end our journey. This is not the final chapter; it is the almost-final chapter. I didn't want to end on sexual abuse; I wanted to end on Freedom. Does it seem unfair that you are here? To be honest, I have put off writing this chapter. It is hard and embarrassing. Yet I want to help you find freedom and joy with your husband. How could I help others if I was still lost? How could I "say run to Jesus" if I wasn't willing to run to Jesus?

I know you may not want to walk into this arena either, but if you don't, you will sin against others. Your self-protective walls or your controlling, destructive sexuality will hurt the people you are called to love. Please note I use the word "intimacy" more than "sex" in this chapter. Intimacy as God designed has nothing to do with the abuse we suffered. It is like comparing a moldy hot dog to a perfectly cooked steak. They may be related—they are both food—but they do not have the same DNA.

Before we get to freedom, we must work through abuse's effects on our sexual intimacy. So let's unroll this tangled web of pain, confusion, fear, anxiety, anger, and childish, stubborn willfulness. First, let's pray. We need to approach the throne of grace to receive help.[358]

Lord, I am about to step into a sensitive, scary, yet sacred place. Give me wisdom, give me insight and love. Please hold my hand as I tackle this area of weakness. Protect my heart as I tear down self-constructed walls of protection. Don't let me settle in this shadowy place of death. Please let Your strength be shown in my greatest area of insecurity, fear and shame. Let me be who You made me to be and not who man made me to be. Give me courage where I

---

[358] Hebrews 4:16

lack, give me grace to do what I fear, hope to change from the inside out, and strength to fight for my freedom. Show me the way out, Lord, and I will follow. In Jesus' name I pray, Amen.

Priorities

Jim and I attended a marriage conference shortly after we began rebuilding our marriage. For a breakout session, the men and women went to separate rooms, each with the assignment to "List 10 ways you feel loved." The woman wrote quickly: talk to me, help with the kids, help around the house, take me out for coffee. When we read our list, the men were shocked. Where was sex? We realized it wasn't even on the list! The men, however, had it as number 1 (and later admitted it was number 2 and 3 as well). Just like the women wanted emotional intimacy, the men wanted sexual intimacy. That day, I realized I needed to "get with the program" because this is so important to my husband and my marriage. I no longer had the luxury of thinking it would all go away. I realized I was making my husband pay for someone else's sin and my heart broke as I saw more damage.

This was not a group of sexually abused women; this was a cross-section of normal women, and not one thought to list sex as a way they felt loved. This matches my experience in counseling women: they all struggle with their sexual expressions in marriage, but not all because of abuse.

To the Precious Single

Perhaps you are single or single again. You may think there is no need to step into this place. Yet your experience of abuse will affect your relationships too. It may also affect your relationship with your friends as they step into normal dating relationships and you find yourself filled with rage or fear for them. Your heart will scream *danger, danger* but it is not true. It is simply God revealing wrong thinking about intimacy. You need to learn what sexuality should have been, not what it was. You too need to renew your mind and wrestle with your emotions. You too need to see the past effects, then look at the good future. If God calls sex *good* (and He does because He created it) then we should too. So let's look at sexuality and drop fear and pain.

Sexual Purity

He chose us in Him... to be holy and blameless in His sight. (Ephesians 1:4)

If ever we need a "but God..." moment, it is now. Because you were abused sexually or responded sinfully to the abuse, you may believe Satan's lie that you are tainted, ruined, damaged goods, or only good for sex. God says the opposite: we can be "reborn and renewed," even in the area of our sexuality. The most tender spot in your soul, the place where it hurt the most, can be healed by the Wonderful Counselor.

1 Corinthians 6:9-11 compares the past with the present:

*...neither the sexually immoral nor idolaters nor adulterers... will inherit the kingdom of God. **And that is what some of you were. But you were washed, you were sanctified, you were justified in the name of the Lord Jesus Christ and by the Spirit of our God.***

God, the Restorer and Redeemer, washes and cleanses us from our sin stains, and makes us white as snow, holy and blameless in His sight (Isaiah 1:18). God calls us to not be sexually immoral, but to be pure in our sexual expression. I believe that means complete abstinence for singles and fullness of sexual expression for marrieds. Our bodies are a temple for the Holy Spirit to dwell in, so we should use our bodies in holy ways.[359] For singles, that means honoring God by keeping your body from sinful sex. In marriage, that means honoring God by loving your husband sexually, fulfilling his sexual needs and having your needs fulfilled.

Yah, Right!

For years, sex was a purely physical action I hated. Cris repeatedly said that intimacy should bring me pleasure. I *knew* she was wrong: "You want me to say something terrifying is good." I said that if you are frightened of roller-coasters, it doesn't matter if your friend says "it's fun," it's always a fear-filled ride for you. I didn't get it and I felt she was pressuring me. We weren't even talking about the same thing. My ride was an old wooden ride, where the car lurched from side to side as I boarded. There were no seat belts, so every bump jerked my body. When I reached the apex and looked to the tracks below, I had no confidence that the car would hold or that I could hang on and not be thrown to my death. Her ride was a different roller-coaster, like one at Disneyland; clean, smooth, fast—tight seat belts, padded headrests and a fun ride. They are both roller-coasters, yet one instills fear and terror, the other excitement and pleasure.

The wooden roller-coaster represents abusive sex; distorted, jarring, frightening, even cruel. The Disneyland roller-coaster is like sweet intimacy; starts with tenderness and excitement, then evolves to exhilarating fun and passion. The scary track was about fear and power and pain. The new roller-coaster is about shared enjoyment. So how do we move from pain to pleasure?

---
359 1 Corinthians 6:19-20

Fixing Your Mind

First, renew your mind in the area of intimacy. You need new thoughts. I know from years of habit that you can't go into this arena with old tapes running in your head. You have to face head-on that you have believed lies about yourself, the abuse and the abuser. You may not feel like doing this, but if you are married, you have to fight it. Fight your thoughts, your feelings and your fear, and move past them into peace. Let those emotions talk to you, but don't be controlled by them.

Little Carla made a decision about Uncle Frank's laughter, but her answer was wrong because she didn't have all the facts. If you were sexually abused, I guarantee that you do not have all the facts. Sexual abuse negatively warps your sexuality. You have twisted-wire thoughts that need to be untangled and old fears that are invalid now. You were not responsible for the abuse but you are responsible for your attitudes, thoughts and reactions today. Can you bring God's answers into the picture?

Thinking New Thoughts

I began to question what was good and what was ruined. Rom. 6:11-14 says *I was brought from death to life; so offer the parts of (my) body… as instruments of righteousness. For sin shall not be my master* (abuse, rape, old habit patterns), *because I am not under law* (duty, have to, 180's), *but under grace.* I read good books[360] about sex and replaced my old tapes with God's tapes. I put off thoughts such as "sex is only about pain, power, and perversion" and put on new thoughts like "intimacy is about giving, satisfaction and showing love." The battle for my mind was intense. Old thoughts do not die easily. Deep-seated lies were comfortable. Yet truth had to prevail.

I put my pride in my back pocket. I fought, argued, learned, forgot, took captive, absorbed, experienced, rejected, explored, reasoned, discussed, debated, claimed, contended, resisted, opposed, struggled, challenged, transformed, improved, changed, converted, re-started, repeated, recommended, vetoed, banned, and disallowed my thoughts about sex. Then I did it all again. It was not easy. But I wanted to be who God made me to be and not who man made me to be. So as often as I tripped, I got back up again. I am writing this book is to give you the tools I never had. Your course will run straighter and faster as you draw on God-given resources.

---

360 Intended for Pleasure by Ed and Gay Wheat, Revel Books, Grand Rapids, MI, © 1977
Strengthening Your Marriage by Wayne Mack, P & R Publishing, Phillipsburg, NJ, © 1980
The Act of Marriage by Tim LaHaye, Zondervan, Grand Rapids, MI © 1998

Using Tools

For some, years of lies, heartache, walls, control, and pain have built a sturdy fortress, a well-defended citadel. Satan's hold is strong in this area. You will not overcome this area with a snap of your fingers. Each journey is unique, a personal battle. Start by obedience. Ask God into your bedroom.[361] Fight the black shame and bring God's light and the joy of His love into your bed. I told myself again and again *"this is my husband, it is not my abuser. This is not the same as the past. This is something new, a good experience, a good gift."* I called the battle out. I named the lies. I grieved the things I had lost. I used my tools: *I refuse to be deceived by my flesh and will be led by the Spirit. I am responsible for my own thoughts and actions.* There were times, especially at the start when I had to stop in the middle of making love to run to the bathroom and throw up. My body fought against my plan. Yet, I refused to quit. Learn what you need to learn. Be thankful if you are not stuck in an area.

Loving Intimacy

...a man will leave his father and mother, and be united to his wife, and the two will become one flesh. This is a profound mystery—but I am talking about Christ and the church. (Eph. 5:31-32

The Bible often uses word pictures to explain deep concepts. Ephesians 5 compares a husband's love for his wife to Christ's love for His bride (the church = you and me. Let's look at intimacy through that lens. In the ideal act of intimacy, at the moment of ecstasy, the moment when your emotions and body rise up in union, there is a mystery of mutuality. Husband and wife both give and receive with freedom and joy and openness. There are no winners and losers. There is no shame or fear, no secrets, no walls, and no running. There is no joy mixed with sorrow, no pleasure mixed with pain, no good mixed with bad. We receive while giving, we delight while pleasing, we enjoy while thrilling. In that moment of ecstasy, the world around us ceases to exist, or to press in on our consciousness. We look beyond ourselves and within ourselves at the same time.

God designed sexual intimacy. He designed our bodies to respond, and created them so that we would find pleasure in the moments of sweet surrender. Intimacy woos the other to participate; it draws, loves and connects. It is not a moment of power but a moment of sweet surrender to each other. True intimacy brings two people into unity, while they remain distinct. Not diminished by the experience, but enriched and renewed.

---

361 Hebrews 4:16 *Grace and mercy to help you in your time of need*

The mystery in the uniting of man and woman is a picture of Christ's love for His church. I believe those moments are a taste of heaven, a shadow of the future reality. As Father, Son and Holy Spirit are in total communion, with freedom, joy and openness to be themselves—separate yet joined in perfect unity—I believe sexual intimacy is the main place that concept is seen in this world. It is a good thing, a sacred thing. It is the first glimpse of the wonder that is ours *when self has died, yet we are fully alive in Christ.* (Col. 3:3-4 God wants to pour love into us, in part through sex with a loving husband/wife.

I think that is why Satan has worked so hard to destroy the freedom, deprive the joy, and deceive us of the openness of intimacy. Friend, Satan has won in this area for years. It's time to resist the devil so he will flee from you. Sweet freedom awaits.

Five Facets of Sexual Unity

There are five areas of intimacy that were damaged by the abuse. First there is an **emotional** aspect of sex. Lovers want to express their love, and sex is a primary way. Sex is a unique God-honoring way that expresses deep affection to one's spouse. Proverbs 5:18-19 says, "May your fountain be *blessed*, and may you *rejoice* in the wife of your youth. A *loving* doe, a *graceful* deer—may her breasts *satisfy* you always, may you ever *be captive by her love*." Do you see sweet, loving intimacy in this verse? Or do you feel used, ashamed, empty and trapped? As a victim of abuse, I absolutely missed the emotions. Sex was a duty, an expectation or an obligation. Intimacy out of love for Jim was not in my toolbox. It's hard to be intimate when you are walled-up tight.

Second there is a **spiritual** aspect, which the Bible explains as *the two become one.*[362] God designed sexual intimacy as a gift, like a glue that binds a husband and wife together. A married couple has a unique connection in the spiritual realm, and a special blessing from God over their relationship. While this is good news for marriage, it is horrible news for victims of sexual abuse. Sinful sexual contact also forms a spiritual connection. I didn't want to be one flesh with my abuser, but I was?

This quote from Chapter 4 also applies to abuse: "To us (demons, a human is primarily food; *our aim is the absorption of its will into ours, the increase of our area of selfhood at its expense....*"[363] I felt like a weaker vessel absorbed into the stronger vessel. The abuser's personhood increased while I was destroyed. I disappeared, and was a non-person. I was not valued or cherished; I felt violated, lost, overpowered, destroyed and ravaged. I hated the connection of the present to the past. I avoided it and fought it every step of the way. It

---

[362] 1 Corinthians 6:16
[363] The Screwtape Letters, C.S. Lewis, Touchstone/ Simon and Schuster, New York, NY, © 1961

explained why I had trouble letting go of the abuse, but it also made me mad. Yet staying mad wouldn't set me free. I asked God to sever the connection. Perhaps you should stop now and ask God to break any unholy spiritual bond between you and the abuser. Write a certificate of divorce because the union was impure. Read it outloud.

Seen and Known

Third is the **relationship** aspect of intimacy. The biblical word for intimacy is *to know*. Gen. 4:1 says and *Adam **knew** Eve his wife; and she conceived*. Jesus described a close, intimate relationship with God the Father in John 17:3: "*This is eternal life: that they may **know You**, the only true God, and Jesus Christ.*" Intimacy is a good thing, connected with being known, being seen, and being touched. Doesn't your heart cry out to be known? Not in the way you were hurt, but the way that God created you to desire Him and know Him? Intimacy is a taste of that.

The fourth area of sexual intimacy is **physical sensations**. Because I had stopped feeling my body years ago, I had to re-train my body and my mind to feel hot, cold, tiredness, pleasure, even itches. I was completely disconnected from normal sensations. I rubbed my arm but felt nothing. I held my husband's hand and tried to feel his fingers in mine. Some of you were so confused about the changes that took place in your body and the abuser's body that you shut down your feelings. Or your body responded positively to the touch, but you were horrified at the pleasure, and shut off your feelings. Perhaps you didn't have the capacity to process all the sensations, so you "shorted out" and stayed there. One way to change is to pay attention to the sensations your body feels. (I put them on a scale of Good 1 to 10 and Bad -1 to -10.) Maybe you can keep a journal and be encouraged when it feels good more often than bad. Remember, baby steps.

One of the gentlest moments of healing in my journey came when I realized Jesus was betrayed by a kiss. A close friend and companion betrayed Jesus with intimate touch. Jesus sympathizes with betrayal.[364] He knew the heartache and destruction yet entrusted Himself to God who judges justly.[365]

The fifth area of intimacy affected by abuse is **memory**. The body has memory, skin has memory and the mind retains memories in "files" of events. In the beginning, I changed my actions during sex, doing the best I knew how. My husband received it as a gift and a sacrifice. Then, as I cleaned out past hurts (by facing them honestly, forgiving, renewing my mind), my thoughts about sex changed. I realized there was no **shame in**

---

364 Hebrews 4:15
365 1 Peter 2:23

sex with my husband; he didn't feel shame, and he thought I was beautiful. I could keep myself intact (I didn't have to self-protect by going away). Then I began to feel pleasure too, so I felt like my body was normal. My feelings and reactions changed, which drew us closer, which made it easier the next time. I replaced old memories of abuse with new, sweet, pleasant memories, which I could think about the next time we were intimate.

All five parts are affected in abuse. They all can be changed to be normal in good sex. Sexual abuse is sin. Sin destroys, causes fear, robs and leaves us in pain. But abusive sex is *not* intimacy. Baby steps toward intimacy and trust in a God who calls it "good" brought me these truths.

Christ-like Intimacy

"As a Christian physician, it is my privilege to communicate an important message to unhappy couples with wrong attitudes and faulty approaches to sex. The message is this: **"You have God's permission to enjoy sex within your marriage."**[366] (quoted from Intended for Pleasure)

When Jim is intimate with me, he is very gentle, very considerate, patient, tender and sweet. Does that sound like the fruit of the Spirit? Could this also be a picture of Christ's love? He doesn't force, he draws. He pays complete attention, he is fully present. He desires to draw me to intimacy. His desire is to be in me, one with me. Doesn't Christ desire those same things? For us to open our hearts to Him that He may dwell in us? That we may be one with Him as He is one with the Father? He wants us to receive with open hearts all that He has for us; to receive the gifts that He gives.

From the husband comes the seed of new life. Isn't that a picture of God's gift of new life? Is his release a picture of God's release of power that creates something new in us? Are we not new creations?

As women we often don't have the same desire as our husband. Isn't that a picture of us not having the same desire for intimacy as Christ has? Aren't we often cold to His love, too tired, or bored? Aren't we often distracted by the world—our kids, our jobs, household chores? Don't we often give Christ leftovers rather than our first fruits?

Could the sexual tension between a man and a woman reflect the tension between Christ and us? Rarely at the same intensity, Christ always in pursuit, Christ always available?

---
366 Intended for Pleasure, Ed Wheat, Revel Books, Grand Rapids, MI, © 1977, page 14

Could the woman yielding to her husband's tenderness be a picture of the church yielding to Christ? Is her willingness to say yes to her husband a picture of us saying yes to God? Is her willingness to be persuaded to be intimate a picture of our willingness to be persuaded by God?

Could the sweetness of the union be a picture of the unity we have with Christ? Could the desire to please her husband be a reflection of our desire to please Christ? Could the desire for relationship in a woman's nature reflect our need for a relationship with Christ?

Could the urgency we feel reflect Christ's urgency to see us mature, to come to completion? Could the sweet surrender to the passion be a picture of the willingness of Christ at the cross, the passion of Christ? Could the explosion of joy be a picture of true joy in His presence? Could the sweet tenderness and closeness you feel after intimacy be a picture of the rest you have in Christ? Could the bond you feel be a picture of the security we have in Christ?

These new thoughts left me reeling. Yet they also gave me great hope. It was a Joshua 5:14 moment: *"then Joshua fell facedown…in reverence and asked Him, "'what message does my Lord have for His servant?'"*

Christ with Skin On

Can you look at intimacy through the lens of Christ loving the church? When Jim makes love to me, he is a picture of Christ's love for me. He is being Jesus to me "with skin on." His love, His kindness, and His gentleness are being displayed to me through Jim's touch, his words, and his treatment of my body. Making love with me, Jim is being Christ-like at that moment.

Perhaps your husband is not kind, gentle or loving. Perhaps he does not desire to be intimate; he pushes, demands, is selfish or rejects you. Perhaps he does not represent God's love or desire to you in any way. Let me help you with that. Often, as abused women, we tend to choose our mates through the lens of pain. Did you choose a quiet man because you never wanted to be overpowered? Did you choose a violent man who recreated the abuse in your home?

Jim came from an alcoholic home and was pretty distant from me emotionally for years. If you married before you dealt with the effects of your abuse, there is a good chance your husband has issues of his own. If your husband is not kind, do you know a friend who is kind? Is your pet gentle? Is your sister loving? If you had children, do you remember the desire your baby had for you and you alone? God always provides other ways for us to understand His love. Look for ways God reveals Himself to you through others. Can you speak into the situation and ask your husband to change? Can you address what he does that hurts you, and tell him your preferences?

You should know that as I changed and Jim did not, our marriage was difficult. I reminded myself that I had changed, so I kept loving him, growing and following God. Over time, Jim has joined me, not because of nagging, or anger, or put-downs, like in our early years, but because God worked in his life too.[367] You as a wife don't carry the whole weight of responsibility for the quality of the sexual act. Your husband needs to do something—be kind, patient, or woo you, say "I love you," understand your body, etc. But your husband doesn't read your mind. You will need to tell him.

If you will not reconsider intimacy in the light of what God intended it to be, you won't change. If you wait to change, you never will. Weeks become months, months become years, years become decades and you will never enjoy the sweet wonder of God's gift.

I learned to wake up my body and wrestle with my thoughts. I questioned and was pushed.[368] I did it wrong and learned to do it right. I took risks and was stubborn. But friend, I can tell you with certainty; it won't come to you without effort, without Jesus, without His power or without your obedience. Remember the children of Israel spent forty years in the desert because they were afraid to obey God and fight for their promised land. Have you spent forty years in your sexual desert because you are afraid to be on God's side? Like Joshua, God isn't going to join you on your side; He is calling you to His.[369] Will you choose to fight this battle God's way? Will you march around your Jericho? Will you obey the call of God?

Being Connected

When I detached intimacy from its God-given purpose of love, closeness and mutual pleasure, I missed out on God's plan. It was just an action with my body but there was no spirit-to-spirit connection. When I was sexual with Jim but wasn't really there (either by going away or pretending), I detached the action from the relationship. It was simply a performance or a duty. Can you see Satan's trick there? I did the hard work but missed the blessings; I got nothing out of it because my heart was closed. *Shut up and do it* was an old tool that never worked for me. Intimacy requires a death to self, to 'my way,' to

---

[367] Some major marriage issues will surface as you change. Getting good Biblical counseling for these issues is essential.
[368] I would have never have found freedom in this arena if Cris had not consistently, persistently, persuasively challenged my thoughts and attitudes. It has taken me years, but I pray your trip will be much shorter than mine.
[369] Joshua 5:13-14

lies, habits, survival techniques, rules, pretending, and every trick in your survival kit. Freedom only comes when we give up so we can graciously, generously give to another.

Sometimes I asked Jim if I could initiate instead of him for several months. When it seemed like it was always "on the table" I felt agitated, annoyed and out of control. I committed to him that I would initiate twice a week. That way, I could have easy days, knowing that nothing was going to happen. On the days I decided (or had waited so long that it was deadline time I had time to prepare myself, to talk to myself, to run to Jesus and ask for His healing. I used several of my tools at that time: *I have a choice and a will* tool, *the Bible is the source of Truth* tool and *renew my mind* tool. Was it easy? No. But I began to experience the difference between intimacy and sexual abuse.

In order for intimacy to be the best and to honor God there has to be a connection between everything; body, soul, and spirit. Marriage brings opportunities for dependence, trust, faithfulness, words, communication, knowing each other, being able to ask for something or tell each other your needs, give-and-take, encouragement, teamwork, joy, laughter. Marriages as God designed them are a picture that enable others to understand the Father's love. The fruit of the Spirit, love, joy, peace, patience, goodness, humility, faithfulness, and self-control will mark our relationships. Gone is the hatred, despair, enmity, impatience, evil, pride, perversion and selfishness of our previous lives. We are ambassadors for Christ, revealing the true nature of a loving God to a fallen world.

Aroused Too Soon

Daughters of Jerusalem, I charge you… **do not arouse or awaken love until it so desires.** (Song of Solomon 2:7, emphasis mine

The past brought another problem: God does not want sexual intimacy to be aroused until the time is right, but abuse awakened us (turned on our "light switch" too young—before we had the tools to know what to do with the feelings, before we had the right words or the power to make decisions. God's plan is for married adults to be sexually intimate, but we experienced sex outside of both marriage and adulthood. How does this affect us now? Many sexually abused women are tigers in the bedroom before marriage and cold fish afterwards. They were turned by something illicit (forbidden and now struggle to be satisfied in routine sexual relations.

Pretending

We are also plagued by deep-rooted pretending. We pretend enjoyment when we hate it; connection when we aren't present; satisfaction when we are filled with distrust and disgust. We pretend we don't feel the shame, abasement, degradation or fear when we are really choking on it. As a child, I pretended the abuse didn't happen. At school, I pretended nothing had happened the night before. I pretended my home was normal and I was normal. Abuse silenced me, and locked me in a prison of lies. I kept the secret. As a married woman, I drank to endure. The numbness of alcohol relaxed me. Once I stopped drinking, I had sex with my husband because it was my wifely duty; it was important to him. So my ways were checking out, pretending, then drinking, then duty.

All my detective work finally revealed a terrible truth: fear of rejection had bound me. I kept doing the same things and hating the result. But I was terrified my husband would reject me or humiliate me as my father had. That big fear led to all the other fears; punishment, being seen as less than, fear of the unknown, fear I would be like my parents. It was the puzzle piece that made all the others fit. I saw the foundational lie in this. My husband loved me and we could work together to find the new life.

What is your way? Do you check out, plan shopping lists, honey-do lists, trips to take, friends to call? Do you solve work issues or kid concerns? Do you take it, waiting for it to end? Do you denigrate it to match the blackness in your soul, imagining rape, torture, or being watched? Do you squeeze your eyes shut and cry? Do you make up rules to hide yourself? Do you pretend it's someone else? Do you numb your soul with alcohol or drugs or cut later to punish yourself? You have other tools my friends. None of these things are good tools.

Flesh or Spirit?

The flesh, the world and the devil have a mighty victory in this arena. You can't walk down the street without seeing some twisted picture of the world's sexuality. I heard Beth Moore say that young women struggle with the same issues she fought in her sexual abuse, but they haven't been abused. Her answer? Our *culture* has abused our women—from TV shows to rap music, teen magazines to casino billboards. Sex bears little resemblance to the sweetness God intended. Internet pornography invades. TV programs flash skin and innuendoes; presenting sex as seductive power. Advertisers know sex sells. The flesh distorts and degrades our sexuality. It pulls toward lewdness, impurity, debauchery, and immorality.[370] The flesh twists what is good and distorts it towards bad. The pull of the flesh is real and needs to be mastered. Sex is a tool of destruction in Satan's hand but is a gift of love in God's. Satan distorts what God meant for good.

---

370 Galatians 5:19-all deeds of the sinful flesh.

When my son was in private Christian school, a new boy enrolled because two girls from his public mid-high school were already pregnant. Sexting is Satan's game: young girls taking naked pictures of themselves, sending them into the world with no understanding of what can happen. How could these young people know what they are throwing away? They are giving away precious gifts and gaining nothing. That has Satan all over it.

A Precious Gift
"Woe to him who quarrels with his Maker.... Does the clay say to the potter, 'What are you making?' Does your work say, 'He (the Creator) has no hands'?" (Isaiah 45:9)

I was angry at God for making me a weak, vulnerable girl. I believed Satan's lie *if only I had been born a boy I wouldn't have been abused*. Yet God created women different than men. Different does not mean less than, it just means different. Women are weaker vessels[371] physically and emotionally, yet we have equal value to God. God's design is for men and women to complement each other, not compete. The cross is the great leveler: no matter what anyone says, we are all the same at the foot of the cross. A wife is God's gift to her husband, as well as God's representative to him.[372] We are receivers, who respond well to being loved.[373]

I believe as we receive the precious gift God has given us, our femininity, with open hands, we will be shocked at the wonderful gift He has bestowed on us. Abuse often robs us of our womanhood, closing our hand to what God has given us as a priceless blessing. There really are only two choices. Be the woman God made you to be; tender, vulnerable and giving, or become like a man, hard, powerful, and controlling. Will you receive the priceless gift of being a girl?

As you change, your spouse may be pleased with the changes he sees, or he may be very unhappy with you. Either way, I encourage you to keep moving forward. God will heal you, mature you and call you to wholeness. Maturity in Christ will help you be a better wife and mother.

As I have fought the battle towards freedom, God revealed another stronghold: denial. I told Jim I needed to hear encouragement; that he could see the changes I had worked so hard to make. So he complimented me about one of our intimacy times. A normal person would be encouraged, but I freaked out. Poor Jim, I had asked for words, but reeled when I heard them. As I prayed about it, it became clearer. Pretending was such a deep-seated

---
371 1 Peter 3:7
372 Genesis 2:18- *helper* A study of the Hebrew word is of incredible insight to our role in our marriage
373 The word *husband* comes from the word *husbandry*, to tend a garden. We respond well to good gardening.

habit that a word of truth cut through the deception. When Jim complimented me, I had to look at the truth: **I *am* a sexual being.** God wouldn't let me *pretend* to change; God wanted me to see that I *had* changed. I didn't need to hide behind the wall of protection anymore. I am a woman, deeply loved by God and her husband, and wired, by God, for intimacy. I could believe truth and change. I could speak truth and live.

Desire

One morning, during a serious discussion on intimacy in our little group, one gal mentioned how deeply our husbands desire us. By 5 pm I was "gone" and I had to unpack my reaction. What made me go away (in fear) was thinking about Jim's desire for me. That was the last thing I wanted. Desire was the enemy, the reason I got abused. I hid myself from desire, just as I did as a child. To be desired meant that I was going to be destroyed, become an object, be used, overpowered, and plunged back under the icy waters of despair. Yet after years of punishment, Jim still desired me! The desire has never stopped. Jim desires intimacy with me; it is in his very nature. His desire for me is a picture, a reflection, of how God desires intimacy with me.

It was a *red rose moment*. I had to examine what had happened. Why had God created man to desire intimacy? So that I could see a picture of Christ. How grateful I am that God never quits. He pursues and pursues and pursues. We blow it and run away yet He calls. We build walls yet He still woos. Jim's desire is a picture of how Christ desires. That consistency, that steady craving, is not a bad thing. So what went wrong? Why did I fear it? Desire is not wrong, but lust is. Lust is a fleshly twist on the good thing God created. It is right to hate lust, and say no to it. But God wanted me to think differently about Jim's desire. It is not evil; it is a sweet example of God's desire for us.

I have argued with God about how He made Jim. I have wanted Him to take Jim's desire away, and remake him without desire. I have lived thinking that *all* desire was bad and needed to be eliminated. But I know a woman who has a loveless marriage where her husband doesn't desire her in any way. Do you want to have a marriage like that? Would you really want to be married to a man who no longer desired you? For years I wanted to be Jim's roommate, not his wife. But now, having a biblical picture of sexual intimacy, with new thoughts, new understanding, and new insight, I am sad that I almost missed out on what God wanted me to learn about His love.

Mindful Change

One week Cris began to ask me some tough questions. Since I could never remember them, she finally typed them out. These questions were forged out of our hard conversations. I know you will feel embarrassed by some of them, as I did. But again, anything worth doing well is worth doing badly. So grab your will, join hands with Jesus, and read:

Pick maybe two to concentrate on every time you make love:

What do you hear? Even small sounds
What do you feel?
What is one sensation?
How does your husband smell?
What does his skin taste like?
Is the taste different on his neck or his chest or his back?

How does your skin feel?
How does it change?
How do your lips feel and change?
Do your husband's lips feel different after kissing for a while?
What does the inside of his mouth feel like?
What does his tongue do?
What movements do you like the most?
What is your level of arousal?
Do your desires change?

Which do you like better, when he touches you with his hands or his lips?
Does your husband kiss your neck differently than your breasts?
What are your hands doing? Are you feeling what they are touching?
What makes you the most excited to touch? Your husband's back, hair, face, hands, lips, private parts?

How does your body move?
Does that change from beginning to end?
How does your voice sound? Relaxed? Frustrated? Teasing? Frozen? Childish? Sexy?
Does that change from beginning to end?
How relaxed are you? Any tight muscles? Release and relax them
Does movement make the pleasure more intense or shut it down?
What does your breathing sound like? Does it get faster or slower?
What does his breathing sound like? Does it get faster or slower?

How long does it take for the feelings to fade away afterwards?
How does your body feel different afterwards? Trusting,
    thankful, happy, satisfied, tired, needy, disappointed?
Do you feel closer to your husband after?
How does your spirit feel after? Stronger? Peaceful? Feel God's joy over you?

What are your thoughts during, after? At what point does it change from duty to delight?
What do you think about, and how does that intensify or reduce the pleasure?

When you review the intimacy, what are the highlights you dwell on?
What do you say your husband after?
Does your conversation change?
Do you encourage him in what he did well?

Whew, bet you're glad that list is done. Well, as you know, it isn't about reading and knowing (head knowledge) it is about doing and knowing (heart knowledge). So these assignments may take time to complete. Maybe you will not need the detail. I am thrilled for you. But there are some, like me, who need great help in this area and this list will move you. Friend, you do not have to arrive today. You don't have to succeed in every area. My motto is simple: I don't want to be the same person I was 6 months ago. I want to change, heal, grow and mature. Our goal is not perfection but direction. Our goal is No More Excuses. No more blame-shifting. It's time to move forward to truth and freedom. Wewant to glorify God in every area of our life and that includes intimacy.

Going Away

During the course of my journey, I realized that I "check out" during sex. I just disappeared. I went (I thought) to a safe place, deep within myself. I began to understand that during abuse, in the moment of terror, the basic instincts of fight-or-flight take hold. If you can't physically fight and can't physically take flight, the only option is to take flight within your mind. That is what "going away" does. It takes you to another place. However, over time I began to realize that being checked out is not God's way. In fact, I realized that the only voice I heard in my "safe place" was the voice of Satan. Only he talked in my distant land.

Going away was a very deep-seeded habit. What began in the bedroom had spread, in true black-dot form, into much of my life. If I was frightened anywhere, anytime, I went away. Hardly the response of a warrior princess of the King! So I renewed my mind. I asked the Holy Spirit to show me when I was going away and when He did, I made the choice to stay. The Holy Spirit would hold up a mirror and show me I had zoned out again. Once I realized I had gone away, I had to look at the situation that had caused fear to erupt. Once I saw it, I took the tools and applied the truths I was learning. I stopped running, turned and fought for freedom.

If you have ever watched the movie *The Matrix*, there is a time when Neo stops running from the agents, turns and starts fighting them. No one had ever fought the agents before without dying. Yet Neo, finally understanding who he is (the One), fought for his freedom. In many ways, this whole book is an attempt to teach you to fight God's way rather than run away. Remember, the only way out is through.

Focus

Once aware of these bad habits, I began to isolate the feelings. Did I hate everything or just some things? This is where Cris' list of questions really helped. Rather than an overall "I hate sex" mentality, I focused in on my body and my feelings. What really made my skin crawl? What was pleasant? Here's an example: it frightened me to make love at night. Once I realized that, I spoke with my husband about it. What do you think his response was? Yes, he was 100% in: he wanted to help any way he could. We tried making love in the morning, or adding candles, or planning for the middle of the afternoon. I hated being woken up to make love (no surprises there) so we worked together to make things easier for me.

Remember, you are not alone in this battle. Once they understand, most men are very willing to help. It may take some awkward discussions but it will help immensely. Small changes may help you in huge ways.

Speak

On my journey to freedom, God's command to "Speak" was a constant challenge for me (Prov. 31:8). Speak at work, speak to my son, and finally, speak in the bedroom. I wish I could tell you it was easy for me to talk to my husband and I enlisted his help right away but I didn't. Remember, I am a teacher. I teach Bible studies and accounting at a local community college. So you would think I could speak about sexual things with my husband. Ha! Freedom did not come easily. Yes, abuse victims are strange creatures: inconsistent, indestructible, intense, insecure, injured, and inspiring.[374] It is this strange mix that confuses those around us. If you are confused, imagine being someone who loves you! So if you struggle to speak, take baby steps. This book was written to give

---
[374] And anyone who knows you, and reads this, says, "Amen!"

you words and word pictures to help you explain what has happened. Perhaps you could have your husband or friend read this chapter and say, "That's me." If that is too hard, underline what is true about you and give it to them. My prayer is to open up the lines of communication and save you years of pain. I don't want you to miss out on God's gift to you because you can't get over the wall of fear.

As a child my nickname was "Chatty Kathy" but as an adult, I rarely spoke about things that mattered to me. Only in moments of abandon would words come easy. When someone hurt or scared me, I was paralyzed–unable to speak into the situation. Cris challenged me to talk to Jim, to discuss things about intimacy with him. It felt like climbing Mount Everest. Very slowly, I began to have simple conversations with him. In the dark bedroom, when I couldn't see his face, I told him very small things. Just to say "I don't like when you put your full weight on me" felt impossible. Yet I was able to get through those small conversations, and graduated to bigger ones.

One victory came when I realized that I don't always have to use words. I could make sounds to tell my husband that I liked something or turn my face if I didn't like it. I could pull him towards me or push him away. I had to choose to sound foolish (put my pride in my back pocket) and admit that I really didn't know simple things. I had to explain my feelings when I felt nervous or curious. I chose to fail, then try again. I recently realized there is no failure in this area. My husband is pleased and content, and doesn't look at me as "less than" or as a disappointment. He appreciates my every effort. Pleasing him sexually is one of the easiest things I do.

Excuses

I also had to fight my excuses. *I'm too tired. I've had a hard day. I'm too stressed about the kids. There are people in the house. I have a headache. I'm mad at him. There is too much going on. I don't like it. It takes too much energy. I'm exhausted...* Friend, I am sure you have a few as well. Yet as much as we try to think they are valid reasons, bottom line, these are excuses because *I don't want to.*

Friend, how would you feel if your husband said to you, "I don't want to love you or be kind (or compassionate or gentle or merciful) to you"? You would be devastated. Yet, somehow, we justify our selfishness with "I don't want to." I know this sounds hard, friend, but it is not about what you want but about what God wants. And He says "Yes."[375]

---
375 1 Corinthians 7:3-5

Headway

Along the journey I realized that I had trouble "starting my engine," getting the pump primed. I knew that women were slow cookers and men were microwaves but my slow cooker wasn't even plugged in. I was tempted to go back to old tapes, old tricks, and old methods but I knew it was wrong. So how did I prime my pump?

Go back to where it went wrong. For me that meant the very beginning. Genesis 3:25 says *the man and his wife were both naked, and they felt no shame.* So I worked to get used to my husband's nakedness and my nakedness without feeling shame.

I also realized that I needed to think about intimacy throughout the day rather than five minutes before bedtime. If you are a planner, plan for intimacy that night. If you are fun person, think about how much fun it will be. If you are a doer, plan to do. If you are someone who "goes with the flow," then jump into the flow during the day. Slow cookers need time! The more I planted thoughts about our intimacy all day—what I would say to Jim, how good his hands would feel, how my body would respond, how we would cuddle afterwards and talk from our hearts—the more I looked forward to what I had imagined.

After I had some victories, I realized I needed a spark of electricity that flowed through my body to plug in my slow cooker. That spark, the moment I felt "turned on," was a normal and good thing. You may know that, but for someone like me, so confused in this area, even the "doing what comes naturally"[376] did not come naturally. I leaped forward when I moved from T-shirts to pretty lingerie (on special occasions). I always thought it was to excite him, but I was surprised when a pretty nightgown really helped me fire up my slow cooker—and it makes me feel beautiful. One of many nice surprises with sweet intimacy.

It's a Party

I asked God to give me His picture of intimacy. He reminded me of my baseball team after we won Provincials: jumping up and down, hugging, joy on our faces—a huge celebration. I immediately saw the contrast: my locker room was deadly serious, silenced by the heartache and disappointment of a humiliating defeat. I approached intimacy as a death, instead of something that could bring me life. Intimacy is like a wedding not a funeral; like a party not a wake; like a fun-filled day of skiing, not a stressful day of taking final exams.

---

[376] A song in my Poofy file from the movie, *Annie Get Your Gun.*

Perhaps, instead of being serious like I was, you are annoyed, bored, hard or depressed. You don't have to tell the winning team to smile, to hug each other, or jump for joy. The party flows freely from within. Good intimacy is high-fiving, hugging, back-slapping, inside joy that bursts out. That's your goal: to celebrate!

Associations

After a while, I did not feel shame being naked and I worked on celebrating. But I still had a major hurdle: my thoughts were self-destructive. During intimacy I thought about random things—work, kids, cleaning, laundry, shopping or taxes. I took those old thoughts captive but what thoughts should I put on? I didn't want to go back to bad old habits so I looked to the Bible, the Song of Solomon, which describes married sexual love with sweet word pictures:

Let him kiss me with …his mouth – (his) love is more delightful than wine (1:2)

Foreplay—His left arm is under my head, and his right arm embraces me (strokes me) (2:6) Your lips drop sweetness as the honeycomb, my bride: milk and honey are under your tongue (4:11)

Feeling beautiful—Come north wind… and south wind… Blow on my garden that its fragrance may spread abroad. Let my lover come into his garden and taste its choice fruits. (4:16)

After sex—I have come into the garden, my sister, my bride; I have gathered my myrrh with my spice. I have eaten my honeycomb and my honey; I have drunk my wine and my milk. (5:11)

Playfulness—I am my lover's and my lover is mine; he browses among the lilies (6:3)

Passion—Your stature is like the palm, and your breasts like clusters of fruit. I said, "I will climb the palm tree; I will take hold of its fruit." …your breasts (are) like the clusters of the vine, the fragrance of your breath like apples, your mouth like the best wine. May the wine go straight to my lover, flowing gently over his lips and teeth. I belong to my lover, and his desire is for me. (7:7-10)

This is just a sampling, there were many more. I memorized these, not to know them, but to pull thoughts into my mind to help me prime my pump. What a difference it made when I thought of my husband as a gardener enjoying tasty fruit, or browsing among my lilies! I still ponder the joy of belonging to my lover, as his joy for me is evident. I like to think about my breasts as grape clusters that intoxicate my husband. These sweet word pictures arouse delight, joy, and pleasure over a sweet union. Amazingly, thinking about kissing, fruit, wine, and honey helped a whole lot more than the latest crisis at work or my son's newest problem.

Fall Forward

I watched a movie called *Hope Springs*, about a couple who has been married 30+ years and are trying to bring intimacy back. They start out as quiet, dead roommates: no intimacy, no touching of body, soul, or spirit. After some counseling, the husband plans a romantic evening in a fancy room with a fireplace, wine, chocolate-covered strawberries and special music. Yet despite his efforts, it was a colossal failure. Frustrated, broken and defeated, they sat on the counselor's couch the next day. But rather than calling it defeat, he saw victory. "When I met you, you weren't even on the playing field. Last night you fumbled the ball on the 1-yard line. Good job!"

Your intimacy is not going to always be successful. Intimacy is like life; good times and bad. Sometimes you will have great strides, like an 80-yard pass, but other times, you will grind out some plan and lose 5 yards. The most important thing? Stay in the game! Don't throw up your hands or punish yourself for your failure. Don't say you're done and won't try again. Don't sulk or stomp around because it is hard, or pout because it wasn't as sweet as you wanted it to be. Call out to Jesus. Run into the throne of grace and ask for His help, in your time of need. Fall forward into your Savior's arms rather than back into the pond of despair. As Gary Thomas said in *Sacred Marriage*,[377] "If you are going to fall, fall forward." If you fall—and you will—fall forward. Keep moving, keep trying. God is on your side. You will eventually experience victory.

Losing Yourself

I want to talk to women who experienced abuse over a long time. This is not for the one-timers but rather for the women who were caught in that hopeless trap of repeated abuse. The three years of abuse with my dad was unrelenting, overpowering, and deadly. Under its pressure, I lost my sense of being, hope and purpose. I became an object. I existed more like an unwanted dog than a child. In that place, I fought for a measure of control, and found it. I realized, with childish thinking, that if I "helped" my dad, I could make it go faster. I couldn't stop it, but I could control the length. That tiny measure of control meant everything to me. It gave me life, hope and purpose; a reason to live. I remained a separate person rather than being absorbed into my father's

---
[377] <u>Sacred Marriage</u>, Gary Thomas, Zondervan, Grand Rapids, MI, © 2000

will. A lie was planted in my heart that control in sex means life, personhood, and protection. So how open do you think I was to losing control in sex? Giving up control meant being absorbed, overpowered, used up, then disappearing. So a brick wall was built around that childhood lie. No amount of reason, persuasion, argument, or love could penetrate that wall. What did you do to keep yourself during the abuse? What gave you a measure of control? Can you turn it over to God?

Honoring God in Intimacy

For from Him, and through Him and to Him are all things. To Him be the glory forever! (Romans 11:36)

Barb's paraphrase: For from Him comes intimacy, and through Him flows intimacy, and to Him is intimacy, for His glory.

Let our intimacy bring us closer to God. If you are married, let the time with your husband be a gift of worship to God. If you are single, your heart can be sweetly drawn to your Heavenly Husband. May we draw near to God as we would draw near to our husband. May we be open and yielded and enjoy our time together as we would drink in the sweet fellowship of communion. May our love be a taste to the world of God's love. We are ambassadors for Christ; does that calling extend to our bedrooms? May every aspect of our lives be lived for Him.

Friend we are moving from duty to delight. That can only come when our thinking is right, our will is engaged, and we are fully surrendered to God. I know it will take time. Let us yield ourselves to Him, let us submit to God, let us say yes to Him. Let's fight with His weapons, with His power, for His glory.

So why is there sex? My childish explanation was so that there would be babies in the world. My adult explanation is; to display the mystery of Christ and His love for us.

Bottom Lines:

1. Use your tools in this area.
2. Sex and intimacy are different.
3. Intimacy is a taste of heaven, a picture of God's love for us.
4. Take baby steps.
5. Find joy.
6. Fall forward.

Discussion Questions:

1. How do you glorify God with your body (as a married or a single)?

2. Is there an area in your life that keeps you at a distance from your Heavenly Father? Can you address it now and forgive the sinner and draw closer to God?

3. Which of the five areas in sexual intimacy were affected during your abuse? Can you pray for God to restore a godly understanding of all five?

4. What parts of this chapter do you need to forgive your abuser(s) for? Can you do that now, and give them to God?

Friend of the Traveler:

1. If your friend trusts you enough to talk about this chapter, you should be happy. Listen to her questions or confusion and re-read what we have written, or see if you can answer her questions from your own intimate experiences.

2. Remember that intimacy has been twisted for her. Try to untangle the wires-in-a-jar, and remind her that sex is supposed to be a sweet blessing, not torment.

3. If she is single, help her understand why God wants her to be celibate (have no sexual contact). Show her the blessings from obeying God in this area.

4. If she is married, help her come up with a plan to change one or two areas. Encourage her a lot! Don't get mad or frustrated if she drags her feet. Remind her that her sexual experiences can change if she takes little steps.

Worship Song: ***Draw Me Close to You*** **by Kelly Carpenter**[378]

---

[378] Draw Me Close to You, by Kelly Carpenter, performed by Michael W. Smith. © 1994 and 2004, Mercy/Vineyard Publishing, www.youtube.com/watch?v=B2q5SrprcvY

Chapter 14
Open Road Ahead—Freedom

So if the Son sets you free, you will be free indeed. (John 8:36)

I believe every Christian has a desert experience. We pass through the punishing heat, and finally stand at the edge of the Promised Land. We scope it out—we see its fruit and its wonders, but we also see how the way is blocked by powerful people and fortified cities.[379] Do you look but never enter the Land and take it; never walk in the freedom God has for you? Christians must learn the lessons that can only be learned in the desert: God is Sovereign and in control. God's ways are not our ways. God will lead: our job is to follow Him and trust Him.[380] God will discipline us along the way.[381] God provides and wants us to remember His provision, and not become proud.[382] God drives out our enemies, not only by our power, but often in spite of us.[383] God wants us to fear Him, obey Him and walk in His ways.[384] When we cross over the Jordan into the Promised Land, He will give us rest.[385]

Friends, our goal has been to walk you through your desert. Now it is time for you to use the tools you've learned to cross over the Jordan River and into your Promised Land.

Are We There Yet? Yes ... and No

One summer years ago, I lay on a blanket and felt the sun's warmth on my face. I pondered my long spiritual journey. God had lifted me out of the pit of despair, and I had worked hard to learn things that helped me get out. Now I could bask in the warmth of His love, resting on the soft ground. Just then, God revealed a mountain ahead of me. *Good grief* I thought, *what is that mountain?* I realized it was the mountain of maturity, the journey of every saint. My climb out of the pit had brought me to the place where most Christians *start* growing. I was weary of climbing, yet I wanted to ascend the mountain. "Yes, Lord" was my answer to His call from the peak.

---
379 Numbers 13:27-28
380 Deuteronomy 1:29-33
381 Deuteronomy 8:5
382 Deuteronomy 8:6-14
383 Deuteronomy 9:3-6
384 Deuteronomy 10:12
385 Deuteronomy 12:10

As I began to climb, an interesting thing happened: I passed other Christians—women who had grown up in the faith. They stumbled over small obstacles. A harsh word from a friend turned their ankles. A snub for a promotion was a chasm that they could not cross. A hard marriage, a rebellious child, or a financial downturn left them stuck on a cliff, paralyzed. Yet, onward I climbed toward maturity. *Why?* I wondered. *Why me but not them?* Then I realized the answer. *Because the tools you use to get out of the pit are the same tools you need to climb the mountain of maturity.*

One woman described her life as "walking in a river of poo." She wanted out of it like I wanted out of my pig slop. Desperation pushed me to move. Other Christians with an easier life couldn't handle minor suffering because they had never matured through a major suffering. My anguish had become a blessing. When I needed to forgive a harsh word from a friend, I had already forgiven my dad—how hard was it to forgive that friend? When I was snubbed for a promotion, I had already learned that I work for the Lord, not for man—how hard is it to be passed by? When I lost the chance to adopt more children, I had already learned to be content in the circumstances of barrenness; this was just another disappointment.

My Life, From the Other Side

My testimony in Chapter 1 was written so you could relate to me. I wrote it from my perspective, and I tried to build a bridge from *you to me*. Using a lot of "sanctified guessing," my testimony in this chapter is written from God's perspective. I hope it will build a bridge from *you to Him*.

God placed me in a hard family of unbelievers, so I could drink my fill of the world's solutions to problems. He let me feel the sting of harsh rebukes, sharp criticism and hateful words, so someday I would temper my words. He had created me to react to injustice and violence, which I did, but not under His control. That would come later.

God planned for me to go to church, not a "real" church, where His Son was known, but a church where I had seeds of Bible truths planted in my heart. They stayed in my heart and grew, but they did not in the rest of my family. In the suffering of my home, God called me to Himself.

God saw my mother reach for me out of a drug-induced fog. He heard my soul make its first vow: *no matter what it takes, I will make my mother love me*. He called it good that I craved love, and saw the time years later when I would feel real love. He created me to be stubborn and strong; a pioneer.

God saw my father come into my dark room and take me, wound me and terrify me. He marked that abuse on my father's soul and cried at my sin scars. He saw my weak state, He heard my pitiful cries and He comforted me through my soft cat and my special safe tree. He knew Satan would throw everything at me so I would to be strong in the Lord, not weak. He called me to Kingdom work so I had to be a tenacious fighter with a will of iron.

He showed me the evil heart of all men, not just my dad, when the neighbor boys trapped me. I went too far and called all men "evil" (and most women) but I needed to know by experience, not just words, that all people have sin natures. He knew I learned better living through it than just listening to words.

Then His Gifts

He brought me joy by making me good at sports, even though I'm short. Sports gave me a way to get out of the house, and feel good for something. Playing games let me express my strong passion in acceptable ways. He taught me how to work with others as a team—useful in the church.

He orchestrated my life so I would find Him, placing a girl who loved me and loved to tell the gospel next to me at work, two summers in a row. He knew I would respond to His invitation to be loved. He showed me the answer isn't in the church people; it's in Him. He wooed me, taught me, rebuked me, corrected me, and trained me in righteousness. He knew I would believe the lies of the world—that my problems were from without—but He loved me so much that He allowed me time to discover my real enemy; the enemy within. He called me to point others to Him.

He knew I would learn my lessons the hard way. *Why listen to someone else when I can do it my way* seemed to be my motto. He knew I would fall, but He called me to get back up again. He called me to persevere, keep moving forward. He did not waste my tears, or my life. He called me to share those tears with you, to reach out to all who suffer from the scathing effects of sexual abuse. He knew I would meet many with skinned lives and skinned hearts. You wouldn't want to hear easy answers, spoken from an ivory tower but you would listen to someone who had been down the dark alleys of life and found they were nothing but dead-ends filled with spiders and snakes.

He used my anger to keep me alive, even in a smoke-filled garage with the car's motor running. As long as I was angry, I kept attacking people's words, trying to get to the core of their faith. I examined their beliefs until I found truth. I held truth and compared it to other true truths, opened my Poofy File and applied it to my huge stack of "Unknowns." Then He let me struggle to conquer my anger and let it die, replaced by kindness and compassion that reflects His nature, not mine.

When I chose to marry Jim out of a desire to seem normal, God smiled because He knew that many of my lessons would be learned with him. He knew how often He would bless me through Jim, and how I would humble myself and change to be more loving. He was excited that I would receive love and pass on my love to our son. He knew my son and my husband would help me knock off the rough edges of pride, anger, control and selfishness. He knew that my last big struggle would be in the bedroom, where I learned that intimacy was His expression of desire and love.

A New Family

He sent people to help me. Not perfect people, but women who faithfully led me to Christ; Melanie, my Moses, and Cris, my Joshua. They saw my good and my bad. They called me to life, to love, to Him. They prayed when I gave up, "spanked" me when I powered up, counseled me when I rose up, and loved me when I messed up. He taught me (through them) that no one goes the whole way with you. God knew I would be part of your journey. Some people water, some plant, some fertilize, and some pick flowers. I know I am only one of His helpers in your journey to freedom. I have prayed, pushed, counseled and loved you. I want to help you find Him too. Whether I am your Moses or your Joshua, I pray I have helped you find your way to the Promised Land.

He let me go down the path of Christian psychology and find its dead-end. He wanted me to be able to compare it to the power of His Word and the changes through the Holy Spirit. He knew you would be blinded by it too, so I had to be able to take off your mask.

He created me to be a teacher. He knew that once I tasted the freedom of forgiveness, I would never stop telling others. I consistently, persistently point people to Christ so that they can find the freedom that forgiving their abuser brings. I am a one-string guitar with a one-word chorus: Forgiveness.

My Abundant Life

I cannot change the heartache of my life. I cannot change yours. But I can call to you, "Come and see that the Lord is good." See how God has used my heartache for my good and yours. Where Satan has stolen, God has restored. When man has hurt, God has healed. Where I have fallen down, God has lifted up. I hope you can see *the wonder of Christ in me... the hope of glory*. (Col. 1:27)

> I am not a victim of sexual abuse; I am a victor in Christ.
> I am not a secret keeper; I am a truth speaker in Christ.
> I am not a scared little bunny; I am a risk-taker in Christ.
> I am not a mess; I am a messenger of Christ.
> I am a willing vessel, once broken but now renewed.
> I am a willing voice, once silenced but now proclaiming strong.
> I am a willing servant, once paralyzed but now well-used.

Freedom's Daily Effects

The remarkable thing about God is that when you fear God, you fear nothing else, whereas if you do not fear God, you fear everything else. (Oswald Chambers)

Here is my description of Freedom now:

- I can ask for forgiveness quickly. When God convicts me during the Bible study that I have sinned, I can take correction from teaching, listen with discernment, and repent. (Psalm 119:33-40)
- I see how God stops me from sinning. He sends "stop signs." I speak my frustration in the quiet and don't blow up and take out people in anger and frustration. (Jude 24)
- I can receive correction when I sin. When God convicts me, I can quickly repent, turn away, and do the right thing. (Prov. 12:1)
- I don't have to hide. I don't feel condemnation, shame or guilt. I don't have to pretend or put on a mask so that people don't see me. I am free to be the new Barb—Christ in me. (1 John 4:18)
- I am not afraid of failing. I don't fear being known, or making a mistake or being seen as less than or having my sin revealed. I am free to take risks. (1 John 2:12)
- I have joy and peace. I have contentment in my circumstances and joy every day. My starting point every day is joy. I am free to enjoy life. (Phil. 4:4)
- I can run into life rather than running from life. I can step into difficult situations, not be dominated by feelings, but led by God. I am free to be His ambassador. (2 Cor. 5:19-20)
- I have more capacity to do things. I do not carry heavy loads of unforgiveness or other people's suitcases. I am free to run with my backpack of responsibility. (Gal. 6:4-5)
- I know what the Word of God says and I want to obey it. I don't do it out of guilt or duty or fear. I am free to obey God because I love Him. (James 1:22-25)

- I can see situations more clearly; I am less deceived, more teachable, and more knowledgeable. Life is less confusing, less grey, more clear. I am free to think biblically and willing to listen to the counsel of others and the Word. (Psalm 119:18)
- I can self-counsel. I don't listen to the lies, I tell myself God's truth, I am not afraid of what lies ahead because I know Who lies ahead. I am free to walk into life. (Psalm 119:29-32)
- I have died to self. I don't live for me. I don't trust my heart. I don't believe my own press. I am free to live for Him. (Gal 2:20)
- I don't hold the world so tightly. Jobs, health, friends, family, finances, and fame do not own me. I am free to love God with my whole heart. (Matt. 6:19-33)
- I no longer trust in my own heart, my own thoughts, my own desires. I am free to trust Him with my life. (Prov. 3:5-6)
- I can talk about my sexual abuse without shame, fear, lies, pretending or anger. I know it is in the past, I have forgiven it, I do not carry it any more. I can use the lessons I learned to help you get free. I can use my life as examples of good choices and bad ones. I am not a victim anymore. (Phil. 3:13-14) I was sinned against, and have forgiven.
- I can make love with my husband without shame or fear. I know I am a sexual being. I know I glorify and honor God when I share myself with him sexually. (Song of Solomon)
- Freedom is Christ—His love, His life, His power, His goodness, His mercy, His grace, His humility, His tenderness, His compassion. Just Christ. (1 John 4:16)

I have learned that staying free takes as much diligence as getting free. How do we stay free? By continuing to deepen our understanding of our position (children of the King), our power (Holy Spirit within us), our process (maturity through suffering) and our purpose (to glorify God).

Freedom From Inside

I used to believe freedom came from outside—freedom from pain, heartache, sin, drama, and bad people. I thought I would be happy if my life were free from trials. But happiness is not a godly goal. The root word of happiness is *happenstance*—the circumstances of life. When my happenstance was good, I was happy. When it was not good, I was not. Yet God wants us to live beyond our circumstances. He wants us to live in joy in freedom. But our world is not getting better, it is getting worse. Things will not improve, they will continue to decline until Jesus returns. Freedom comes in our response to life, not life itself. Freedom is a choice. It is an inside job, a heart issue.

Freedom Means Finding the Righteous Way Through

No temptation has seized you except what is common to man. And God is faithful; He will not let you be tempted beyond what you can bear. But when you are tempted, He will also provide a way out so that you can stand up under it. (1 Corinthians 10:13)

Freedom comes from *knowing* God will provide a righteous way through every trial. God will provide the way; our job is to find it, walk in it; drawing on His strength, His power and His nature so He will be glorified as we walk. God doesn't take away the trials; He grows us in the trials. Our prayer is not, "Lord, take away the trial;" the prayer is "Lord, how can I glorify You in this trial?"

Freedom – No Longer Tossed To-and-Fro

Freedom is having the anchor that holds in the storm. Ephesians 4:11-16 says:

(He gave different gifts) ... to prepare God's people for works of service, so that the body of Christ may be built up until we all reach unity in the faith and in the knowledge of the Son of God and become mature.... Then we will no longer be infants, tossed back and forth by the waves, and blown here and there by every wind of teaching and by the cunning and craftiness of men in their deceitful scheming. Speaking the truth in love, we will in all things grow up into Him who is the Head, that is, Christ. From Him the whole body, joined and held together by every supporting ligament, grows and builds itself up in love, as each part does its work.

When we are anchored to Christ, He holds in the storm. He fastens in the light of false doctrine. He joins us as we love others and work together to serve Him.

Freedom is Living All-Out for Jesus

Therefore, as God's chosen people... clothe yourselves with compassion, kindness, humility, gentleness, and patience. Bear with each other and forgive whatever grievances you may have against one another. Forgive as the Lord forgave you. And over all these... put on love... Let the peace of Christ rule in your hearts...and be thankful. Let the Word of Christ dwell in you richly... teach and admonish one another in all wisdom... sing, psalms, hymns, and spiritual songs with gratitude in your hearts to God. And whatever you do, whether in word or deed, do it all in the name of the Lord Jesus, giving thanks to God the Father... (Colossians 3:12-17)

God's love flows through us because Christ lives in us. We are no longer the empty cup screaming to be filled; we have broken out the bottom of the cup so God's love can flow through us to others. We are no longer paralyzed victims, walled sufferers, or vengeance-filled women. We learn to live as God made us to be. We practice forgiveness daily and live in the wonder of being forgiven. We love others. We let Christ's peace rule in our hearts. We are thankful. The Word dwells in us richly and we speak with wisdom. We live for Jesus alone. Our identity is not broken mirror, but a brand-new mirror. We no longer crawl but are free to fly for Him.

God's Process – Maturing Through Hardship

What causes us to grow? Is it age? Do you know older people who are still petty, mean or hard? Is it Bible knowledge? Do you know smart people who are sarcastic, bitter, and arrogant? Is it business success or finances or fame?

In the chapter on Emotions, we looked at our emotional response to suffering. Here, we look at suffering as the means God uses to bring us to maturity.[386]

In bringing many sons to glory, it was fitting that God…should make the author of their salvation perfect through suffering. (Hebrews 2:10) The word "perfect" comes from the root word *teleios*, which means adult, full-grown, maturity. Christ was brought to perfection by suffering, and we are being conformed to His image.[387] So, God uses suffering as a tool to help us grow. Responding to suffering in a godly way will bring maturity.

Paul Tripp writes that there are five sources of suffering:[388]

> We suffer because *we live in a fallen world* plagued by disease, natural disasters, dangerous animals, broken machinery, etc. We suffer because of *our own flesh*…we make choices that make our own lives painful and difficult. We suffer because *others sin against us*…from subtle prejudice to personal attacks…We suffer because of *the Devil*…the enemy in our world, a trickster and a liar who divides, destroys, and devours. He tempts us with things that promise to give life but actually destroy it. We suffer because of *God's good purpose*. God calls his children to suffer for His glory and for their redemptive good. (all italics added)

We cannot, and should not, try to avoid suffering. Escape is futile. An easy pain-free life is not reality. The world doesn't have an answer for suffering. The world runs from it. Yet God embraces and uses suffering. You probably know Romans 8:28 but do you

---

[386] James 1:2-4
[387] Romans 8:28&29
[388] Instruments in the Redeemer's Hand, Paul David Tripp, P & R Publishing, Phillipsburg, NJ © 2002, page 144

know Romans 8:26a? It says the *Spirit helps us in our weaknesses.* God told Paul, *'My grace is sufficient for you, for my power is made perfect in weakness.'* (2 Cor. 12:9-10) Paul got it, and said, *"I will boast all the more gladly about my weaknesses, so that Christ's power may rest on me. That is why, for Christ's sake, I delight in weaknesses, in persecution, in difficulties. For when I am weak, then I am strong."* Maturity means we can approach suffering from God's perspective, through God's power, and with God's purpose in mind.

God's Goal for God's Girls

Praise be to the God...the Father of all compassion and the God of all comfort,[389] who comforts us in all our troubles, so we can comfort those in any trouble with the comfort we have received from God. For just as the sufferings of Christ flow into our lives, so also through Christ our comfort overflows. (2 Corinthians 1:3-5)

Friend, each journey will look different but the goal is the same: maturity in Christ, so you can do the good works God has preplanned for you. God has work for you to do. He didn't heal you just to be healed. He matured you to do His work. I don't know the work you will be called to, but I know *the nature* of the work: *Comfort others with the comfort you have received.*

Sin remains. Women are hurt. Be part of the solution, friend. Extend a hand of grace to a stumbling sister. Teach her what you have learned. Shorten her journey, lighten her load, and give hope to her weary heart. Melanie told me early on my journey that she held one of my hands so I had a free hand. I could grab the hand of someone behind me and lead them to God. Now, I speak often, openly and honestly about my past. Why? Not to tell of my pain, but to proclaim my God. Teaching and speaking are ways to grab *your hand* and show you how to really live.

God has placed you in that Sunday school class or Bible study or with that neighbor whose marriage has failed, or with that young girl whose life reminds you of yours at that age. You can speak into her life with the confidence of one who knows the journey. You can tell her there is hope ahead and lead her to the Hope-Giver. You can use your gifts, your experience and knowledge to draw her to the One who redeems and restores. Be Christ's ambassador of love to a lost and broken one. Listen for the language of pain and speak the Language of Mercy. Take her by the hand, be Christ incarnate in her life.

---

[389] The Greek word for comfort is *paraklesis* (Strong's #3874): "The act of calling toward or hither to help, begging, and also exhortation, encouragement toward virtue. (All) Scripture is a *paraklesis*, an exhortation, admonition, or encouragement for the purpose of strengthening and establishing the believer's possession of redemption ...to strengthen their faith." The Complete Word Study New Testament by Spiros Zodhiates, AMG International, ©1991

Once I sat with a young girl who was raped two months earlier. I asked, "How do you get out of the pain?" She had no idea. So I taught her about forgiveness. I urged her, loved her and held her heart as I spoke difficult truths. Can you imagine the years of hurt she will escape if she chooses forgiveness? What joy there was to take the hand of someone so young and lead her to God's truth, love and power. Freedom in months, instead of years! My sisters, you have the opportunity to be God's hands and feet, His voice and His heart, to a suffering people.

You will pass many butterflies who are crawling instead of flying. I pray you will stop on the way and help those dear sisters who are paralyzed or in despair, and give them hope to be a transformed butterfly. Point them to God and His ways. As we share our stories—proclaim our Savior and Lord—our maturity will call them to do those hard things; to take risks, to jump in faith, to follow Him. Changed lives and true maturity give others hope. Women often tell me it is my good life that encourages them to keep trying. Your walk, your ability to say, "I *know* forgiveness is hard, I know the struggle and the heartache but I *also know* the freedom and the joy" can bridge the gap for those who are on the other side of pain. Your words are not empty, your life is not shattered, your hope is real, your faith is functional, and your love is deep. Bring them to the other side, God's side, of suffering. At least point the way.

Leaving the Chains Behind

Not that I have already obtained all this or have already been made perfect, but I press on to take hold of that for which Christ Jesus took hold of me. Brothers, I do not consider myself yet to have taken hold of it. But one thing I do: Forgetting what is behind and straining toward what is ahead, I press on toward the goal to win the prize for which God has called me heavenward in Christ Jesus. (Phil. 3:12-14)

Many Christians quoted "forget what is behind" or "forget the past," when I tried to talk about my sexual abuse. Man, it frustrated me! I had tried to forget the past but it kept being my present. I tried to press on toward the goal but the chains of pain held me back. I strained toward Christ but I stumbled over sin. One night in desperation, I called out to God. "Lord, this verse must be true because it is in your Word, but I don't understand it. Help me!" In my spirit, I heard *Read the next verse*. So I looked at Philippians 3:15: "All of us who are *mature* should take such a view of things." When you are mature (*teleios* again), you will be able to forget what is behind. Not that I never remember it, but in the sense that it is part of *your past*, not your future. Your future is to press onward towards the goal God gave you in Christ Jesus.

Friend, God's goal is to bring you to maturity, forget what is behind and press on toward the goal. You will no longer be chained to the past or burdened by the pain. You will be free—gloriously free—to proclaim your Redeemer who has worked wonders for you.

Growth and Change

I believe at the start of your journey the abuse consumed your thoughts. Now it's not a pot bubbling on the stove, but more like a picture hanging on the wall. You can show others the picture; describe the people, the location and the background. But it is only a picture of the past, not a scene from your present life. There are days you walk by and don't even notice it. As you walk in a godly way through the trial of abuse, it fades into the background. You don't go back and wrap yourself in the chains.

Take a look at your life before you read this book, and after. Hopefully you have moved more toward the right:

Curses_____Blessings
Bondage_____Freedom
Shame_____Grace
Confusion_____Choices
Disobedience_____Obedience
Angry at God_____Love for God
Tricked into Satan's will_____Following God's will
Victim_____Victor

Release From Captivity

Jesus said: *The Spirit of the Sovereign Lord is on me, because the Lord has anointed me to preach good news to the poor. He has sent me to bind up the brokenhearted, to proclaim freedom for the captives and release for the prisoners.* (Isaiah 61:1, Luke 4:17-19)

Our prayer, Friend, is that your broken heart has been restored, your prison walls of fear are down, and you have been released from the prison of pain. You are out of the pit. You can feel the solid ground beneath you. You have powerful tools and have tasted God's goodness. But God has even more for you…

…to proclaim the year of the Lord's favor and the day of vengeance of our God, to comfort all who mourn, to provide for those who grieve in Zion – to bestow on them a crown of beauty instead of ashes, the oil of gladness instead of mourning, a garment of praise

instead of a spirit of despair... be called oaks of righteousness, a planting of the Lord for the display of His splendor. (Isa. 61: 2-3)

My friend, God wants to proclaim the year of the Lord's favor on you, called the Year of Jubilee.[390] In the Old Testament times, the Jubilee was a whole year of celebration, every fifty years, where land was returned to original owners, slaves were released from their bondage, mortgages were erased and debts forgiven. The land rested and the people celebrated freedom all year.

Right after the "Year of Jubilee" this verse proclaims "the day of vengeance:" God will take revenge, and judge those who have sinned against us without repenting. He removes the ashes of past pain, despair and grief. We can leave it in His hands, so that our hands are free to receive the crown of beauty, the oil of gladness and the garment of praise.

Instead of their shame my people will receive a double portion, and instead of disgrace they will rejoice in their inheritance; and so they will inherit a double portion in their land, and everlasting joy will be theirs. (Isa. 61:7)

God will give a double portion, remove your disgrace, the painful inheritance and you will rejoice in your inheritance as adopted children of the King. Everlasting joy can be yours.

Staying Free

It is for freedom that Christ has set us free. Stand firm, then, and do not let yourselves be burdened again by a yoke of slavery. (Galatians 5:1)

My picture of freedom is this: God has given us a huge playground, many acres in size, with wonders and fun and places of rest and places of meaningful service. The playground is covered by His grace. Around that playground is a huge fence called Love that protects us from Evil, outside the fence. Evil and Sin clamor to get in; deceive us to come out. What joy and peace there are within the walls of Love. Yet for most of us, the pull of Evil draws us away from peace and joy to heartache and strife. Freedom is living within the Borders of Love. It means living in the Land of Grace, and speaking the Language of Mercy.

You have everything you need to live in the Land of Grace. Your heart has grown to God-sized. You know how to renew your mind so you can be transformed. You have learned to take your thoughts captive to the obedience of Christ. You can do the Word, obey it and

---
[390] Leviticus 25:13

practice it. You know what parts you are responsible for and what parts God is responsible for. You can choose forgiveness over anger and bitterness. You trust God. You love Him more. You are free to worship Him with all your heart, soul and mind. You surrender to Him and live for Him. You have found freedom–true freedom: freedom in Christ.

Keep doing these things. Keep on standing firm in the faith, and don't let yourself be pulled back into your old habits. Don't carry that old yoke of slavery for even one minute. Don't toy with familiar "favorite bad feelings." If you slip back into the old chains, I think you will find you don't like it anymore; old sins don't feel good when you have tasted Freedom.

Climb That Mountain

He will lead you up the mountain of maturity in the same ways He pulled you out of the pit. He will straighten your path[391] and level the ground.[392] You will be clothed with strength and dignity, and can laugh at the days to come.[393] Your life will reflect the wonder of God's power and purpose. You will be a living testimony that God reigns.

> So what began with a crawl has become a race we can run well.
> What began as a step has become a journey.
> What began with fear has become faith.
> What began as a heartache has become a heart-beat.
> What began with our effort has become His provision.
> What began with 30 bad days a month has become 28 good days a month.[394]
> What began as a broken spoon has become a garden tractor.

I love you my Friend and I'm so proud of you for having the courage to go on this journey. God will bless your socks off! Be an ambassador of hope to others. Live well, love deeply, and light the way. Proclaim His mighty power. Welcome to Freedom!

Bottom Lines:

1. Suffering purifies and grows us
2. Submit to God's purposes
3. Help others to find Hope and Freedom
4. Put the past behind you

---
391 Proverbs 3:6
392 Proverbs 4:36
393 Proverbs 31:25
394 You know your number, this is mine ☺

Discussion Questions:

1. What descriptions of Freedom can you relate to? Are you there now? What description of Freedom speaks to you the strongest?

2. How do you respond to suffering? Review the explanations of suffering on pages 258-9 and make a plan to practice one.

3. What does Christian maturity mean to you? How do you see yourself growing and maturing?

4. How has God comforted you? Who is in your life today that you could share this godly comfort with? Will you call her or meet with her this week?

Friend of the Traveler:

1. Freedom is a continual process. Your friend may find freedom in one area, while remaining chained in others. Rejoice with her, and keep praying. Are you ready to go through the book again, so she can find more freedom?

2. Give a small gift or momento to celebrate finishing the book. Sign and date it.

3. Praise her when you see her enduring suffering in godly ways—it's a very good sign of growth. Pray together and look for ways God answers her/your prayers.

4. If she is done with her journey (either because she's free, or because she wants to stop), you have a free hand to be able to help someone else. Pray and look around at who is in your life. Offer her your hand, and open Chapter 1….

Worship Song: *Take the Shackles Off My Feet* by Travis Cottrell[395]

Song of the Stone Wall (Helen Keller, 1910)

I understand the triumph and the truth
Wrought into these walls of rugged stone.
They are a miracle of patient hands,
They are a victory of suffering, a paean of pain;

---

[395] Shackles by Erica Atkins-Campbell, Trecina Atkins-Campbell, and Warryn Campbell Copyright: © EMI APRIL MUSIC INC. © IT'S TEA TYME MUSIC © THAT'S PLUM SONG © WET INK RED MUSIC performed by Travis Cottrell, album Travis Cottrell

All pangs of death, all cries of birth,
Are in the mute, moss-covered stones;
They are eloquent to my hands.
O beautiful, blind stones, inarticulate and dumb!
In the deep gloom of their hearts there is a gleam
Of the primeval sun which looked upon them
When they were begotten.
So in the heart of man shines forever
A beam from the everlasting sun of God.
Rude and unresponsive are the stones;
Yet in them divine things lie concealed;
I hear their imprisoned chant:--

"We are fragments of the universe,
Chips of the rock whereon God laid the foundation of the world:
Out of immemorial chaos He wrought us.
Out of the sun, out of the tempest, out of the travail of the earth we grew.
We are wonderfully mingled of life and death;
We serve as crypts for innumerable, unnoticed, tiny forms.
We are manifestations of the Might
That rears the granite hills unto the clouds
And sows the tropic seas with coral isles.
We are shot through and through with hidden color;
A thousand hues are blended in our gray substance.
Sapphire, turquoise, ruby, opal,
Emerald, diamond, amethyst, are our sisters from the beginning,
And our brothers are iron, lead, zinc,
Copper and silver and gold.
We are the dust of continents past and to come,
We are a deathless frieze carved with man's destiny;
In us is the record sibylline of far events.
We are as old as the world, our birth was before the hills.
We are the cup that holds the sea
And the framework of the peak that parts the sky.
When Chaos shall again return,
And endless Night shall spread her wings upon a rained world,
We alone shall stand up from the shattered earth,
Indestructible, invincible witnesses of God's eternal purpose."

The Language of Mercy	The Language of Condemnation
Authority	**Authority**
-Christ has all authority yet uses it for the good of others not himself. Authority is a gift to protect and to serve.	*-The abuser has all authority. He calls the shots and the shots are all about what he wants, when he wants it, and how he wants it.* Authority is my right to use and to destroy without question.
Brokenness	**Brokenness**
- When I am broken, God will lift me up. God doesn't want me to be broken so that I am defeated and useless, He wants me to get to the end of myself so that He can help me. He wants me to call out to Him in my brokenness so that He can be my strength in my weakness.	*- You are defective, useless, hopeless, a waste of time.* You are of no value. You should quit trying and die. Nobody cares for you. You are unworthy and unwanted. You are such a loser. You can't do anything right. You are broken and can't be fixed. Give up. Nobody wants you. You are all used up.
Correction	**Correction**
– To help someone who is on the wrong path, to lovingly put your hand on theirs and teach them the right way to go.	*– To be yelled at, to be hit, to be screamed at that you are wrong again and again.* Correction has no moral compass, it changes with the emotions of the one in charge. What was right yesterday, may be wrong today. You are such an idiot, you are beyond help. You don't need to be corrected, you need to be destroyed because you are wasting space.
Daughter	**Daughter**
– A sweet term of endearment for a female child. Lovingly close.	*– A person forced to be in relationship with an angry man because he is her father.* A trap with no escape.
Discipline	**Discipline**
– Discipline is loving correction. It is training and teaching so that the harmful behavior is not repeated. It is explained and modeled so that one being corrected can mature.	*- Discipline is punishment.* It is harsh and mean. It is removal of good things with the explosion of bad things. It is physically and emotionally volatile.

Father	Father
-Father is a wondrous term. He is a defender, protector, provider, and anchor of the family. He never stops loving us. He is selfless and wants what is best for us. He uses his power to protect us. He would die for us.	*– Father is a frightening term.* He is the accuser, the decimator, the stealer, and the destroyer of our family. He never stops loving Himself first. He is selfish and only wants what is best for himself. He uses his power to get what he wants. He will kill us to get what he wants.

Failure	Failure
- Failure is part of life, part of learning. We often learn more from our failures than from our successes. Being human means we will fail. Anything worth doing well is worth doing poorly first.	*- You are a loser.* You will never succeed. You should stop trying. You should be ashamed of yourself. You have embarrassed me by your failure. You are such a disgrace, I wish you had never been born.

Forgiveness	Forgiveness
- *Forgiveness is a gift.* It is a choice you make to not remember the sin done to you. It is not conditional on the sinner's repentance. - *Forgiveness is handing the offense over to God.* It is receiving His payment for the debt, and releasing the obligation to Him.	- *Forgiveness must be begged for.* You have to prove to me that you will never do this thing again. I will only forgive you when you do it right. *– Forgiveness means I will let it go right now but I will bring it up later when I need to.* Forgiveness means that you will always have to pay in the future. It is not removed from you permanently, only temporarily. I have the right to bring it up again when I need to.

Forgiveness of sins	Forgiveness of sins
- Paid for once for all. Jesus paid the penalty of all our sins, all our sins, once for all. We don't have to do penance or add anything to what Jesus has paid. We are asked to repent, to turn from the sin, but we don't have to pay for the sin. God looks at as with love, even when we fail.	*- You must condemn yourself for your sin.* You have to run away from Jesus until you have beat yourself up enough to show him how sorry you are. You have to condemn yourself and punish yourself for your sin. God sees you as a failure and is disgusted that you still can't do it right. He expects you to pick yourself up by your bootstraps and try harder.

Justification	Justification
- *God sees me just as if I had never sinned.* Jesus paid it all. **Noah** In theology, remission of sin and absolution from guilt and punishment; or an act of free grace by which God pardons the sinner and accepts him as righteous, on account of the atonement of Christ.	- *God secretly holds my sins against me.* He says that He forgives me but he never ever forgets. He has a big stick and can't wait to let me have it when I sin.
Kindness	**Kindness**
- *It is a fruit of the Spirit, God's love to us.* It is gentleness extended to us, not because we have earned it but because it is in the heart of the person giving it to us.	- *It must be earned.* I will be kind if you deserve it, if you have earned it, it I feel like it.
Love	**Love**
- *Love is a gift, it is not earned.* It is in the heart of the Giver. Love flows out of the heart of the giver, it is not what is earned by the other person. If someone doesn't love you, it tells you about their heart not being able to love, not your worth of not being lovable or your inability to earn their love. God loves because it is His nature. God loved us while we were still sinners. Jesus died for us while we were caught in our sin. The Father in the Prodigal did not turn his face from the son but watched earnestly for him. His heart was moved with mercy and tenderness towards his prodigal son. - *God's love woos me to Himself.* God loves me unconditionally in spite of knowing all about me. Rather than condemning me for my sin, he paid the penalty of my sin so that I could run to Him. Once wooed by his love, I show my love to Him by choosing to obey Him. There are no strings attached with love. There is no fear in His love.	- *You have to earn my love.* You have to perfect for me to love you. If I don't love you, it is your fault. You have to perform for me to love you. My heart is hard and mean unless you do something to soften me and make me love you. If you do it wrong, love will be removed from you. - *Love demands.* Love punishes. Love yells. Love is jealous. Love is envious. Love withholds. Love manipulates. Love overpowers. Love is selfish.

- *Love gives.* Love gives the benefit of the doubt, love believes the highest, love covers sin. - *Love protects.* True love will die for another, in another person's place. Jesus died for us.	- *Love takes.* Love believes self, love looks for fault, love exposes your sin for all to see. - *Love protects self.* If you loved me, you would do take the hit for me.
Sanctification	**Sanctification**
- *Christ lives in us therefore we are sanctified.* We are fully sanctified because Christ lives in us. God sees us as whole sanctified because He sees Christ in us. God wants us to live so that what is in us flows out of us. **Noah** The act of making holy. In an evangelical sense, the act of God's grace by which the affections of men are purified or alienated from sin and the world, and exalted to a supreme love to God.	- *I have to try harder, work harder, pray harder, read my Bible more, sacrifice more.* It is all that I can do for God. God may have forgiven my sins before I was saved but it is up to me and my strength and my knowledge to live the Christian life. I must work harder.
Enemy	**Enemy**
-*Someone who puts their desires ahead of God's and pulls you away from God and His love.* We have few true enemies.	-*Anyone, anytime, anyplace. One who was close can become one in the twinkling of an eye.* Trust no one, never, ever. All have potential to be your enemy if you have what they want.
Obey	**Obey**
-*God's call of our life. He gives commands and as His servants desires that we will lovingly obey them because they are best for us.* God knows us and loves us and wants what is best for us and knows that if we will follow His ways our life will be blessed.	-*A demand from an enraged adult. The commands change with the wind and are unreasonable but as a child you must obey as the decrees are what is best for the adult.* The adult doesn't care what is best for you, only what is best for him and he wants it now. Period. NOW.

Submission	Submission
-A choice made by a person of equal value to willingly agree to the authority of another for the order and peace of God's kingdom. It cannot be demanded or it is not submission. It cannot be forced or it is not submission. It is a willingness to agree to the role God has called you to. **Noah** *The act of submitting; the act of yielding to power or authority; surrender of the person and power to the control or government of another.*	*-You are lesser, stupid, a moron, without knowledge and ability so you must submit to me as God has made me higher than you. God says I am in charge so you are sinning if you don't submit. You don't have a right to a voice, a concern or an opinion. Do what I say and shut up.*
Will	**Will**
-Being given the free choice to do something. God loves us so much that He has given us a free will. We can choose a course of action, we can choose our thoughts, we can choose our belief systems, we can choose to obey, we can choose to worship, we can choose to give, we choose. You cannot be coerced and manipulated and tricked into a free will choice. **Noah:** *We reason with respect to the value or importance of things; we then judge which is to be preferred; and we will to take the most valuable.*	*-Being tricked, coerced, ensnared, manipulated, overpowered, and trapped into doing something that you don't want to do but feel that you can't get out of. Being swept down the river by other people's choices or being trapped into a chute by having all your choices removed until there is only one path. You have no choice, my will is your will. You will do it my way, you will be happy doing it my way, and you will be silent.*
Truth	**Truth**
Jesus Is Truth. Jesus tells us true. God cannot lie. We can take God's Word to the bank. It is inerrant. God speaks truth in love so that we may grow in Him and walk in truth. Truth brings freedom.	*You are stupid to believe the Bible. Trust me when I tell you that this is right. Only I know what is best for you. Don't trust your feelings, trust me. You are told to ignore other voices, other concepts, other truths, and only believe what that one person is telling you. Only they know you well enough to speak into your life. Nobody else knows you like they do.*

Mirror	Mirror
James 1 tells us that the Word of God is a true mirror for us. As we listen to the Word and do what it says, we will see ourselves correctly.	*I am the only one who knows you. You must listen to me because I know you best. You can fool others but you can't fool me.* You are being seen through the eyes of a carnival mirror and you will become distorted in your view of yourself if you believe what they say.
Motive	**Motive**
But if I have not love, I gain nothing. 1 Corinthians 13:3b God not only cares about the what but also about the why and the how. I cannot use anger or ungodly means to accomplish God's goals.	*The end justifies the means.* It doesn't matter why you did it, it matters how it turns out. You can use force, selfishness, anger, anything to get what you want.
Choice	**Choice**
God gives you a choice. You are a victor. Christ lives in you and you have a new heart which gives you the power to move, grow, and change. Christ in you, the hope of glory.	*You don't have a choice. You are a victim.* You need to wait to have someone rescue you. You are powerless to move, grow or change. Someone else must fix you. Your life is useless until you are healed.
I can	**I can't**
I can do all things through Christ who strengthens me. Phil 4:13 God knows we can't do it right – only in His power and out of His strength am I able to do what He calls me to do.	*I can't change. I can't be loving. I can't be kind.* I have tried and I have failed. There is no way to do what God calls me to do so I give up.
Redeem	**Redeem**
To purchase back; to ransom; to liberate or rescue from captivity or bondage, or from any obligation or liability to suffer or to be forfeited, by paying an equivalent; as, to redeem prisoners. God redeems us because He loves us not because we have earned it.	*If you show yourself to be worthy* I might give you a chance. You have to prove that you are worth the effort and the time and the price I pay. You have to earn it. You have to perform for me. Work harder, try harder, and serve me and then I might give you a crumb from my table.
Gift	**Gift**
God gives good gifts to His children because He loves us. Gifts flow out of God's heart of love to us. He showers us with his gift of compassion, love, eternal life, Holy Spirit. God is a giver of good gifts.	*You owe me if I give you this gift.* There is a price tag for this and I will call in my marker when I want to. I can always take away any gift I give you if you don't appreciate it enough or don't thank me enough.

Permission to Behave Badly*

*Terms and Conditions: Behaving badly may have severe negative consequences on your life and relationships, including, but not limited to: loss of relationships and intimacy (including God), loss of trust, lack of peace, inability to pray or worship, physical consequences (illness and disease, STDs, migraines, stress diseases, insomnia, ulcers, pregnancy), spiritual consequences (including grieving the Holy Spirit, inability to hear God's voice, allowing evil spirits of rebellion, disobedience, pride, rejection, guilt and many more access to your soul, lack of strength in resisting temptation, general weakness, mental confusion, inability to make God-pleasing choices, inviting life-dominating sin patterns into your present, spiritual blindness and self-justification, spiritual pride), emotional consequences (including shame, guilt, depression, confusion, despair, suicidal thinking, anger, fear, worry, etc.) and other life-altering effects such as removal from church fellowship, loss of friends and family, divorce, bankruptcy, joblessness, homelessness, loss of reputation, loss of trust, sickness, death and others.

Use at Will

Signed, Satan

Appendix C
Psalm 18 to Face Terror

During the end of my journey, as I struggled to face the issues of sex and intimacy to finish this book, God revealed yet another deeper layer of pain in my soul. This is not the average garden-variety pain, this was a demonic side of ritualistic abuse and it planted terror in my soul.

This is not in the body of the book because it is not the norm. It is in the back of the book to help those who need to know what to do, if this is a problem in your life.

I had done all that I knew to do in the area of sex. I understood intimacy, I had tasted intimacy and I liked it. But I had a problem. It was clear that I was stuck— I couldn't get going. I knew that I could go back to old tapes and tricks and old methods to get me going, but I wanted to learn how to prime the pump God's way. So as I began to look at the issue I felt the "I won't" rise up within me. That is often a red flashing light, warning me that I have fallen for a lie of Satan.

Deeper Revelation

So Cris and I revisited the last situation. The man was a Mason. He cut me and drew blood. We realized it was not just sexual abuse, it was ritual abuse. I felt terror in mysoul. It wasn't fear; it was cold life-ending terror. I realized that when I consider sex itis 'deadly serious'. And I mean Deadly. Serious. No fun, no joy, no enjoyment, no love, no intimacy or tenderness. It was being called into the principal's office – not the time to play or party but to be silent and serious.

I realized that I could not overcome my foe, he was stronger, older and wiser. He had planted terror in my heart—a long taproot of terror.

I prayed and God reminded me of when I was a little girl and the neighborhood boy (who was a little older than me) kept bullying me. Finally I told my mom what had happened. She gave me permission to fight back. The story goes that I ran out of the house at full steam, picked up a stick, and beat him all the way home.

God's Solution

As Cris and I prayed, God told me to read Psalm 18 outloud. Here are some of the highlights of that Psalm that God used to set me free:

The cords of death entangled me; torrents of destruction overwhelmed me. The cords of the grave coiled around me; the snares of death confronted me. (Psalm 18:4-5) Were the cords going to hold me fast and the tsunami going to sweep over me or was I going to walk in the freedom of Christ and realize He has already set me free. I can walk in freedom because He who is in me is greater than he who is in the world. Would I believe the lie that I was forever entangled or the truth that I have been set free, redeemed by Christ's blood.

In my distress I called to the Lord; I cried to my God for help. From his temple he heard my voice; my cry came before him, into his ears. (Psalm 18:6) I cried out to God, I called for help. I needed His strength, His power, His wisdom.

Smoke rose from his nostrils; consuming fire came from his mouth, burning coals blazed out of it. (Psalm 18:8) I sensed the indignation of my God. I felt the strength of His covenant with me, my enemies were His enemies.

He rescued me from my powerful enemy, from my foes, who were too strong for me. (Psalm 18:17) I felt the power of God assuring me that He had me in the palm of His hand. He would go before me.

You save the humble but bring low those whose eyes are haughty. (Psalm 18:27)
I understood that God stands against the proud, He would bring him low because his eyes were haughty.

You give me your shield of victory, and your right hand sustains me; you stoop down to make me great. (Psalm 18:35) I knew that God was fighting for me, His righteous anger was swelling and He was stepping in for me.

I pursued my enemies and overtook them; I did not turn back till they were destroyed. I crushed them so that they could not rise; they fell beneath my feet. You armed me with strength for battle; you made my adversaries bow at my feet. You made my enemies turn their backs in flight, and I destroyed my foes. (Psalm 18:37-40) I had a picture of me picking up the sword of the Spirit and rather than parlaying the sword, I was hitting my abuser over and over with it. As he ran, I pursued, much as I had done with the neighborhood boy, chasing after him with my Father's permission to fight.

He is the God who avenges me, who subdues nations under me, who saves me from my enemies. You exalted me above my foes; from violent men you rescued me. (Psalm 18:47-48) I felt triumphant and free.

Therefore I will praise you among the nations, O Lord; I will sing praises to your name. (Psalm 18:49) I sat humbly on my couch, praising God within as I saw the freedom that He had brought me as I fought for my freedom with His strength and His weapon.

Yes, that little terrified woman who had been held captive for years, heard her Father give her permission to stop the bully. I ran at my enemy picking up my sword and defeated them by the Word of my testimony and by the power of His hand. *Praise God the Father, who sets the captives free!!*

Bibliography

The Act of Marriage by Tim LaHaye, Zondervan, Grand Rapids, MI © 1998

The Attributes of God, A.W. Tozer, Christian Publications, (c)1997

Big Girls Don't Whine, Jan Silvious, W Publishing Group (div of Thomas Nelson), Nashville, TN, © 2003

Blue Like Jazz, Donald Miller, Thomas Nelson Publishers, © 2003

Breaking Free, Beth Moore, Lifeway Christian Resources; Workbook edition © 1999

Changing Your Thought Patterns, George Sanchez, NavPress, Colorado Springs, CO

The Complete Word Study New Testament, King James Version, Spiros Zodhiates, editor, AMG International, © 1991

Counsel From the Cross, Elyse Fitzpatrick and Dennis E Johnson, Crossway Books, Wheaton, IL © 2009

The Cross-Centered Life by C.J. Mahaney, Multnomah Books, © 2002

Dorie, The Girl Nobody Loved by Dorie Van Stone with Erwin W Lutzer, Moody Press, Chicago, © 1979

The Enemy Within, Kris Lundgaard, P & R Publication, Phillipsburg, NJ, © 1998

Experiencing God, Henry Blackaby and Claude King, Lifeway Press, © 1990

Fool-Proofing Your Life, Jan Silvious, Waterbrook Press Multnomah, Colorado Springs, CO, © 1998

Free Indeed, by Dr Richard Ganz, Shepherd Press, Wapwallopen, PA, © 2002

Growing Kid's God's Way, Gary and Anne Marie Ezzo, Growing Families International © 1998

Growing Up Born Again, Patricia Klein, Fleming H Revell Co © 1987

The Hiding Place, Corrie ten Boom, Chosen Books, © 1971

I Don't Want Your Sex for Now by Miles McPherson, Bethany House, Minneapolis, MN © 2001

Intended for Pleasure by Ed and Gay Wheat, Revel Books, Grand Rapids, MI, © 1977

Inside Out by Larry Crabb, NavPress, Colorado Springs, 1988

Instruments in the Redeemer's Hand, Paul David Tripp P & R Publishing, Phillipsburg, NJ © 2002

Intercessory Prayer, Dutch Sheets, Regal Books, Ventura, CA, © 1996

Journal of Biblical Counseling, Dr. David Powlison, editor, Christian Counseling and Education Foundation, © 2005

Knowing the Heart of God, George MacDonald, Bethany House Publishers, Minneapolis, MN© 1990

Leaving Yesterday Behind; a Victim no More, William Hines, Christian Focus Publications, © 1997 reprinted 2002

The Lord of the Rings trilogy, J.R. Tolkein, Houghton Mifflin Co, New York NY ©1954

My Utmost for His Highest, Oswald Chambers, Barbour and Company, Uhrichsville, OH: 1935

The Peacemaker, by Ken Sande, 2nd Edition, Baker Books, Grand Rapids, MI, © 1991, 1997, 2000

Putting Your Past in Its Place by Steve Viars, Harvest House Publishers, © 2011

Real Marriage, The Truth about sex, friendship & life together by Mark and Grace Driscoll, Thomas Nelson, Nashville, TN © 2012

Redeeming Love, Francine Rivers, Waterbrook Multnomah Publishing Company, Colorado Springs, CO, © 1997

Runaway Girl, Carissa Phelps, The Penguin Group, New York, NY © 2012

Sacred Marriage, Gary Thomas, Zondervan, Grand Rapids, MI, © 2000

The Screwtape Letters, C.S. Lewis, Touchstone/ Simon and Schuster, New York, NY, © 1961

Step-by-Step Discipleship Workbook, Biblical Counseling Foundation, Palm Desert, CA

Strengthening your Marriage by Wayne Mack, P & R Publishing, Phillipsburg, NJ, © 1980

Strong's Exhaustive Concordance by James H. Strong, Baker Book House, Grand Rapids MI, reprinted 1991

The 3 Questions Bible Study, Anne Graham Lotz

Thin Places: A Memoir by Mary DeMuth, Zondervan, Grand Rapids, MI © 2010

TrueFaced, by Bill Thrall, Bruce McNichol and John Lynch, NavPress, Colorado Springs, CO, © 2004

Vine's Complete Expository Dictionary of Old and New Testament Words: With Topical Index (Word Study), W. E. Vine (Author), Merrill F. Unger (Contributor) © 1996

Webster's 1828 Dictionary http://1828.mshaffer.com/

What Did You Expect? Paul David Tripp, Crossway Books, Wheaton IL, © 2010

When People are Big and God is Small, Ed Welch, P & R Publishing, Phillipsburg, NJ, © 1997

Why Christians Can't Trust Psychology, Ed Welch, Harvest House Publishers, Eugene, OR © 1993

Will Medicine Stop the Pain? Elyse Fitzpatrick and Laura Hendrickson, MD, Moody Publishers, Chicago, 2006

Word Studies from the Greek New Testament by Kenneth S. Wuest, Wm. B. Eerdmans Publishing Co, Grand Rapids, MI, © 1966

The Wounded Heart, by Dan Allendar, NavPress, Colorado Springs, 1990

About the Authors

Barb sees her experiences of incest and childhood sexual abuse as a bridge to walk across to reach hurting women. A CPA by profession, her passion is to teach the gospel of grace to anyone who will listen. "When women come to the church asking for help, let's take them to Jesus." She is a certified counselor through the Association of Certified Biblical Counselors (ACBC). As the Director of Biblical Guidance for a large church in Albuquerque, NM, she counsels and trains Christian women to be lay counselors in churches. Barb is married with one grown son.

Cris was Barb's second counselor, her "Joshua;" who led her into the Promised Land—a full Christian life. Cris felt God's call to be a counselor in junior high school while helping a suicidal friend. In many years as a Bible study teacher, women's ministry leader and biblical lay counselor, she considers helping Barbas her greatest challenge and highest honor. Now friends, they share a common passion for helping hurting women. In addition to counseling at her church, Cris is a writer and an editor. She is divorced and has two grown sons and a grandson.

www.ingramcontent.com/pod-product-compliance
Lightning Source LLC
Chambersburg PA
CBHW080214040426
42333CB00044B/2658